DESIGNING LARGE-SCALE WEB SITES

A VISUAL DESIGN METHODOLOGY

Darrell Sano

DESIGNING LARGE-SCALE WEB SITES

A VISUAL DESIGN METHODOLOGY

Darrell Sano

WILEY COMPUTER PUBLISHING

WILEY

JOHN WILEY & SONS, INC.
New York • Chichester • Brisbane • Toronto • Singapore

Publisher: Katherine Schowalter
Editor: Diane Cerra
Managing Editor: Susan Curtin
Text Design & Composition: Pronto Design & Production, Inc.

Library of Congress Cataloging-in-Publication Data:
Sano, Darrell.
        Designing large-scale web sites: a visual design methodology / Darrell Sano.
                p. cm.
        Includes bibliographical references and index.
        ISBN 0-471-14276-X (paper: alk. paper)
        1. World Wide Web (Information retrieval system) 2. Hypertext 'systems. 3. Graphic Arts I. Title.
TK5105.888.S26   1996   95-46312
005.75—dc20   CIP

Printed in the United States of America
10 9 8 7 6 5 4

C o n t e n t s

Eight pages of full-color illustrations follow page 130

Graphic design is essentially about visual relationships—providing meaning to a mass of unrelated needs, ideas, words, and pictures. It is the designers job to select and fit this material together—and make it interesting.

Paul Rand, *A Designer's Art*

PREFACE

This book describes a working process and applied design methodology for the effective production of HTML pages for the world-wide-web. The methodology discussed utilizes principles drawn from the disciplines of visual communication design, and user interface or interaction design. Certain fundamental visual design principles are readily applicable to the design of web pages, and can immediately enhance and improve communication effectiveness, while adding positively to a user's experience.

Establishing a web site requires the understanding of designing interactive software applications and navigable content, and therefore overlaps into the domain of interaction design. For example, support for secure financial transactions on the web means that full-featured, interactive web applications are designed much like shrink-wrapped software. An understanding of user interface design principles can only help in this exciting new area.

The principles outlined in this book play an integral role in the methodology designers use when solving complex communication-oriented problems. A main focus of this book is to describe these principles in relation to the unique characteristics of designing for the WWW, and to describe an effective web design methodology:

"Preliminary Design Preparation" describes initial considerations involved in designing a web information space. A look at "what's out there" is insightful and always worthwhile. In all likelihood, similar web sites already exist, and some general categories of web sites are described with screen examples.

It is also important to have a thorough understanding of the limitations and constraints inherent in web publishing *prior* to any design activity. Misunderstanding characteristics of the web can cause serious bottlenecks later in the production process. Undesirable consequences include extensive reworking of artwork, budget and schedule overruns, and web site pages failing to meet client expectations. Also necessary is the ever challenging task of keeping informed of new tools, technology, and innovation. Keeping up with the fast pace of technological developments will remain a challenge for everyone. Fortunately, information about new developments are usually found on the web in the first place.

The fundamental purpose, intention, and goal for establishing a web presence is clearly articulated, thought out, and communicated to the development team. The perceived *need* of the organization to publish information or provide services on the web should be realized, while establishing simplicity as an early paramount design goal. Conclusions reached at this early stage prescribes the direction for all future activities.

"Designing the Organizational Framework" begins the iterative design process as content is grouped into related categories, and organized using precedence, hierarchy, and frequency of access, until an obvious structure emerges. The goal of this stage is a formidable one, requiring revision and refinement. Completing quick sketches and diagrams help to test the structure for the most efficient route through the information space. This verifies user pathways through various operations and user scenarios. Early "paper prototypes" expose structural flaws and convoluted pathways prior to any production commitments. Later, HTML pages provide verification of the structure and an early indication of visual requirements for production.

"Applying Visual Design for the Web" applies communication design techniques to translate the organizational framework into a tangible user experience. The major goal is to establish a comprehensive visual language for all elements on every web page. Many techniques are directly transferred from the graphic design discipline, but also important are user interaction principles, and an awareness of the limitations and constraints in web design. Major objectives at this stage include designing much needed identification cues and navigation controls for users. A well designed page also provides aesthetic appeal and furthers a users perception of quality and attention to detail in relation to the entity establishing the web site. HTML 3.0 tags which support good communication design and efficient page layout are illustrated with numerous examples.

Finally, the "Visual Design Workshop" provides Netscape Navigator HTML constructs for tables, grids, and many of the example pages found in this book. Pages with various organizational layouts are illustrated and clearly marked with accompanied HTML tags. This chapter should provide a helpful quick reference for those interested in applying the techniques discussed in this book to their own HTML page designs. Hopefully, the need to know HTML will dissappear as direct manipulation authoring tools support the full range of functionality and extensions found in browsers such as Netscape.

This book is not intended to function as a comprehensive HTML reference. A subset of HTML tags which are useful and support good visual design are discussed. Chapter 5, Visual Design Workshop, concentrates on the HTML as implemented in Netscape Navigator. However, not all functionality is discussed. More information specific to Navigator may be found on the Netscape home pages.

The reader should already be somewhat familiar with the web, surfed around, and hopefully has some novice experience authoring HTML documents. This book will primarily benefit those individuals involved in establishing large-scale information spaces on the web, and who do not have visual or user interface design experience. The complexity and size of such an endeavor as establishing a web site, I believe, requires a design methodology to insure that the result is a highly *useful* web experience.

I firmly believe in the power of cross-disciplinary collaboration, and have been fortunate to work with individuals invaluable for their contributions to many of these projects illustrated in this book. Specifically, the opportunity to design the WorldCupUSA94 web server while at Sun Microsystems, Inc., would not have been possible without the efforts of several individuals. The combined effort of talented employees from across the business planets of Sun is proof to the effectiveness in cross-disciplinary collaboration and design. I especially would like to acknowledge Regina Schumann, Carl Meske, Will Shelton, Hassan Schroeder, Jim Remmel, Colleen Choy, Judy Lindberg, and Shane Siegler. I would also like to thank Rick Levenson for support, and a special thanks to Jarrett Rosenberg.

The many examples in this book would not have been reproduced without the cooperation from the following individuals: Bruce Koon, San Jose Mercury News; Barbara Kuhr and Ross Van Woert, HotWired; Omar Ahmad and John Sanford, Discovery Communications, Inc.; Jeff Dachis and Craig Kanarick, Razorfish; Rory O'Neill and Eden Muir, Cybersites, Inc.; Bill Alaoglu, En-Linea; Jason Olim, Geoff Jackson, CDnow! The Internet Music Store; Robert Newton,

Bank of America; Tom Eastwood, Sportsline; Doug Turner, Apple Computer Corporation; Dan Miley, Marc Trimuschat, Silicon Graphics, Inc.; Trevor Kaufman, Voyager.

At Netscape Communications Corporation, I would like to thank Jim Sha and Hrishi Kamat for early encouragement to complete this project; Per Thomsen and Hugh Dubberly for reviewing the manuscript; Emil Scoffone for advice; and of course, everyone at Netscape Communications Corporation.

I would also like to thank Jean Orlebeke for additional comments.

Finally, a very special thanks to Diane Cerra at John Wiley & Sons, Inc.

*I feel we are living
in a phase of social
development in which
we have come to realize
more and more that
information is power—
and in which we must
realize more and more
that no one may be
debarred from it.*

Karl Gerstner, *Compendium for Literates,*
A System of Writing

INTRODUCTION

1

The fantastic growth rate of the web attests to its potential value and empowering appeal. Beyond just a passing fad, businesses, institutions, and corporations believe the web provides more than an avenue to sell goods or services; it also functions as a strategic resource for their own employees, members, or student body. In the commercial sector, information has become a valuable commodity in today's competitive marketplace. The investor who views the latest up-to-the-second investment figures, the employee who reads public reaction about the company's product on bulletin boards, or taps the many other information sources (including a competitor's home page), are better informed and enabled to formulate intelligent decisions based on acquiring and evaluating timely information. One of the major advantages of publishing on the web is the distributed nature of the Internet and the ability to access timely, updated information.

A company contemplating the decision between establishing a web presence versus, for example, CD–ROM distribution of information, should consider issues related to the *timeliness* of the information from each source. CD–ROMs must be manufactured, physically shipped, and delivered to users. Like a printed book or magazine, a CD–ROM cannot be updated dynamically; it is therefore less effective for the delivery of time-critical information. The content scope is fixed within the size limitations of CD–ROM technology. CD–ROM content must also be programmed for each specific target platform, an expenditure requiring enormous human effort and funds for cross-platform availability. This fact has been a major production headache for many multimedia companies, some of which choose to focus on Windows only, typically releasing the Mac version months or a year later (UNIX users are usually out of luck for most popular CD–ROM titles).

Content published on the web, on the other hand, is available instantaneously, can be updated dynamically by the second, and may link to relevant information residing on servers located anywhere around the world, 24 hours a day. Web pages can also access huge databases of documents or graphics, incorporate live news feeds and services, and generate custom pages based on personal user interests or needs.

Most importantly, web pages are authored once and then viewable on multiple platforms connected to the Internet.

Another major advantage of web publishing over traditional book or CD–ROM publishing is that little overhead or expense is required for the author. Everyone cannot master a CD–ROM or afford to print a book. In the case of the web, potentially anyone can publish a "home page." The tools required are minimal, lightweight, and inexpensive. In fact, most browsers are free for downloading for personal use and are inexpensive for commercial users. Contrast this with traditional multimedia authoring software products which cost significantly higher, and the price does not include the steep learning curves (or hefty upgrade fees). It is no surprise that the web has experienced such explosive growth. The minimal required configuration for an individual or small business to publish information on the web is a computer, web browser, server software, text editor, a paint program, perhaps a scanner, modem, and an Internet connection through a service provider.

Another area of extreme interest to web publishers is the adaptation of existing television cable lines for Internet connection. The connection speed, at 10mbps (megabits per second) is multiple times faster than most corporate networks using T1 connection (1.5 mbps). ISDN lines are beginning to make inroads into the consumer market, but even cable (80 times faster than ISDN) will no doubt deliver true, distributed multimedia, supporting rich interaction and dynamic displays with video, animation, images, and virtual reality.

At the same time, browsers are becoming more powerful and extensible. For example, Netscape Navigator 2.0, a "next generation" browser, supports multiple "frames" or windows within a single browser pane. This provides a dramatic leap forward in design capability and presentation possibilities for web pages. An entire page does not require reloading when a designated area or frame is updated or referenced. Important contextual information and levels within a hierarchy can now be exposed to the user in an efficient manner. Other technologies, such as support for Sun Microsystems Java language and Quicktime movies inline, pushes the envelope of browser technology closer to full-fledged multimedia delivery environments.

As the capabilities of web publishing further evolve into dynamic interactive environments and applications, the stakes of failing also become higher. Careful planning, familiarity with the medium, and paying attention to user needs will result in an enriching, successful web site. As with any new technology, an initial period of experimentation will eventually give way to intelligent applications in the new medium.

The Urgency of "Getting-it-on-the-Web"

Many web sites today appear, from a design perspective, as if they were hurried onto the net, disregarding users' needs and requirements. Also evident is a low level of visual design competency or the command of a formal visual vocabulary reflecting the design standards users are accustomed to in print. An overall lack of planning, coupled with a new-found fascination for hypertext linking, usually results in a tangled mess of web pages, contributing to users being hopelessly "lost in hyperspace."

Designing a large-scale web site requires thoughtful planning and cycles of refinement, initiated by gathering background information *before* any HTML pages are authored. The high-pressured "get-it-on-the-web" approach is counter-productive because it precludes essential planning stages and thoughtful design revisions required to ensure that the *right* information is included at the *right* time for the *right* user.

Hype and hysteria feed the flame of urgency, as organizations without a web presence feel "out of it" and must now throw human effort and monetary resources at the problem to quickly alleviate this problem. The result can be a blatant reuse of material originally not meant for the web, as content is quickly imported from printed materials, converted into HTML pages, including gargantuan graphics easily reproduced in print, but a burden to download on the web. The distinctive advantages of web publishing are unnoticed and undiscovered, as is an understanding of the behavior and expectations of users who browse the net.

The onslaught of quick-start books for web publishing is very reminiscent of similar publications during the early days of the desktop publishing revolution. Marketing dollars and misleading advertising promoted false claims and expectations that anyone could produce beautiful books, brochures, and newsletters with a few clicks of the mouse. The advertisements forgot to mention that various skills are required to design those beautiful pages. The rush to desktop publish brought the predictable onslaught of truly bad design, followed by the slow adoption of the technology by those skilled to use it best. At the same time, the gradual rise in design sensitivity by those not versed formally in design or publishing increased to an adequate level.

Today, the buzz word "desktop publishing" has all but disappeared from the newsstand, along with the many desktop publishing design companies that tried to capitalize on the hype. The technology has matured and is now ubiquitous in the communications design industry. Individuals and organizations with the skills best to use it (and with something to say) have adopted desktop publishing technology to solve real-world communication design problems.

A similar situation exists today with the web. The novel characteristics, newness of the technology, and seductive lure to reach millions of people have led to an explosion of web sites. Early attempts appear to be experiments rather than fulfilling any real need. Spending an hour surfing the net can be an hour wasted downloading huge, unattractive graphics or reading useless, irrelevant text. Personal home pages have become particularly popular, but some of these efforts do not even present interesting, entertaining, or imaginative content which reflects an interesting facet or glimpse into the individual publishing the page. The number of personal home pages now available on Yahoo (a very useful and popular index for web subjects) exceeds a phone book for a small town. Most, unfortunately, aren't worth the wait to download the page.

Another instance of poor web publishing is the naive misuse of hypertext linking. Overusing hypertext links presents a user with too many bewildering choices; these are especially bothersome when they lead to irrelevant, unrelated information, as illustrated in later chapters. Worse yet are instances where links lead to countless further links, towards no obvious end. Overambitious web authors must resist the temptation to provide links *just for the sake of linking*. This stair-step, waterfall approach reflects a more serious, deep-rooted problem, indicating flaws in the underlying organization. Such designs actually inhibit usability by requiring the user to traverse too many levels for needed information.

In the commercial and business sector, the web site should fulfill a particular function and role, and therefore provide the needed information, product, or services. In large companies, the web site has become an extension of the total corporate communications strategy and provides an important two-way communication conduit to their customers. Many individuals, start-up businesses, and corporations have invested resources in the future of the web as a delivery medium for their information and services.

As the web matures, better uses and applications of the technology will eventually surface. Many web sites today are vastly improved over those found on the web a year ago. Contributing to this end is the collaboration between various disciplines. The new technology has also defined new roles and responsibilities.

Design Collaboration for Web Publishing

Designing a large-scale web site essentially requires a collaborative team involved in a design activity, working closely together on a continual basis, yet dependent on differing skillsets. The design activity never ends, for the web is a living, evolving entity, open to change, improvement, and technological innovation.

The necessary team members with their specific skills include:

1. Computer programmer—familiar with Internet technology, database architecture, CGI scripting (common gateway interface scripting, which customizes the functionality of web sites), and Java programming.

2. Visual designer and user interface designer—knowledgeable about the limitations and constraints of designing interactive applications and able to organize and structure large-scale information projects

3. Editor and writer—familiar with hypertext and its implications for structuring documents; familiar with on-line documentation, search engines, and query methods

4. Marketer—understands the strategic power of the Internet and can identify opportunities and future markets and applications. An example of disciplines and contributions to a Web project is illustrated in Table 1.1.

The working arrangement between the team members is highly interdependent and contingent on each other's skills. For example, the technical know-how required to write a Java applet to process user input from a fill-in form and provide dynamic feedback to the user is in the realm of the engineer, who must communicate functional possibilities to the visual designer, who can then incorporate this functionality within the framework of the design. The designer at the same time must drive the implementation to support the design from the user's point of view and hide aspects of the underlying technology. Ideally, the close working arrangement between the visual and the technical allows experimentation in areas totally new. "What if . . ." scenarios are explored within a cooperative, knowledge-sharing environment.

Trained designers are familiar with the working arrangement described here, for they are used to functioning not only as the designer, but as managers of service bureaus, contractors, manufacturing resources, and so forth. Designers develop project budgets, estimates, and schedules; supervising production through delivery. Expertise is hired as needed, fulfilling a specific project requirement,

TABLE 1.1 Disciplines and Contributions to a Web Project

Project Management	Usability Engineering	Visual Communication	Content Management	Engineering
Initial Client Contact	User Requirements	Art Direction	Copyright Release	Hardware Configuration
Business Requirements	Functional Specification	Screen Layout, Design	Contract Negotiation	Software Installation
Project Plan	Task Analysis	Interface Design	Hypertext Editing, Writing	Custom Applications
Contract Negotiation	User Profile, Survey	Prototyping	Filtering	Implementation
Budget	Interface Design	Design Specification	Documentation	Logs, Usage Statistics
Schedule	Testing, Collect Data	Style Guide	On-line Help	Java, LiveScript, etc.
Resource Allocation	Error Handling	Collateral	Resource Allocation	Maintenance
Day-to-Day Project Management	Documentation On-line Help Resource Allocation	Documentation On-line Help Resource Allocation		Upgrades, Enhancements

whether it be a photographer, illustrator, model-maker, or re-toucher. A recognition of personal skill limitations, while having a mutual respect for those with other essential skillsets, is a prerequisite for building an effective, collaborative design team.

The same situation exists when designing large-scale web sites. Depending on project objectives, a variety of skillsets may be required for effective execution. For example, the advent of VRML (virtual reality modeling language) and other new 3-D functionality maps directly to the skills of architects or industrial designers, who can successfully execute designs in this area. The examples from the web game S.P.Q.R. (see color plate 8) illustrate the skill level of the game creators, who are instructors at the Columbia School of Architecture. The quality of the images speak for themselves. Little advantage would result from non-3-D savvy engineers or writers attempting to model and render navigable virtual environments. It is better to leave it to those who do it best.

Conversely, the need to extend functionality or add rich interaction or animation requires engineering to write customized Java or Live-Script for applications. There is little chance a visual designer or artist is realistically suited to this task. The visual designer will have to work collaboratively with an engineer to incorporate this functionality into the page design.

Good marketing and management skills are needed to ascertain the economic implications, return on investment, and staffing the right team to establish the web site. Costs for staffing, equipment, maintenance, and so forth, must be considered and justified. Specific tasks calling for out-sourcing have budget implications and must be calculated into the total cost. HTML editors, artists, scriptors, and so forth, are available for contract work, usually on an hourly basis. In some cases, these skills may be internal to the organization, working cooperatively with an outside design or consulting firm. In any case, a comprehensive project plan covering the web site scope of services and functionality, budget, and schedule is necessary, just as in any large-scale design project.

One method to generate revenue which may impact a project's budget is to charge for advertising space. Today, many sites include some form of advertising or post links to other companies which have a strategic relationship with one another. Fees vary dramatically for this service and, in the best cases, can even pay for the maintenance of the web site itself. Nearly all commercial sites now include advertising on their pages.

An interesting capability with the web is to track user access to certain areas of the site. Special analysis programs can take the log file from the web server and generate detailed reports, revealing computer platform, browser, and IP address of the user. Report data may also reveal the number of requests for a particular document per hour and the total number per day, week, and month. The usage data may alter the organization or priority of information on the web site, affecting the day to day working operation and design. An area seldom visited may be removed, while a popular spot is emphasized. Visual logging software is readily available from various resources on the web.

Clear communication is essential for everyone involved in the design process. Interdependent decisions are made which have implications for individual team members each step further in the development process. This doesn't, however, mean working together in the same room. In today's distributed work environment, the actual physical locations of team members may be scattered across the globe. Email, phone, and even setting up a web-based development bulletin board system, facilitates communication and work-flow through a project, breaking down the limitations of physical space.

In the end, a web site should be held to the same standards of criticism that artifacts from other design disciplines are measured: by utility, functionality, usefulness, and aesthetic quality, whether it be to educate, inform, entertain, facilitate commercial transactions, "chat," or order a pizza. Most publishers and content providers are very demanding with the visual representation of their information on the web. Rapid improvements in browser capabilities, the increase in connection speed and better compression algorithms, along with more computing power, infers the inevitable future delivery of rich, full-fledged multimedia content over the web. Dramatic improvements supporting better layout and presentation are already here in HTML 3.0-compatible browsers, with even greater capability available today in next-generation browsers, such as Netscape Navigator 2.0.

As technology facilitates greater design expression, latitude, and interactivity, user expectations will also certainly increase. The consumer will determine which web sites to visit and which to avoid. Sites that are easy to navigate, provide compelling, changing content, and support a range of activities (chat, forums, etc.) will no doubt outlast those that are confusing, static, and lacking creativity. It is all the more urgent to recognize the benefits a cross-disciplinary web development team offers in this new medium, in order to ensure the best possible experience for users.

The initial thinking about any proposition has to reach a briefing stage, that is to say, aims and problems must be clarified before design—and design should not be taken to imply the individual designer in this context—can begin to operate in drawing up a plan.

Douglas Martin, *Book Design*

2

PRELIMINARY DESIGN PREPARATION

Become Familiar with the Web

Design projects typically begin by gathering a variety of background information. A large part of the designer's job at this initial stage is devoted to research in order to adequately understand the problem and objectives. Without this knowledge, the designer lacks a frame of reference to adequately provide the solution for the client's needs.

From the start, it is important to understand the medium for which the design is intended. For example, designing a story layout for inclusion in a large magazine requires familiarity with the established look and feel, presentation style and formal vocabulary, and also an understanding of the qualities of the material and production method used in the publication. Similarly, an architect must understand the characteristics and stress qualities of certain materials intended in the construction of a building. Multimedia CD-ROM designers must be familiar with their tools, technical limitations, and the production process before any work is started. In all cases, a thorough understanding of the media, materials, and working procedure precedes the design activity. Lack of understanding or designing in a conceptual vacuum may cause serious production problems later, with possible monetary consequences.

As with any design, the existence of previous work in the particular medium provides an instructional repertory of past successes and failures. Bad design usually invokes the wrath of public criticism, providing a warning to others to avoid replicating the same fate. Good design, on the other hand, may spawn legions of imitations, but more importantly, provides an insight into successful techniques or qualities which can be transferred, extended, and perhaps applied to other problems.

For web site design, it is advantageous to become familiar with the technology and understand limitations and constraints which continue to change. The best way to gain knowledge and insight into web design is to surf the web itself.

Browse Existing Web Sites

Communication goals for web sites vary as widely as the nature of the organizations publishing on the web itself. Chances are, however, that a web site already exists with similar content or services as your intended site. It is worthwhile to spend some time reviewing these sites, noticing how difficult or easy it is to access and navigate through the information. Various visual design characteristics, navigation metaphors, interface controls and page layout styles provide useful examples, both good and bad.

Some very general categories of web sites include:

- Information-oriented services (newspapers, magazines, access to government databases, news feed services, information provider services)

- Research and education institutions (K-12 and higher education, universities, continuing education, research institutions)

- Entertainment (games, social activities, sports)

- Marketing communications (corporate communications, product literature, capabilities information, advertising, service and support)

- Retail business and sales (on-line malls, catalogs, purchasing of products, services, etc.)

A review of "what's out there" is well worth the time and effort required to see how different types of business and organizations currently utilize the web as a communication medium. A quick method to access web sites within a specific area of interest is to perform a Yahoo search (http://www.yahoo.com/) to direct inquiries into specific subject areas. The following is a brief description of a few existing web sites with different communication goals and objectives, affecting the presentation and design of the web site.

COMPUTER-BASED AND TECHNOLOGY COMPANIES

Computer and technology companies applied the web to publishing needs early; today, nearly all computer-based organizations have extensive web sites. The usual content includes company background, product descriptions, upgrade and support services, special news or "What's New" columns, employment opportunities, and even access to employee home pages. Overall, the web site functions as an important extension of the total corporate communications and marketing strategy, providing another conduit for communicating information and services to customers. In most cases, the team responsible for the implementation of the site is within the marketing communications department of the technology company.

More than just offering information limited to the individual company, the web frequently provides a more open and cooperative model, producing links to technology partners or related products from other companies. The approach is quite different than the one from traditional marketing communications. These "virtual business communities" across technology partners, alliances, customers, and related products or services link from one home page to another. Finding related, relevant information is a powerful capability of hypertext systems, clearly beneficial to customers.

Figure 2.1 is the Netscape Communications Corporation home page, which displays information found on most technology-based companies' home page. The page is divided into areas containing a graphic identification element with subcategory choices, "What's New" information which periodically changes, and hypertext links to further information.

Since the web is still new to many individuals, information includes pointers to useful material to help new users learn about HTML, download helper applications, find out more about the web, and so forth. Most web-oriented technology companies provide this information to feed the tremendous level of interest. Publishing "how-to" documents makes a lot of sense, since the rapid changes in technology can be reflected immediately in web documents, in contrast to continually reprinting books or papers. Therefore, the web site not only

FIGURE 2.1

Netscape home page.

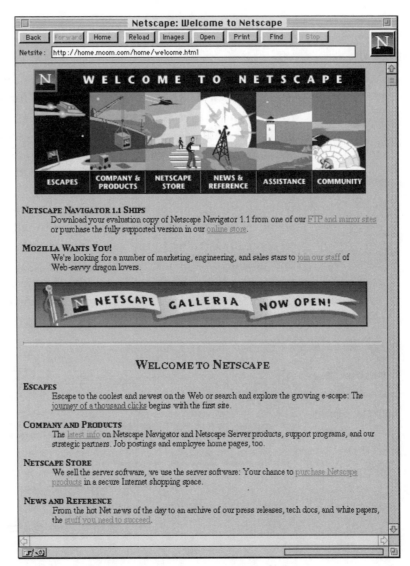

provides information about a company's products and services, but also functions as a learning resource about the web and technology.

Advertising has also found its place on many web sites; it usually appears as a small logotype or graphic included on the page. When selected, the user is typically sent to the advertisers' home page. Monthly fees may be charged for placing logotypes or advertisements, providing a continued revenue stream for the web site. Like the broadcast industry, the more popular the web site, the higher the advertising fee.

Technology-oriented companies may enable users to purchase products on-line or download free trial software for a limited period. Many archival sites allow users to freely download software utilities for free or minimal cost. Software purchases seem particularly well-suited to distribution via the Internet, providing instantaneous downloading for upgrades or bug fixes to customers.

Other goods include promotional products, such as T-shirts and coffee mugs (Figure 2.2). Such items would usually be found in a printed company catalog. In this case, the web offering has supplanted that document. The user browses various products, and then places the articles in a "shopping basket" page, where the items are saved (Figure 2.3) while the shopper continues to browse. The basket may include software, documentation, promotional goods, or anything

FIGURE 2.2

Netscape product page from the "General Store."

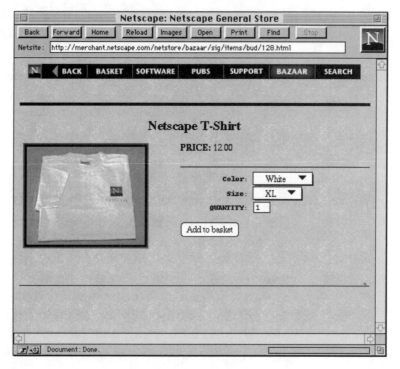

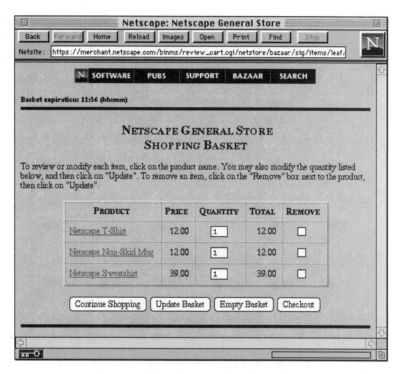

FIGURE 2.3
Netscape Shopping Basket holding items to purchase.

the company wishes to market on the Internet. Once the customer wishes to "checkout," the order is submitted via an on-line HTML form for credit card capture and processing.

Aside from external web sites, most technology companies also have internal servers behind the "firewall," in the safe and secure zone unreachable by the general public. The firewall limits access to proprietary information, which is intended for employees only. Proprietary technology and advanced research must be kept under access control, out of the reach of competitors and the general population. For internal corporate communications, the web functions particularly well as an internal information delivery medium and has repeatedly been referred to in this early stage of evolution as the "poor man's Notes" (referring to Lotus Notes, a program designed for internal corporate communication and collaboration). More importantly for corporations, the internal web site breaks down communication barriers and isolationism, and potentially empowers all employees with improved rapid access to information and internal communication.

Possible information published on internal web sites includes employee benefits and programs, facility services, sales and marketing information, organizational charts, engineering group and project descriptions, advanced research, sports or other recreational activities, company discussion groups, and chat. A major goal of providing an internal web site is to facilitate better communication and information availability for all employees within the organization. This is especially helpful when employees are distributed around the world.

INFORMATION AND NEWS

Numerous news and information services are now on the web; many provide an example for effective publishing of time-dependent information. Various publishers are also using some form of access control or registration for user subscription or profiling. Subscription rates are usually based on a low monthly fee. In some cases, the design of information services replicates the model found in real-world newspapers. Most sites are well organized, probably because publishers have a good understanding of organizing and structuring content.

The Mercury Center Web, in particular, is an example of a very popular web site which allows users to find information based on general, familiar categories, much like the organizational schema of real-world newspapers. A recent survey found this web site to be one of the most popular and frequently accessed. The Main Menu in Figure 2.4 presents very familiar general categories of topics to users, including information on the subscription process itself.

At the top of every page throughout the site, graphics function very much like sectional heads found in real-world newspapers. This provides clear identification for the user's current location, as well as providing two global navigational controls, pointing users to the Main Menu and Directory.

The Main Menu is really the central hub for the Mercury Center Web site. From here, users may access a variety of services and information, including information geared specifically toward the web. The "Today's Newspaper" button points the user to a page with newspaper-like categories of content, as shown in Figure 2.5. The graphic

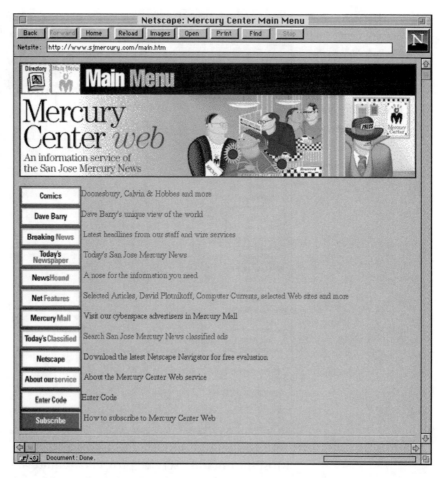

buttons on the left side of the page are accompanied by a short line of hypertext, which describes a lead story within each section.

Selecting the Front Page category would point the user to the page in Figure 2.6, which provides a brief abstract of each news story, similar to headline and by-line copy preceding an article in a real-world newspaper. If the user is interested in a particular story, access is through selecting the appropriate item from the list, and the complete story is served, as shown in Figure 2.7. This structure allows the user to rapidly scan article headlines, read the abstract, then if interested, access the next level of detail to the complete article. It is at this level that the Mercury News requires users to subscribe. The fairly open model allows anyone to freely browse and get a sense of the information space until reaching the actual article level.

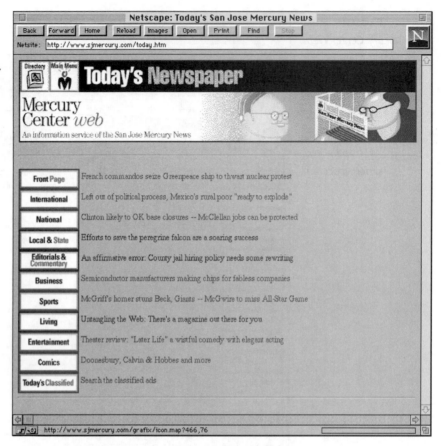

Most information service providers require subscription fees by utilizing some form of access control. In the case of the Mercury Center Web, access control requires users to register and subscribe each month to gain full access to information at the article level. However, the Mercury Web does allow browsing a fairly large area of the web site free of charge. This is important so users receive an idea of the breadth and scope of services provided.

An interesting capability in the Mercury Web includes user preferences. For example, a novel application enables users to select their favorite comic from a menu listing seen in Figure 2.8, and then access a customized comic page, as seen in Figure 2.9. Personal preferences for generating individualized views of the information space are an important feature for news services, especially due to the uncontrollable quantity of information available on the web. Another example using preferences in the Mercury Center is the NewsHound service, which automatically searches stories, news wires, and advertisements for articles matching user profiles. The NewsHound profile searches every hour from numerous sources, sending those which are most relevant to the user. A user may change profiles at any time, depending on current interest or needs. A minimal fee delivers five profiles to the user, who can purchase additional sets of five profiles as needed. Most importantly, the web site delivers the appropriate news to the user, rather than forcing the user to search for it.

FIGURE 2.6

Mercury Center Web Front Page, listing main story headlines. (Courtesy of Mercury Center, @San Jose Mercury News. All Rights Reserved. http://www. sjmercury.com.)

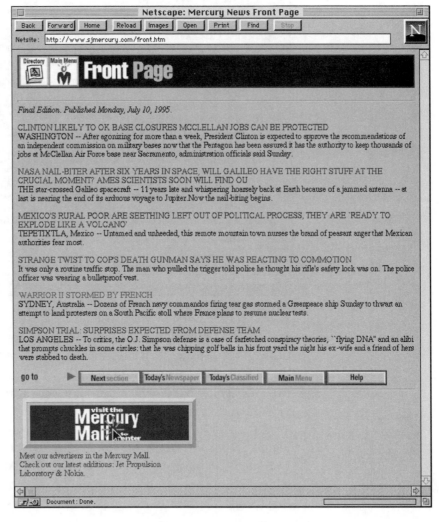

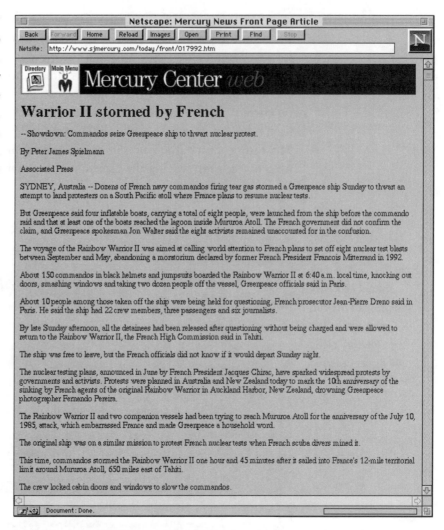

Publishers are familiar with structuring and presenting information and are discriminating when evaluating the appearance and character of the printed page. Web sites such as *HotWired* continue to explore the unique characteristics of the web as a communication medium in itself, designing pages which not only look attractive, but also provide the means for viewer participation with the web site.

Figure 2.10 is the *HotWired* home page, which presents areas of the web site in an informal, colorful graphic ISMAP (an image map, with clickable hotspot regions in the image) and in an Overview textual listing. The text is very important for users who prefer to defer

FIGURE 2.8

Mercury Center comics selection page. (Courtesy of Mercury Center, @San Jose Mercury News. All Rights Reserved. http://www. sjmercury.com.)

image loading in exchange for layout speed. A good practice for designing web pages is to always provide the hypertext equivalent for any graphic or image map, so as to furnish full functionality to low bandwidth users.

The content is grouped into categories assigned imaginative names which relate to the particular subject matter or activity; for example, the "Piazza" is where to go to chat and communicate with

other visitors to the web site. More than publishing static pages of information, *HotWired* offers chatrooms, live special appearances in "ClubWired," and encourages viewer email and contributions to each issue. The two-way communication between web publisher and audience is an important dynamic feature of the web, which takes advantage of the distributed communication powers of the Internet.

Users are encouraged to register and receive special services, such as taking advantage of search functionality and customized home pages. A user is able to select a subset of the entire *HotWired* contents by selecting topic areas from a selection list page (Figure 2.11). This narrows the focus to areas of interest for users and reduces information density on the page. The pages are well designed, fresh in approach, lively in nature, and always inviting to the user.

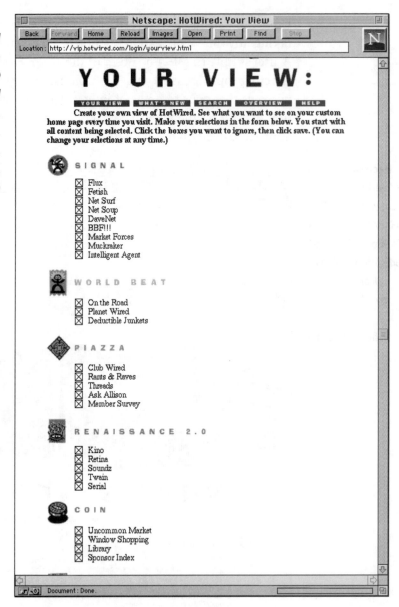

Certain uses of HTML exhibit a clear understanding of the medium
by the designer in order to achieve a specific effect. For example, the
frequent use of the <BLOCKQUOTE> HTML tag provides much
needed margins for the left-hand edge of the page by indenting all
copy between this HTML tag and is frequently used in the *HotWired*
pages. This opens the page design, providing needed empty space to
relieve the dense and overcrowding look web pages assume when

copy is shoved up against the browser edges. The interspersed use of images and HTML text combines to form aesthetically pleasing and interesting page layouts, as illustrated in Figure 2.12.

Web sites are not static, one-time efforts, but require constant updating and dedicated attention, very much as a magazine staff is required to publish a monthly publication. Topics in *HotWired* change frequently and so does the freshness in the visual presentation, which is geared uniquely to the content presented. The various chatrooms and opportunities for user participation also add a sense of community to the *HotWired* site, pushing further into a new

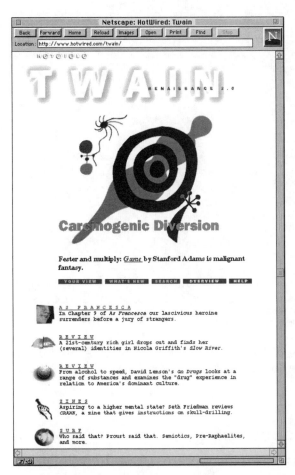

FIGURE 2.12 *Pages from HotWired. (Copyright © 1995 by HotWired Ventures LLC. All Rights Reserved. Used with permission.*

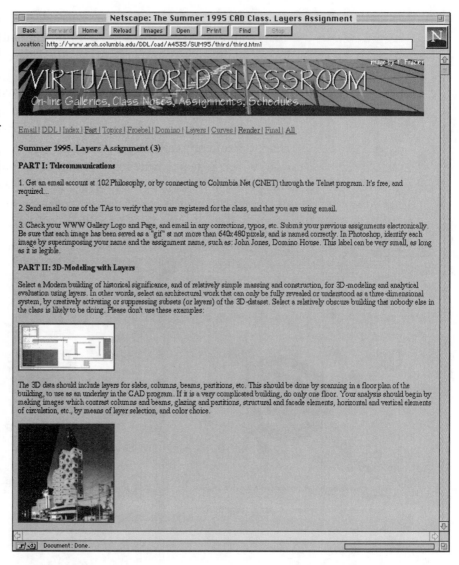

direction. These pages illustrate a variety of web imaging and layout techniques; viewing the source HTML is a good way to learn from the designers.

RESEARCH AND EDUCATION

Research and educational institutions benefit greatly by publishing research documents, journals, newsletters, and bulletins, and by supporting discussion groups, correspondence, and so forth, via a web site. The vast interconnected resources of the web lend themselves naturally to research activities and collaboration, while facilitating communication around the world for individuals having a common research interest.

The "Virtual Classroom" at Columbia University's Graduate School of Architecture is a site which explores the possibilities of "open"

FIGURE 2.14

Virtual classroom student work page. (Copyright © Columbia University, Graduate School of Architecture, Preservation and Planning.)

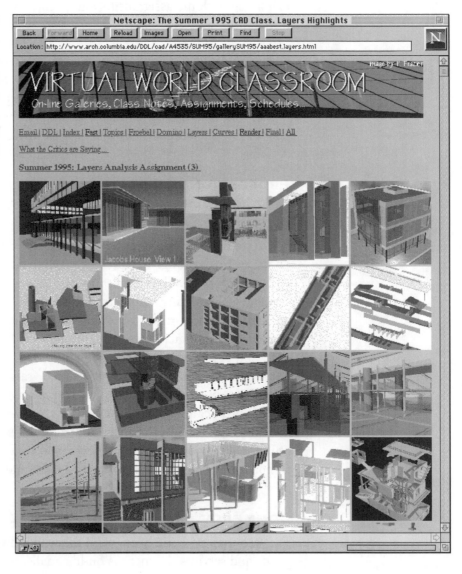

assignments and constructive criticism. Students work on assignments given on web pages (Figure 2.13) and post their work when their assignment is complete. Experts in the field of architecture and computer-aided design may critique the work or contact the student with email for further comments or discussion. The feedback loop and support for communication via the web has noticeably increased student productivity and interest in the subject matter. Individuals in remote locations, with the proper computer configuration, may follow along with the assignments and participate in the class progress through the six-week session.

Once a student has completed an exercise, the work is sent to the university and immediately posted for all to review. Small thumbnails (Figure 2.14) for each assignment are posted on the page, allowing access to the work by anyone interested. Clicking on the thumbnail image serves a larger, completed example to the browser for viewing.

PROFESSIONAL ORGANIZATIONS AND MEMBERSHIP INSTITUTIONS

Thousands of professional organizations which have a geographically diverse membership body are particularly well-suited to publishing on the web. The range of activities may include the delivery of a wide variety of member publications, conference materials and proceedings, maintaining membership directories, facilitating searching through document repositories, job opportunities and classified, local chapter news and activities, collaborative work groups, membership chat, and bulletin boards. Marketing efforts may also include promotional activities to increase membership or raise funds through sponsorship or advertising. Timely news, upcoming calendar of events, and so forth, can be posted immediately, keeping everyone informed. Various information previously printed and distributed via the post office, including membership renewal and fee collection, can now be completed on-line without postage expense and much human effort.

COMMERCE, MARKETING, AND SALES

The web may potentially augment the way individuals purchase goods and services. Numerous on-line malls, storefronts, and businesses provide information about their products through on-line equivalents of catalogs, and also allow users to order merchandise on-line via secure transaction. Items particularly well-suited for on-line purchasing are those which do not depend on the user to "touch and feel" the tactile quality or test-drive the product, such as office supplies and equipment, hardware and tools, and so forth.

CDnow! is a store on the Web selling audio CDs through secure transaction. Since the quantity of audio CDs numbers in the thousands, search technology allows users to query by various input choices, including name, album title, and song title (Figure 2.15). The search returns a listing of recording artists who match the criteria, but also provides links to related artists who have similar styles or are influential to the current artist. Discography information is also included, providing additional information about the artist or music style.

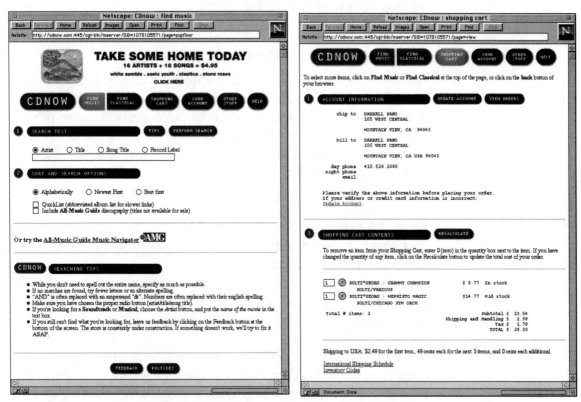

FIGURE 2.15 *CDnow! search page for locating audio CDs and the Shopping Cart for holding purchases. (Copyright © CDnow! All Rights Reserved.)*

The site uses the metaphor of a "Shopping Cart" (similar to the Netscape home pages shown earlier), so users are able to browse through the store, initiate searches, and place items in the basket (See Figure 2.15). At any time during the shopping experience, the user may review or edit the products in the cart, until ready to pay. The shopper enters the credit card number for secure authentication, and an on-line receipt is generated with the order number which can be saved to local disk. The user may also phone in or fax the credit card number if desired. An interesting feature includes the ability for users to save their shopping basket and all contents, so they may continue shopping later or think about their purchases.

On-line commerce is still in its infancy, though the coming advances in web technology should provide a much more robust presentation and experience for potential shoppers.

BANKING AND FINANCE

An area of high activity has been the financial and on-line banking area. The many news headlines mentioning mergers, partnerships, and acquisitions points to the potential explosion in this area of web application development. It is obvious that on-line banking via the web is soon to appear, and with improved security and functionality, quite possibly a revolutionary method for individuals and businesses to complete their financial transactions.

Bank of America, the first commercial bank to develop a website, continues to enhance and add to their site. In 1996 they plan to support home banking functionality via the web. The new Bank of America home page, seen in Figure 2.16, is synonymous to a "virtual bank," and provides useful information for current or potential customers without having to physically enter the bank itself.

Building blocks on the new home page serve as the site's table of contents, and the building block metaphor continues throughout the website and in the "Build Your Own Bank" function. The information on the site is organized to fit the way people make their financial decisions.

FIGURE 2.16

Bank of America home page.

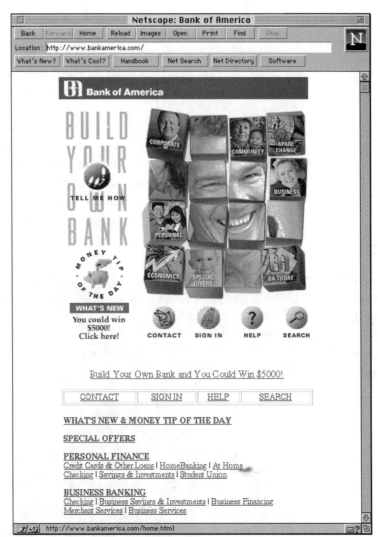

GAMES AND RECREATION

Games, recreational chat, and entertainment sites, such as those for celebrity figures, sports stars, or television fan clubs, provide added information for specific target audiences. Most broadcast and media giants have extensive web sites, providing additional information related to television programs, characters, movies, and so forth. Sports is also an active area well-suited to web publishing, which can take advantage of the immediacy in posting the latest results and scores.

Sports information providers, such as SportsLine, not only provide the obvious posting of scores and game results, but also support a range of activities, including contests, fan club chat, and sports memorabilia marketing. Additional levels of related activities, products, and trivia offer a rich experience for the devoted, die-hard sports fan.

SportsLine has streamlined the page design in order to specifically support access from home users with 14.4K modems. Graphics are therefore used sparingly throughout the site. Since the latest posting of scores or sporting news is of the utmost importance to the intended user, the liberal use of graphics throughout the site would slow down user access to the needed information.

FIGURE 2.17

SportsLine "Baseball Live" page dynamically updating current score. (Copyright © 1995 SportsLine. All Rights Reserved.)

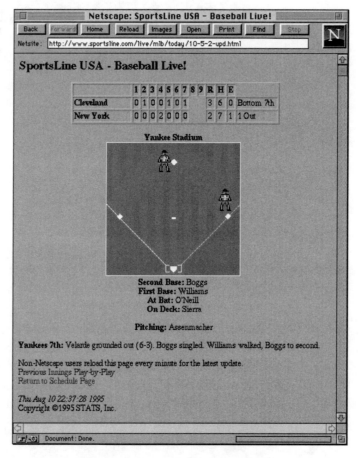

Particularly interesting are the "Live" sports areas, which provide
dynamic score updating during games in progress. For example, the
page in Figure 2.17 indicates the status of a baseball game which is in
progress by using the Netscape "server-push" feature. Game status is
dynamically updated every minute on the page, directly from the
sportsfeed source. Note the graphic of the baseball diamond even
reflects that two players are on base (even wearing the right uniforms).
Subtle cues in the pictographic representation of the baseball field also
communicate the natural grass (with mow-stripes) versus astroturf.

Another example of an entertainment-oriented site, with an emphasis
toward learning activities, is Discovery Channel Online shown in
Figure 2.18. In anticipation of graphics-rich multimedia presentation
capabilities, the Discovery pages use ample imagery and anti-aliased
bit-mapped text, which ensures design consistency and typographic
control. The type appears consistent across platforms, and users cannot alter the font choice or size, since type is actually a graphic
image. The pages appear as if designed within a multimedia author-

ing tool environment. Extensive use of HTML tables controls the placement of page elements within the defined rectangular format.

The web site correlates days of the week with general subject topics, publishing new information for that topic on its given day. The Friday ("Exploration") page, for example, always has new information and stories about the topic of exploring published every Friday (Figure 2.19). After a week, another issue of exploring content supplants the old, while still allowing users to access stories from past weeks. This model ensures that new content is presented on a daily basis. The web site also supports a wide range of activities, such as presentations and chatrooms. The Discovery Channel Online is a good example of how active and dynamic a web site can be.

Since the presentation method ensures that new information is always presented on the web site, opportunities exist to design tasteful pages related to specific subject matter. Each main story for the specific day of the week has an introductory page, as illustrated in Figure 2.20,

FIGURE 2.19

Discovery Channel Online "Exploration Friday" page. (Copyright © 1995 Discovery Communications, Inc.)

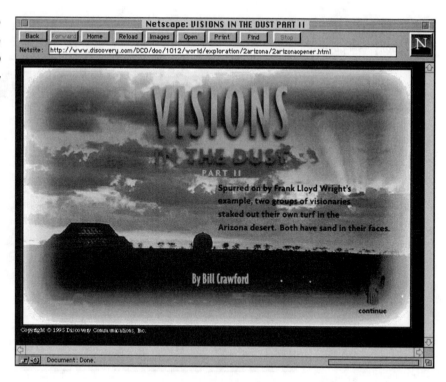

which does not adhere to any strict style or look. The visual presentation is dependent on the content of the story and becomes an area for creative design and interaction. The actual story may or may not continue within the established format, using previous and next arrows to page through the main text, as shown in Figure 2.21.

In the genre of the popular CD-ROM adventure Myst™, S.P.Q.R., created by CyberSites, Inc., is a full-screen navigable game (Figure 2.22). The user travels through beautifully rendered still images of ancient Rome in search of manuscripts or simply browsing and enjoying the sights. The manuscripts are collected and placed on a shelf, located below the image across the bottom of the screen. Such a site is perhaps a precursor of the future capabilities and potential of the web: to provide graphics-rich, interactive multimedia and navigable 3-D worlds.

For the moment, however, response time for users with home modems remains slow. Best results for this particular site are with a

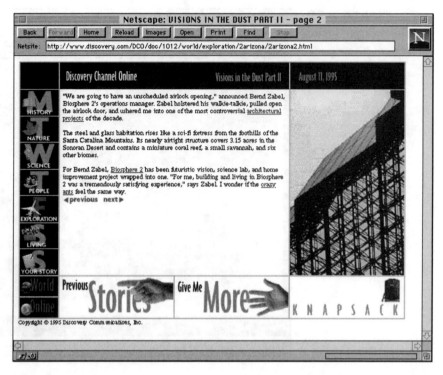

direct Internet connection (T1 or T3), due to the large images which are downloaded with each navigational movement.

Note that the renderings are of the highest quality and precision; they demonstrate the skills and expertise in the creators' own professional background experience in architecture and 3-D computer-aided graphics. Color plate 8 illustrates the extremely high rendering quality in the S.P.Q.R. web site.

Using skilled professionals, such as architects or space planners for future 3-D web applications, provides opportunities for effective cross-disciplinary collaborative work groups. Using individuals with the skills required for 3-D web applications will be imperative to maintain a sense of realism, level of quality, and visual appeal. For example, recent attempts at virtual desktop software environments have demonstrated a naive, ill-equipped understanding of 3-D space, resulting in cartoonish, unattractive office backdrops.

The widespread adoption of web design outside of the engineering community and the coming of easy-to-use WYSISYG authoring tools

suggests that nontechnical, visually oriented individuals with the necessary training and skills will contribute to developing useful, entertaining web applications, using Virtual Reality Modeling Language (VRML), 3-D, and graphics to their fullest potential.

WEB-ORIENTED DESIGN, CONSULTING, AND SERVICES

The existence of the web itself has spawned new opportunities for individuals and organizations to provide services for others wishing to establish a web presence. As the web moves mainstream and becomes a major communication medium for business and commerce, the design activity of producing a web site will be adopted by traditional design firms, advertising agencies, and communications companies. The creative skills found in such companies will be augmented by friendlier web-based publishing tools and possibly staffing employees with a stronger technical background for customizing functionality.

Figure 2.23 shows pages from a company which crosses the line into various disciplines and media. Razorfish provides design and interface services for creating interactive digital experiences for businesses and organizations. The in-house technical expertise and artistic background are reflected in the progressive style of the web pages. The web site also presents a variety of creative work by artists, writers, photographers, and so forth. The experimental approach includes frequent use of Netscapes "server-push" and "client-pull" capabilities. (In server-push, the server sends information to the browser, leaving an open connection. In client-pull, the server sends information to the client browser, which also includes an instruction to perform another action, such as "go to this URL in 10 seconds." After the specified time, the action is performed, as the browser window either reloads the page or sends a new URL to the user. See also Figure 2.29.)

Blue dots dance around the page, titles dissolve on screen, and letters emerge out of blurred backgrounds into crisp, legible words. Subject matter on the "blue dot" page ranges from an unauthorized postage stamp exhibit to a Manhattan address locator. The web site also functions as the company's own promotional e-brochure for potential customers or clients.

As illustrated in the previous examples, the nature of the organization, subject matter, and relation to audience, shape the requirements for the web site design. These sites present different information, communication goals, and supported activities for users; therefore, the design and visual presentation is unique to each. Each example has a content structure, navigation scheme, interface and graphic presentation style, relative to the nature of the content and project goals. A generic, one-size-fits-all approach is obviously inadequate, just as a generic design for all magazines found today in a bookstore is unthinkable. Opportunities for creativity and exploration have only just begun.

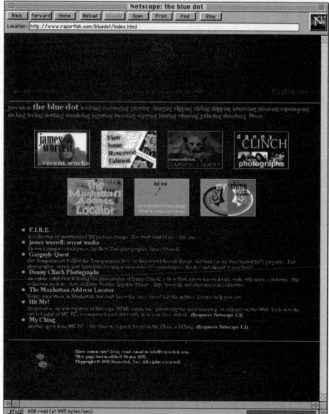

Limitations and Constraints for Web Publishing

Various limitations and constraints should be considered early in the design process. The inherent limitations in web publishing will affect later decisions in the design process. Realizing the unique qualities of web publishing also educates the uninitiated, which helps to avoid costly delays or mistakes made later in the production process. Reworking large amounts of graphic files, for example, negatively impacts the budget and schedule. In all cases, a background knowledge of the various web limitations may save an enormous amount of time, effort, and money.

Designers are accustomed to working within the constraints of the medium, budget, and schedule. Experience enlightens designers in what can and cannot be reproduced through the media at hand. A poster which technically cannot be printed, or a skyscraper which cannot be built, are as good as useless to the general public. The potential consequences may be disastrous, costing hundreds of thousands of dollars to rework a failed product.

Although a disregard of limitations and constraints on the web may not exact an immediate, obvious measurable toll, it can add indirectly to user apprehension, exasperation, and loss of interest in the web site. It may sometimes feel as if the entire web is one big limitation. An understanding of some of the more fundamental issues when designing for the WWW will add greatly to your knowledge base when designing web sites. The rapid pace of development and innovation also demands up-to-the-minute knowledge that enables better results or saves valuable time and effort. The limitations and constraints are broken down into three categories: technical, user-oriented, and content.

It is best to approach web design with this fundamental background knowledge. Since web publishing is a design process, each of the steps has dependencies which greatly affect the final outcome. Being familiar with web limitations and constraints, along with actually spending time surfing current sites, provides an effective starting point for web site design.

UNDERSTANDING TECHNICAL LIMITATIONS AND CONSTRAINTS

As with new technology, it's important to understand characteristics and unique considerations when designing for delivery in this medium. Technical issues include the connection speed, computer platform, display resolution and bit-depth, and browser support.

Connection Speed

Of all the technical limitations that affect web page viewing, connection speed is the biggest factor in performance for users. The performance (and price) difference between a high-end and low-end connection is dramatic. At the low end are home users, most likely using 14.4 or 28.8 modems connected to service providers, who in turn are connected to the Internet. Any connection with a modem below 14.4 is nearly useless for web browsing. Prices for 14.4 modems are continuing to drop. They can be purchased via mail-order catalogs for around $100. This helps to proliferate the 14.4 modem for home users. Often they are bundled with new systems. These systems are targeted for the consumer market and most now include internal modems as standard equipment. The home market segment will most likely continue to grow rapidly in the next few years.

The home user market may or may not be the most important audience for a web site. If it is, inclusion of large images should be avoided from the very early design stage. The larger the image file, the longer it will take to download. Although there are many other technical variables which affect transmission rates (efficiency of TCP stack software, number of simultaneous connections, etc.), a 100K image may require over a minute to display when using a 14.4 connection. Obviously, pages crammed with large graphics will test the patience of any user with a 14.4 modem connection.

Some browsers, such as Netscape, do alleviate some of the pain by supporting continuous document streaming, which displays images as they are transmitted, allowing the user to perform an action before the entire page is decoded and displayed. Prior to this feature, users had to painfully wait to perform an action until the contents of the entire page were transmitted and displayed. Regardless of this feature, scrolling pages filled with large in-line graphics require lengthy delays and should be avoided for the home user/14.4 modem speed audience. Make certain illustration artists and production team members understand the implications of this limitation *before* any conceptual design work (or contract artwork) is done.

Also, keep in mind that the home users may pay their own expenses for connection time (on the net, time *is* money), and will therefore desire rapid access to needed information. Always design for simplicity and directness. The last thing a user wishes to see after waiting a few seconds for a page is a big, useless graphic having no purpose, surrounded by a massive wall of confusing text. Remember that the home user pays a connection fee to the service provider and may also incur a separate subscription fee from individual web sites. Connection fees quickly add up. Quick response time is a major factor for home users; for this reason, image loading is frequently disabled on the user's end.

On the other hand, corporate employees or campus-based university students typically have a higher bandwidth, having either ISDN or direct T1 or T3 connections. Response time is much faster and in-line images do not appear to impede responsiveness. Users having high-end connections may also spend more time on-line, casually browsing, due to subsidized access fees by their company or university. A general idea of the intended audience (home versus working) and connection speed between the two greatly impact the design possibilities of the web site (see Table 2.1).

Regardless of connection type, web publishers should use graphics with care. Reserve images for content that requires illustration or visual description and include the image when it benefits the user. A common technique is to use small thumbnails or miniatures when appropriate, providing optional access to the full-size files if requested by the user. This doesn't force the user to sit through lengthy download periods.

TABLE 2.1 Typical Internet Connection Speed and Audience

Speed	Audience
14.4 modem speed (14,400 bps)	Home users
28.8 modem speed (28,800 bps)	Home users
ISDN connection (128,000 bps)	Business, few home users
T1 connection (1.5 mbps)	Corporation, universities
T3 connection (4.5 mbps)	High end, corporation
Cable lines (10 mbps)	Home users

It is always a good practice to provide a textual link equivalent for any graphic which functions as a link, such as a button, just in case image loading is turned off. When provided, a user is not stranded and can still navigate through the web site. Providing the sizes of images prior to downloading is also good practice, so users have a rough indication of the impending time required for downloading.

Hopefully, bandwidth limitations will begin to vanish as faster connection lines, innovative compression algorithms, and superior browser technology become available. The prices for ISDN line connection continue to drop and phone companies are quite anxious to spread its usage to home users. Pacific Bell, for example, provides various service packages for ISDN connection to business and home users in California. Rates and services are included on their home pages (http:// www.pacbell.com).

One of the most compelling possibilities for high-speed consumer connection is through existing cable lines. At 10 mbps, the sheer speed and power would be unrivaled by current on-line service providers. Tele-Communications, Inc. (TCI) and Kleiner Perkins Caufield & Byers intend to offer nationwide service through their "@home" service (http://www.home.net).

In general, graphics have the most impact on response time for users. The bigger the file size, the longer it takes to receive. Keeping images to practical dimensions is one method to cut down the file size.

Another useful approach is to reduce the colors in an image. For example, a five-inch wide by three-inch high photographic image is 88K at 8-bit, 256 colors, 72 dpi. The same image at 5-bit, 32 color is 66K. The best size reduction is achieved by saving the image as a 33K JPEG file. However, support for in-line JPEG is limited to Netscape Navigator for the moment. Color reduction is easily accomplished in any image processing tool like Adobe Photoshop™ or Equilibrium's De Babelizer™. These are common tools in the multimedia and design disciplines and work extremely well for reducing file sizes through color reduction.

An interesting workaround solution for connection speed limitation is the use of "hybrid" applications which use CD-ROM content for rich, full-screen static graphics, while sending update information (mainly text) through the Internet. Users will typically be unaware of where the information is coming from, either locally off disk or remotely through a service provider. Multiuser games are a possible large application of this approach.

Computer Platform

Computer platform makes a difference to users because certain operations in browsers are processed locally. This includes decoding page layouts and table formatting, tiling backgrounds from GIF texture swatches, and displaying photographs, graphics, and so forth. This also includes the viewing of video, since these files are played locally after network transfer. A page consisting of tables, images, and a background texture is rendered much faster, for example, on a Sun SPARCStation 20 than on a 386 PC. This consideration does impact design decisions, especially if your target audience all use workstation-class systems (designing for an internal corporation) versus Intel 386 personal computers (home users).

If development is on a high-end workstation, it is important to always test your web pages for performance on other less-powerful platforms. In all likelihood, most of your audience will not have high-end workstations. The perceived speed differences in page decoding between high-end and low-end systems is dramatic. Restricting the web page development process to a single powerful platform does not realistically test the pages for response times and page decoding.

Netscape users may increase local performance to some degree by setting the network and disk cache to maximum settings in the user preference options. However, your design should not require or, more importantly, assume users will change their preferences for optimal viewing of web pages.

Display Resolution and Bit-depth

Screen resolution and color bit-depth for a particular computer configuration dramatically alter the visual appearance of web pages. Developing and viewing web pages with a 16- or 24-bit color video display reproduces graphic imagery at its best. Dithering is nearly nonexistent with continuous-tone photography and original colors are reproduced well within expectations. Large flat areas of color look clean and crisp, without any deviation.

However, 16- or 24-bit display capability, though dropping in price, is still not the normal configuration with most users. The 8-bit, 256 color video display is more prevalent and has become the usual standard display configuration sold to most consumers. Users must generally pay extra for an upgrade to enjoy full, true 24-bit color.

Web pages may be designed with a 16- or 24-bit video display, but all pages should be viewed in 8-bit mode to check color, preferably testing images on various platforms. The differences in color palette mapping between systems alter the appearance of graphics which may visually appear suitable on your development platform. Netscape dithers graphics to the color cube found in the target video display, which generally reproduces continuous-tone photography well across platforms. However, areas of solid color may have "speckles" if the computer doesn't have the color which matches the information in the GIF or JPEG image. All of these concerns are nonexistent with 16- or 24-bit color.

On Windows and UNIX versions of Netscape, users may choose a setting in preferences referred to as "Use Closest Color in Color

Cube," which consequently turns dithering off. This causes continuous-tone photographs to have higher contrast with sharp tone differentiation instead of displaying dithered gradations. Flat areas of color remain solid and clean. (Macintosh users do not have this optional setting.)

The variables which influence display color vary from platform video card to settings on a monitor. Two identical systems may display different representations of the same web page, due to variance in monitor contrast and brightness settings. One trade-off in cross-platform information distribution on the web is that exactness in color integrity is difficult to ensure. As with any image processing production task, always try to attain the highest quality original. A bad photo or scan file simply adds to the degradation of image quality, especially when numerous variables are involved.

Resolution varies widely between systems. Identifying the target users' platform may help to determine page size requirements. Designs optimized for 640 x 480 resolution (common VGA and notebook resolution) appear small and undersized on higher resolution displays, commonly used with systems from Silicon Graphics or Sun Microsystems. Likewise, a web page sized comfortably on a 1280 x 1024 high-resolution display will require lengthy vertical and horizontal scrolling by users with VGA or notebook computers. Limiting the horizontal width of your page to 572 pixels or less will ensure full viewing on 640 x 480 displays, as well as on larger screens.

Text in web applications pose an interesting challenge for the visual designer. Exact font specification does not exist in HTML web publishing. Instead, the concept of logical tagging is used. HTML text is tagged in very general formats to ensure cross-platform viewing. For example, headings are tagged as <H1> through <H6>, with the lower numeral representing the largest heading size. However, the exact font cannot be specified by the designer. Therefore, the font used to display text on one system may be Palatino, while appearing in Times Roman on another system, and so forth. Adding to this confusing situation is the capability for users to define a default font of their choice by changing the user preference settings. Figure 2.24

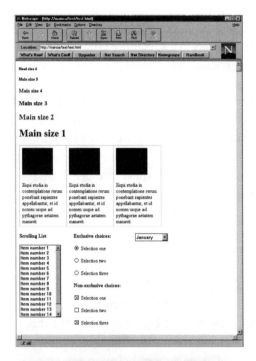

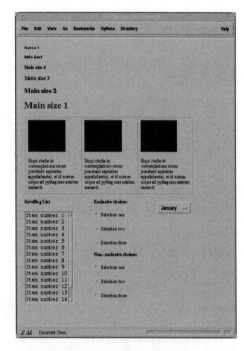

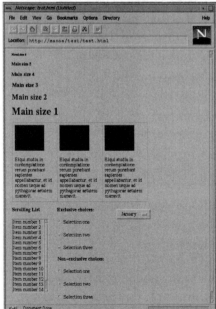

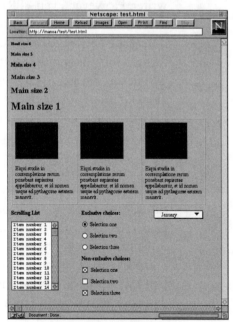

FIGURE 2.24 *Various HTML elements viewed across platforms. Top-left: Windows95, top-right: Sun SparcStation 20, bottom-left: Silicon Graphics Indy, bottom-right: Macintosh.*

shows the same HTML document across various platforms. Notice the differences in text and controls that are specific to the graphical user interface widgets on each particular platform.

HTML does not currently support tabs or effective ways to align text into columns. The implementation of HTML 3.0 tables and alignment extensions found in Netscape, help to alleviate this problem. However, the behavior of HTML text is that it will wrap accordingly as the user resizes the browser pane. Text will therefore break inconsistently and elements will spatially shift depending on the text size and current window aspect ratio, both determined by the user.

The use of the HTML <PRE> tag, which is used to specify fixed-width fonts, allows very limited alignment control, though the method to accomplish this is rather crude and laborious. The benefit is that the text layout will appear somewhat fixed across platforms. Spatial alignment is accomplished by adding blank spaces with the keyboard space bar, much like aligning columns of text using a typewriter. However, even <PRE> type has variances between systems and must also be taken into consideration. Figure 2.25 illustrates the difference between computer platforms displaying the same HTML form, which uses <PRE> text for alignment. The horizontal rule within the form is fixed to an absolute width, which provides a visual comparison for horizontal spacing between platforms. Prior to HTML tables, using the <PRE> tag provided the only means for text alignment into columns, especially for designing legible forms.

The best advice is to always review web pages on various systems and displays prior to release. There are too many platforms, video cards, display resolutions and palettes, and so forth, to ensure complete cross-platform visual consistency for web pages. However, some projects may have a general target platform, for example, home PC users running Microsoft Windows. In such cases, optimization can be made for the chosen environment, simplifying design decisions in relation to platform constraints.

Browser Support

Another important consideration is the type of browser your intended target audience will most likely have. Different browsers offer

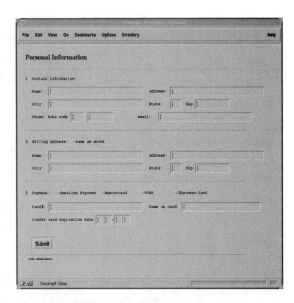

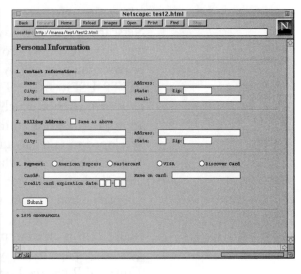

FIGURE 2.25 *Variations in an HTML form viewed across multiple platforms. Top-left: Windows95; top-right: Sun SparcStation 20; bottom-left: Silicon Graphics Indy; bottom-right: Macintosh.*

dramatic differences in page presentation seen by users. Remember, though, that regardless of the browser flavor, connection bandwidth may force users to view pages without loading images, which dramatically alters the page presentation.

Netscape currently offers the richest support for design and layout, and is also the most prevalent Web browser currently used by those on the Web. Advanced layout features include support for tables (multiple column-based layout), frames (separate HTML document windows within a single browser pane), background colors and patterns, client-pull and server-push, support for the Java™ language, and plug-ins, such as playing Macromedia Director™ movies in-line within the browser window. When using these advanced features in a Web site, users who do not use Netscape will not see the effects of this functionality, nor have the same interaction richness as those who do. This is probably why numerous web sites include a tag line recommending "for best viewing, use Netscape" to inform users of the advanced features and capabilities.

It is possible, though time-consuming in the production cycle, to serve specific Web page editions to particular browsers. For example, a Web site may have a version using the full functionality of Netscape, while also having a text-only version for Lynx users, which is a text-only browser. The server is able to determine which browser the user has by what is called an environment variable (HTTP_USER_AGENT) which is provided to the server. A webmaster writes a script which then takes this information and serves the appropriate edition to the user. This allows web sites to be fully developed to take advantage of the rich design capabilities in Netscape Navigator, while allowing viewers of other browsers to see sites which, though not as intricate in layout or as graphics-rich, are still usable and provide the needed information.

Figure 2.26 is an example of two different presentations of the Voyager home page based on the type of browser requesting the URL (Universal Resource Locator, synonymous to the address of the web site). The Netscape version on the left takes advantage of tables for producing a layout matrix, while the non-Netscape version is limited to a single column.

Designing web pages for the corporate setting may not be as troublesome, in that the organization may use a single browser with a site license for all employees. (More importantly, all employees will prob-

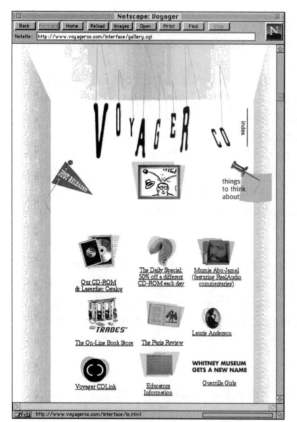
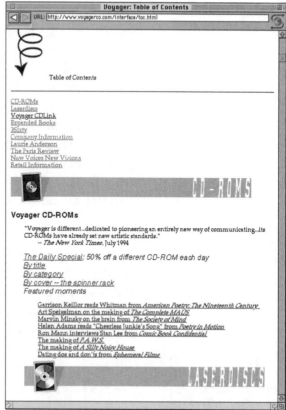

FIGURE 2.26 *Alternate web page presentations (Netscape left, non-Netscape right) for the Voyager web site. (© 1995 Voyager by Trevor Kaufman and Peter Girardi.)*

ably have the same connection speed.) The design of the web page is therefore slanted toward the features available in the particular browser. It's safe to assume, for example, that Netscape employees only view web documents using Netscape, and all internal pages may take advantage of the full features without considering browser dependencies.

To summarize, external web sites must consider a wide variety of users with different flavors of browsers, who may not have the capabilities to effectively view the web pages as intended. However, these individuals may or may not be considered the primary audience. It all depends on the customer base and target market for which the web site is designed. Some of the features of Netscape will briefly be discussed, in order to understand the differences in browser capabilities.

HTML tables, as illustrated in the drawing in Figure 2.27, offer the web publisher similar capabilities found in page layout programs, such as Framemaker or QuarkXPress. A derivative of grid-based graphic design layouts can now be applied to web pages, adding much needed structure to the haphazard, random-like quality of web pages, and providing better control over spatial positioning of content. Tables are especially useful when designing online forms by ensuring alignment and spatial proximity of labels to appropriate input field.

In Netscape, web publishers may specify table and individual column widths by percent or in exact pixel dimensions; in the latter case, they lock the format regardless of browser-page resizing. Additional attribute tags control the placement of graphic elements, form widgets, and typography within each table cell (or column), closely

FIGURE 2.27 *Applying the concept of table-based design to web pages for spatial positioning and arrangements of page elements.*

approximating that familiar multimedia look. For complex data, tables can be nested within tables, each with different attributes for spatial positioning. Extensive examples of table-based layout are in Chapter 5.

Prior to tables, formatting in web pages was nonexistent, as copy and image wrapped from top to bottom in one large page. The entire horizontal width of the display screen can now be partitioned into functional units, which is useful in cases where design is limited to smaller, 640 x 480 screen resolutions. When designed effectively, tables help to eliminate the requirement for scrolling.

Pre-HTML 3.0 browsers do not support tables, and the resulting page appears in a long, single page column, as shown in Figure 2.28. The visual appearance between the pages is dramatic to say the least, affecting the layout and presentation. In some circumstances, textual copy positioned near the associated images is now moved into a location where other elements begin to cause visual interference, contributing to comprehension loss. Note how the page content simply flows in a single, lengthy column down the page.

Many web sites include a message indicating that an HTML 3.0 capable browser is required for "best viewing." However, since table support is an included HTML standard, it seems only a matter of time before all browsers support tables (in one form or another). The user should be informed when the web site takes advantage of HTML 3.0 and pointed to the appropriate vendors for upgrade, purchasing, or downloading of the appropriate viewer. As mentioned earlier, it is possible to produce separate web site pages for different classes of browsers, though time constraints may not allow for this.

Another major feature found in Netscape is the support of "frames." Netscape frames are synonymous to individual, separate documents residing in scrollable or nonscrollable windows, that occupy a specific position within the browser pane. In other words, multiple documents may be viewed within a single browser pane. The frames contain different HTML documents, which may display text, images, video, tables, and so forth. This feature functions like a multi-windowing system within a single browser pane.

FIGURE 2.28 *HTML 2.0 (left) compared with 3.0 (right) layout of the same screen.*

Figure 2.29 illustrates a possible application of Netscape frames. In the left image, frame one functions synonymous to a toolbar and will change the contents of frame five, which is another second-level toolbar. For example, the toolbar in frame one may have general sports categories, such as baseball, football, soccer, hockey, and so forth. The frame five second-level toolbar may provide selection of categories *within* each sport. For example, if basketball is chosen in frame one, frame five may display NBA, College, High School, Local Clubs, and so forth. Selecting a category in frame five may change the contents of frames two, three, and four, displaying the appropriate information for each category within basketball. Making selections in frame three may further change the contents in other frames, as illustrated in the far right example.

Instead of decoding an entire new page with each user selection, only frames which update or reference subsequent HTML pages are decoded and drawn. More importantly, this capability *preserves context* for the user while navigating. Levels of detail can be shown while preserving the global picture of the information. In this example, the user sees the organizational structure throughout the navigational task, as the toolbars provide context for a user's location within the information hierarchy. This is a major improvement over a single, static page which takes over the entire browser pane, destroying all contextual information for users. Multiple viewports into the information space, with rich interactivity and functionality, are possible when implementing frames.

In terms of real-world application, frames have many uses. For example, help can occupy a single frame, without the need to take over the entire browser page. Shopping or commercial web sites may provide multiple views of the same object for comparative analysis. Science or research sites may provide multiple views for the same reason. Work may continue in designated frames, while monitoring dynamic information, such as stock quotes or news feeds, in a separate frame.

Of course, how well this functionality benefits users depends on the proper use and organization of the web site. Using too many frames

FIGURE 2.29
Netscape frames provide multiple documents on a single browser page.

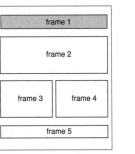
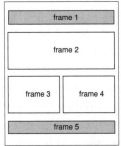
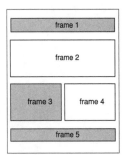

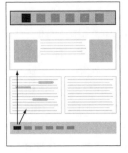
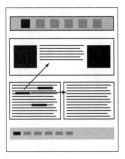

within the browser pane will no doubt be problematic to users, simply because of a perception of more program complexity. Navigating hyperspace with a single browser window is already potentially disorienting. With frames, navigation occurs across separate designated windows within the single browser pane, potentially causing more confusion than before. It becomes even more important to plan the overall organizational framework and user task-flow through the web site when implementing Netscape frames. A well-designed web site, along with common sense, should use frames only when beneficial for user comprehension or to achieve tasks.

An HTML tag is available in Netscape for users who view a page using frames without a frame-based browser. The author must include conventional HTML or explanatory text between this tag, so a non-frame browser may still display page content. The frame's capability is ignored by browsers other than Netscape, so the inclusion of this tag is helpful to those users.

Netscape also allows web authors to alter the color of the browser background. Netscape supports author specification, with hexadecimal values, a different solid background color for pages or underlying textures, which are rendered by wallpapering a small GIF image within the browser pane. These extensions, when used appropriately, can add much needed contextual information, providing users with a stronger sense of place by helping users identify areas within the web site. This helps to counter the "lost in hyperspace" feeling when navigating through indistinct pages in large web sites. However, background colors should always be tested on different displays to ensure color integrity. Also note that this feature may not be available in all browsers, and is not supported in pre-HTML 3.0 browsers. In such cases, the background HTML tags are ignored.

Another interesting capability in Netscape is the support of client-pull and server-push. Until now, web browsers have been asynchronous, requiring a user action to initiate something, such as clicking on a link, submitting a form to a server, or requesting information. With client-pull and server-push, for example, stock quotes, sports scores, traffic conditions, and so forth, could be dynamically updated within specified time intervals, with no user action required. The information would dynamically update, as a new page is automatically seen by the user. Not only text, but individual in-line GIF images can also be dynamically updated. Although far from providing real-time animation, the implications for applications are numerous and range, for example, from pictographic coding for conditions (weather, traffic, surf, etc.) to dynamic advertising. To find more information on dynamic documents, see the Netscape home pages at http://www.netscape.com.

Figure 2.30 is an example of a web site which uses server-push capability in Netscape to produce an interesting introduction to the web page contents. The title page for this section dissolves and emerges from the solid black background, very much like a 35 mm slide show.

FIGURE 2.30 *Examples of server-push in the Razorfish web site. (Designer: Craig Kanarick. Copyright © 1995 Razorfish, Inc. All Rights Reserved. http://www.razorfish.com.)*

The Java™ language from Sun Microsystems, Inc., shifts the web browser from a static, paper-based model to an interactive, behavior-driven environment. The language is intended to create distributed applications across the Internet, and can be viewed on Java-capable browsers, such as Sun Microsystems HotJava™ and Netscape Navigator 2.0.

With the future development of authoring tools and support in Netscape Navigator, Java-based applications are sure to gain in popularity. However, among the non-technical web authors, the need for true WYSIWYG authoring tools is high before there is a widespread adoption of this technology among the general population. Since Java is based on the C++ programming language, it seems unlikely that nontechnical content creators, such as artists or graphic designers, will jump in and immediately author Java "applets" or programs. Extensive on-line documentation on Java is available on the Sun Microsystems, Inc. home page (http://www.sun.com).

Again, not all browsers will support Java; strategies to deal with this fact are necessary if the intended audience includes the widest possible distribution. Testing for browser compatibility, as mentioned earlier, is one such approach.

Other interesting areas of development include VRML (Virtual Reality Modeling Language) and QuickTimeVR™. VRML is a language for describing 3-D multi-user virtual worlds on the web. The WebSpace™ Navigator and WebSpace™ Author by Silicon Graphics (Color Plate 7) are examples of a VRML-capable browser and authoring environment. These products offer intuitive graphical user interfaces to the web authoring process. More detailed information on these products can be found on the Silicon Graphics home pages (http//www.sgi.com).

QuickTime VR uses a 360-degree panoramic photo which finds useful applications for "virtual tours" of architectural landmarks or travel sites. Available for Windows and Macintosh computers, the example in Figure 2.31 is a room-by-room tour of the White House. Users click on a room in the floor plan and launch the QuickTime VR player to pan the view within the selected room. Users may also zoom in and out of the panoramic view.

Another technique available in QuickTime VR is support for object movies, which allows users to examine objects interactively. For example, users in a virtual mall may pick a product up for further examination, rotating the object. The object and panoramic movies can be combined to produce a compelling virtual experience.

As easy-to-use tools become available for this technology and become widely available to artists and designers, useful applications will undoubtedly appear.

Nevertheless, the future of the web is heading toward support for rich interaction and dynamic displays, similar to the type of interaction once only available on CD–ROM-based multimedia products. The web is a volatile area, with technological innovations occurring at lightning speed. An effective way to understand technical limitations and constraints is simply to try to keep informed of developments. Many resources are freely available on the web itself and most technology companies offer documentation or even beta versions of their latest software releases for trial usage. It is well worth the effort to keep abreast of current trends and developments, so as to understand at a higher level, the design directions, possibilities, and opportunities when designing a web site.

LIMITATIONS AND CONSTRAINTS FOR USERS

Users will interact with the web differently than when reading a book or watching television. Considering limitations and constraints from the users point of view will help in designing usable, easy to navigate web sites.

Being "Lost in Hyperspace"

Users can easily become disoriented and lost while browsing web sites precisely because of the Web's main strength: ability to traverse in a nonlinear sequence through information, as seen in Figure 2.32. New users are especially susceptible to the confusion and jarring effect when first navigating a hypertext link. Indeed, in a poorly designed and unstructured web site, a link can throw the user into complete disarray, baffling the user as to how the current page relates to the last and where the next link will go. The Back button on the browser, if known by the user, functions much like bread crumbs left to retrace one's steps through unfamiliar territory.

The main contributor to confusion is that an obvious organizational structure of the information space is lacking. Even within a small

FIGURE 2.32

Being "lost in hyperspace."

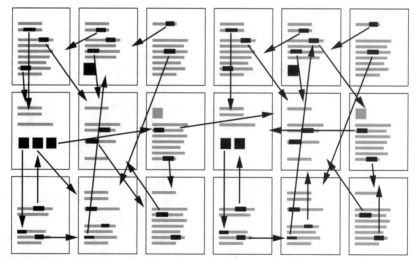

collection of documents within a single web site, users may lose their sense of place and resort to clicking back repeatedly to retrace their steps. Extra effort should be allocated upfront to ensure that users always knows where they are in the web site. Obvious location cues and contextual information must be a designed into the web site for the benefit of users. Various techniques help to alleviate the disorienting "lost in hyperspace" effect, including the design of an obvious structure, providing location cues and identifiers; all are discussed later in detail. Users who enter into a maze-like web site will seldom linger or explore further, but "backout," probably never to return.

Web Surfing versus Reading Printed Materials

Reading a book or magazine is a much different activity then browsing the web. A book is generally linear in its organizational structure and viewed in various physical positions for the reader. The portable nature of print supports reading in a multitude of postures. The content is confined between the outer book covers, with an obvious beginning and end (Figure 2.33). Individuals surfing the web, on the other hand, are more likely sitting at a desk, staring directly into a glowing computer monitor. The surfing activity is more likely to be fragmented and quick, rapidly clicking through pages, restlessly scanning "chunks" of copy and images, then moving on, traversing web sites which dramatically differ in visual quality, colors, metaphors, navigation, and content. The attention span is likely shorter and the desire for needed information great; consequently, the patience for

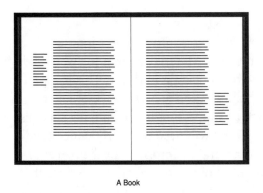

A Book

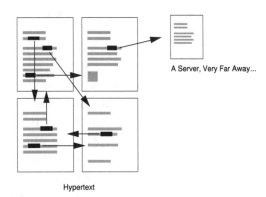

A Server, Very Far Away...

Hypertext

FIGURE 2.33 *Reading a linear book versus hypertext.*

poorly designed web pages is low. Lengthy scrolling windows of endless copy directly imported from printed materials or confusing, crowded pages fail to support this user behavior associated with web surfing. Most important, the true power and advantages of web publishing remain unexploited to their fullest potential and benefit.

To begin with, content should be filtered into smaller units of related content. Information is reduced to concise, conceptually related units, facilitating rapid scanability, with access to greater detail if so desired. This technique is referred to as progressive disclosure or providing levels of granularity for users. This allows users to drill-down to greater detail without having to parse through overly crowded pages of text. Everything cannot fit on a single page; therefore, it is much better to organize the information into smaller, comprehensible chunks.

Another basic reason for brevity and conciseness when designing web pages is simply the difficulty of reading text on the computer screen versus print. The glowing CRT screen tires eyes and the physical posture in sitting upright in a rigid position cannot compare with the flexible reading positions available with printed materials. The end document may be a lengthy research paper or journal retrieved from on-line archives, but the user is still more likely to save the document to the local hard drive or instead, immediately issue a print job. Connection fees from various service providers may also compel users to quickly browse-and-save interesting content, rather than read it on screen.

The same principles used when designing software user interfaces apply to handling text for web pages. Material written for web applications should be straightforward, concise, and direct. This is especially important when the web application is highly task-oriented, requiring user interaction, such as supporting home banking services, shopping, or user registration. Users will need to clearly understand the information required for input and be informed of their success or, if encountering a problem, told how to remedy the situation. If unsuccessful, messages should be constructive, positive, nonjudgmental, and advise the user as to how to correct the situation. The user should be given the steps needed to fulfill the task in a direct, affirmative statement. The example dialogs in Figure 2.34 are useless and in the latter case, fairly threatening. These messages do not communicate any useful information to the user or present a course of action.

When designing fill-in forms, keep labels short and clear. As former colleagues once said, long sentences and help text scattered throughout the window are an admission of failure in the interface.

Users Alter Page Characteristics

Unlike printed or multimedia CD-ROM products, web users may dramatically alter the appearance and layout of web pages by changing attributes in their user preferences file. Graphic designers and publishers who are extremely sensitive to the character and specification of page layouts must now understand the implications and dynamic nature of the web presentation. For example, resizing the browser window border can dramatically reformat text and graphics, wreaking havoc to the original intended layout. In Figure 2.35, a fill-in form provides fields for user input with labels and identification text for each section of the form. The field and labels have been aligned by visually adding spaces with the keyboard space bar, the only method

FIGURE 2.34
Poor choice of wording in dialogs does not provide constructive information to users.

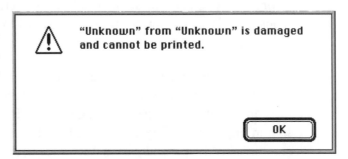

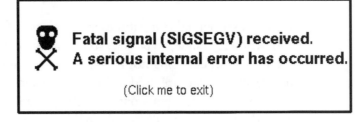

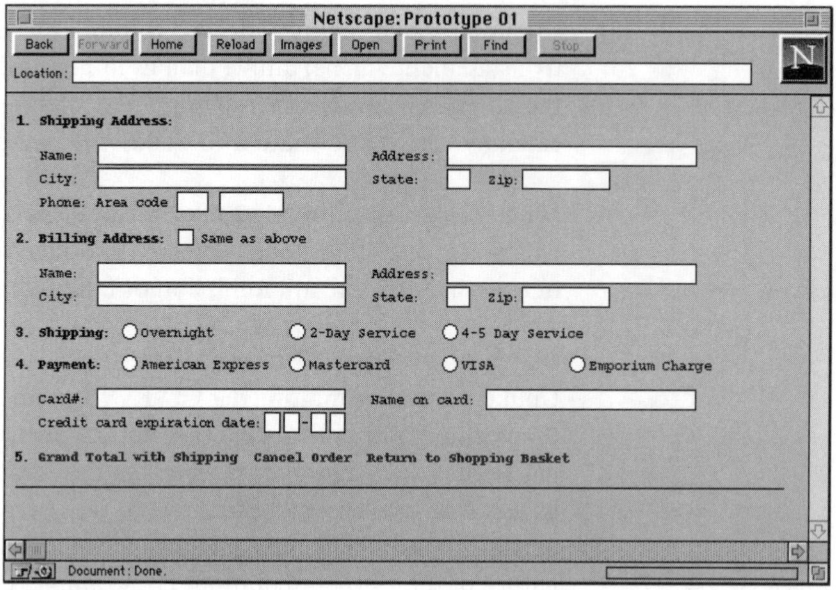

FIGURE 2.35

A fill-in form page with clearly defined sections and labels.

for alignment without using HTML tables. Input fields are sized consistently, in order to induce regularity and visual grouping.

In Figure 2.36, the same form has been resized by changing the aspect ratio of the browser window; the resulting page has become disorganized and cumbersome to fill out properly. Fields are spatially repositioned away from the appropriate labels and the care taken to induce regularity and order is destroyed.

User changes in type sizes also push input fields out of alignment, breaking copy in awkward places, causing disjointed sentence structure, and creating a longer scrolling window for smaller displays, as seen in Figure 2.37. Though still legible, the exact spatial alignment, accomplished by painfully using the space bar and <PRE> HTML tags, has now been shifted off-kilter.

Various user-definable attributes in Netscape affecting page presentation include changing type size, style, background color, link color, and of course, choosing not to load images, among others. Publishers and designers who are used to locking in exacting design specifications and assuming total control of the presentation should understand the implications of user-definable attributes to the final presentation. Don't expect web pages to look exactly as they appear on the single development platform. Always review designs on as many different hardware configurations as possible.

When using tables in Netscape, absolute pixel dimensions fix column widths and can be used when the information requires positioning elements in proximity to each other. For example, the page in Figure 2.38 retains its layout regardless of browser window resizing. Relationship between image and text is ensured. In Figure 2.39, the tables do not use absolute pixel dimension and stretch horizontally to fill the browser window. In very general terms, absolute pixel width for tables is useful when the content of the page is controllable and fixed—for example, for tables of contents or icon arrays. When the amount of information is undetermined—for example, a document returned from a search query—it is better to avoid the constraints of applying absolute table widths. This provides more viewing flexibility for the text, attributes of which are mainly user-definable anyway.

FIGURE 2.36

The same form in Figure 2.35 has now been resized by changing the aspect ratio of the browser window, causing a re-ragging of input fields and copy.

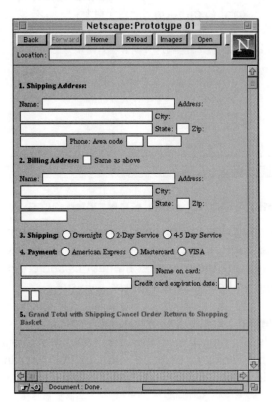

LIMITATIONS AND CONSTRAINTS WITH CONTENT

Preparing content for distribution on the web involves issues such as
access control, charging for information, and copyright infringement.
Considering these content limitations and constraints impacts the
design and organization of the web site.

Internal versus External Audience

Goals and objectives may differ when providing information to an
internal versus an external audience. With traditional printed communications, large corporations usually provide an external (public)

and internal (employee-only) printed company magazine. In such cases, the external piece usually has an emphasis on public relations, with potential shareholders included in the audience definition. Budget requirements are sometimes higher and production teams are usually larger. Internal corporate communications focus more on the everyday workings of the organization and its component parts, departments, employee-specific activities and programs. In both instances, the intended audience and communication goal differ, thus influencing the finished product.

Designing a webspace for the corporate enterprise has similar requirements in differentiating between the external and internal audience. Additional information may be provided on the internal

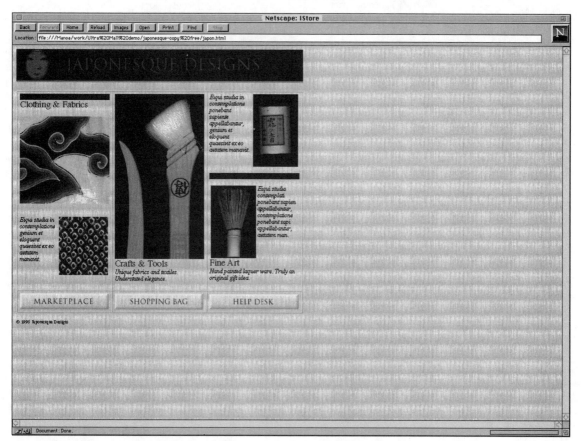

FIGURE 2.38 *Resizing a browser window with a table using exact pixel widths.*

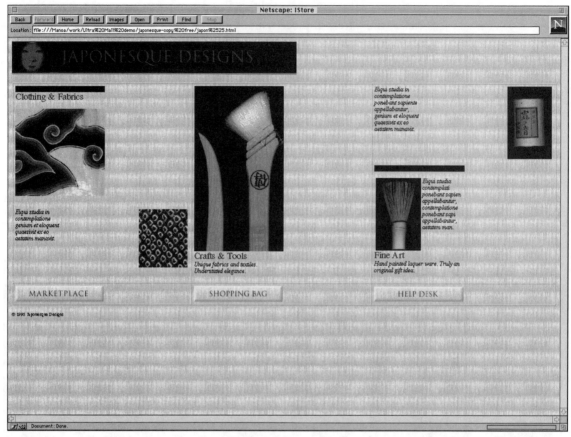

FIGURE 2.39 *Resizing browser with a table using percentage.*

server which must remain inaccessible to the general public. The most common method of assuring security for the corporate enterprise is to establish a proxy server outside the firewall, while developing internal, company-only accessible information on an internal server behind the so-called firewall. It is also possible to establish access control on a single server, requiring users to register and login in order to gain access. This may be the case even within the internal corporate enterprise. Information specific to certain groups within the organization—for example, financial data—may be accessible only to those within the finance department.

The different needs and requirements between an internal versus external server for the corporate enterprise are great and have immediate implications on what can and cannot be included in the web sites. Obvious general areas of differentiation, such as proprietary information, research, or advanced product development, will most likely not be included in the external server. Internal information will probably include most information previously distributed through print, such as benefits and program enrollment, organizational charts, employee directory, recreational activities, and so forth. Individual employee home pages may also be included internally as well as externally. Certain information is therefore included in a web site based on the particular audience for which it is intended.

Charging for Information

Commercial applications on the web may include the capability of charging users fees for information access. Certain information or services may require various charging models, implementing one or a combination of the following: flat-fee, hourly-fee, metered access, and per-document subscription. In the flat-fee model, users are given access to the service for a monthly charge, much like current on-line services. An additional hourly fee, ranging from $2 to $5 per hour, may be charged. This charge is usually added after the user exceeds a minimal number of hours per month. Metered access charges the user a set amount for each hit the user accesses information. For example, a news service may charge $.50 for each article access. Per-document subscription is synonymous with a real-world book store, where documents are purchased outright and users receive unlimited access.

A free browsing area is usually provided, so as not to lock out the curious potential customer. A 30-day trial offer or partitioning certain free-zones may also be defined within the information space. Information spaces which require access fees need additional effort in the planning and implementation of pages to provide details to users, such as pricing options, user registration, password login provision, reviewing account status, and error detection.

Access control-based services must handle a variety of user scenarios and conditions. For example, users with knowledge of the URL who attempt to enter a section of the information space under access control must be informed that they do not have access privileges to the information. Users should be given the choice to subscribe or exit the system, or hopefully be given more information as to what they are expected to receive for their money.

Different member classes may require various fees. For example, a service provider may have levels of service defined as Gold, Silver, or Bronze, with users paying a premium for the Gold service, which entitles them to full access or special services, while the Bronze service is cheaper with minimal advanced functionality. Member classes may also be defined by the existing member classes found in the organization itself. For example, corporate members may pay a higher fee and receive different information, than individual members in a professional society or membership institution.

A current, growing trend is to provide a totally free Web site, with revenue generated solely by advertisements using a graphic banner, or perhaps an animation, audio, or video commercials embedded into the browser page. This avoids the burdensome task for users to complete the registration process for multiple Web sites.

Copyright

It's important to assure copyright release on all content included in a web site. Stock photography and clip-art resources generally have liberal reproduction policies for print; however, some explicitly prohibit the posting of their images on the net. The usage policy (*read the fine print*) is usually unambiguous and clear. This is true with most popular stock image CD-ROM resources. Be advised that although the advertisement may clearly indicate "Royalty Free," this policy is usually in reference to printed materials and does not extend to posting images on the Internet. If there are any questions or doubts, contact the legal representatives at the source and verify usage restrictions. It is well worth the trouble to consult their legal representatives if any questions do exist.

Try to obtain a written release form for any images included in your site. Contract photographers, illustrators, or artists will most likely place conditions on the use of their work within the confines of the

web site and charge fees accordingly. The web site is liable for what
it publishes and will be held responsible if copyright protected work
is published. Make sure your content sources create original material
that can be published.

Of course, it only takes a few seconds to copy an image out onto a
local hard drive; artists and designers should be aware of this.
Netscape is particularly well-endowed for users copying out images
to their local disk, as illustrated in the handy pop-up menu in Figure
2.40. A nifty logotype or graphic image will be copied, and probably
end up on someone's home page somewhere. A healthier attitude to
have is to assume your graphic will be "saved as" by someone out
on the net, as it is nearly impossible to enforce a totally secure copyright.

When permission is given for on-line inclusion of photography or
illustrations, certain restrictions may be enforced for web reproduction. For example, a size limitation may be imposed by the agency.
For the WorldCupUSA94 server, participating team and action photography supplied from the sport photographic source could not

FIGURE 2.40
*Copying images found
on the web is one
click away.*

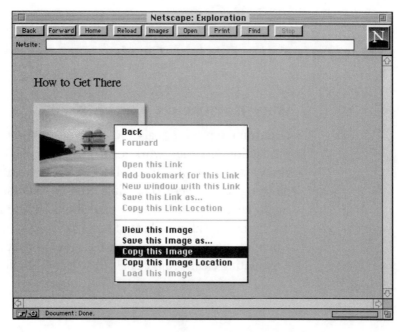

exceed a 100K size limit. GIF and JPEG formats compress well, and most of the imagery posted remained well below this stated limitation.

For rapid prototyping and creating demos, stock image catalogs on CD–ROM are invaluable. The Photodisc™ series includes a three-ring binder with printed thumbnails of all images available in their CD–ROM products. The accompanying CD–ROM sampler has images from a variety of subject categories, including the ability to search with specific keywords. For visual designers and multimedia authors, this resource is invaluable for client presentations and rapid prototyping.

Along with the hundreds of books available today covering the web, there are numerous publications which are dedicated to copyright protection. A few are mentioned in the bibliography of this book for further reference. Also, the Copyright Clearance Center (508-750-8400), Interactive Multimedia Association (410-626-1380) and Software Publishers Association (202-452-1600) may provide additional information regarding copyright issues.

Determine the Project Goals

WHY ESTABLISH A WEB SITE?

Determining project goals and objectives are initial steps which precede production or design work for the web site. An overall project goal clearly states the fundamental reason for establishing a web presence, directing further activities, while keeping the design focused toward a single, central goal. A project plan should be communicated and understood by all members of the development team. This establishes a tangible goal for everyone on the development team to work toward. Articulating clear project goals from the beginning also aids in removing ambiguity when determining project functionality and content for inclusion in the web site.

First, however, there should exist a recognized *need* by the organization or business for establishing a web presence. The fundamental question is: "Why provide a web site?" A clear reason may at first seem obscure, due to ill-formed logic—for example, motivated by a competitor's current web offering and, therefore, feeling the pressure to get on at all cost. In this early stage of the web, the lure to establish a web site for the sake of its own existence is great. Unfortunately, the result usually provides a less than useful experience for users, due to a lack of planning and clarity in its primary role and function.

Once project goals and objectives are determined, appropriate content and functionality that support these stated objectives are identified. Information should always be considered for inclusion in a web site by its relevancy to the overall project objectives and goals. Clear articulation of objectives early in the design process enables the development team to trim extraneous, irrelevant information from the proposed content listing and also functions as a constant filtering checkpoint. Attention is focused on the real information needed by the users or activities which support users' tasks. Sheer information quantity should never be the goal of a web site. Less is more—when it's exactly what the user needs.

Table 2.2 lists various web site applications and the high-level goals which define the major project objectives. Though greatly simplified, the listing illustrates clear goals within each category, which should be articulated to all members of the development team.

Goals and objectives vary greatly depending on the nature of the web site. Possible web applications are limitless; with future advanced features and capabilities they will afford greater potential for an enriching user experience. However, attention should focus first on the user, not features or functionality.

TABLE 2.2 Web Site Applications and Their Goals

Category	Example Project Goals
Education	• Increase student involvement in all subjects and activities • Support distributed student collaboration and exchange among schools • Host "virtual" science fairs, field trips, expeditions, etc. • Support international "virtual" student exchange
Professional Organization	• Increase membership by reaching areas geographically dispersed • Reduce mailing expenses on membership materials, publications • Support on-line registration, membership renewal, purchasing publications • Function as main communication medium for all chapters
Corporation/ Business	• Augment corporate collateral communication strategy • Provide investment, financial information for shareholders • Publish company magazine, newsletter • Provide open forum for customer feedback, suggestions, support
Merchant	• Establish "virtual" storefront, expand name recognition • Provide product and product information • Support purchasing of goods on-line • Provide access to partner businesses

DETERMINE THE PRIMARY AUDIENCE

Web applications will typically be relevant to a certain segment of the population. For example, a web site for a computer company will no doubt be of interest to its current customer base and others interested in technology, including the competition. Based on this profile, this web site provides the appropriate information (such as product specs, announcements, etc.) and activities (tech support via email, user bulletin boards and chat, etc.) for the intended audience. The many television stations available on cable are an example of content directed towards a particular audience, whose interests may be sports, cooking, animals and nature, politics, comedy, and so forth. Magazines on a shelf display a wide range of subject matter, with the content, structure, visual presentation, and style intended to satisfy a particular reader audience. In short, the message is shaped toward the target user.

For a web site, a similar situation exists. Index resources, such as Yahoo, quickly illustrate the breadth of subject matter currently available on the web. With so much information overloading users, it is even more critical to communicate in an economic, streamlined manner, as directly and clearly as possible to the intended user. An ambiguous, tentative web site, catering to too many interests or trying to "do too much," overwhelms users, loosing focus, clarity, and understandability.

Nothing can take the place of careful planning and forethought. Time and attention to review existing web sites, becoming familiar with the limitations and constraints of the web, and thinking about the project before rushing into the web design activity will benefit the end user. From a practical and economical perspective, the user is, after all, the customer who will largely determine the success or failure of the web site. Above all, keep it simple.

The greater effort and longer time dedicated to the development of the structure pays off in the end because it makes detail work so much easier.

Karl Gerstner, *Compendium for Literates, A System of Writing*

3

DESIGNING THE ORGANIZATIONAL FRAMEWORK

A large part of a designer's job is to make the complex understandable. Achieving understandability requires the communications designer to *organize* and *structure* information *before* making decisions which determine the exact visual style or presentation. The source content may arrive in a multitude of formats from different sources, with the designer's challenge to organize, prioritize, and then integrate the components into a cohesive communication design solution. An overall plan must be developed first, which then guides the design through the later production stage. Thus, this important phase in the design process determines the visual presentation and style, communicating the information in an organized, cohesive manner.

Web sites may differ greatly in degrees of required user interaction. A research document repository may only require a few user tasks, such as filling in a search query window to subsequently access needed documents. Other web applications, such as home banking, shopping, or financial investment, require specific interaction sequences, as the user interacts with the system, providing input for processing. It is imperative, especially in highly interactive web applications, that the organizational framework supports the intended functionality, based on identified user tasks, goals, and needs.

The iterative design process begins with the overall high-level organization before focusing on page details. Repetitive cycles of "rough" visualization followed by further refinement ensures that the design attained is the most appropriate solution possible. The working process is similar to an architect planning a building. The architect must clearly understand the needs of the public, the constraints of materials, characteristics of the building site, and overall functional requirements of the project. Most importantly, the architect must take into account the human aspect of the building structure and ensure that the scale and overall design fit the requirements of the future inhabitants. The architect then later develops, refines, and evaluates drawings; in the end, these evolve into an exacting final blueprint that meticulously specifies the structure and visual character.

All possible uses, activities, and situations must be anticipated and accommodated by the architect, planned for inclusion in the structure, and specified through the blueprint. Sometimes, the plan calls for an extensible architecture to allow further expansion and development. The extensive planning and exacting specifications found in the architect's blueprint precedes the physical activity of construction. Without a blueprint, there is no plan and no building.

Of course, an architect's working process is quite a bit more complex than previously described, but the analogy should illustrate the importance and advantages in using a design process and careful planning to reach the final goals of a project. Similarly, the web designer of large-scale information spaces needs to *pre-visualize* the web site, organizing the information or activities into an obvious, navigable structure for the user. Like an architect's blueprint, the web designer progresses through repeated stages of sketching and visualization which, in the end, become the organizational framework for the virtual information space. The framework functions as the blueprint, shaping the information space and all later steps in the design process. This includes the visual design and style considerations, which should communicate an obvious framework to the user.

There are many examples of effective organizational structures in the real world which function much the same way as an organizational framework designed for the web. A well-designed floor plan, for example, allows individuals to locate an office or room easily. Corridors and hallways are designed to provide direct access to a given destination. Effective signage throughout the building floor plan is positioned in needed, obvious locations to reinforce an individual's place in the context of the entire space. If needed, viewing a floor plan map with the familiar dot and "You are here" designation provides an *overview* when lost or confused. In some cases, floors within the building site may even use color or other visual attributes to clearly differentiate one level from another.

The web is frequently referred to as the "information highway." The use of clear highway signs illustrates how important it is to know where one is going. These signs are taken for granted by all of us, but could you ever imagine a road trip without signs or maps to aid in navigation? Interchange exit numbering provides needed orienta-

FIGURE 3.1

Highway exit numbering and signage for driver orientation.

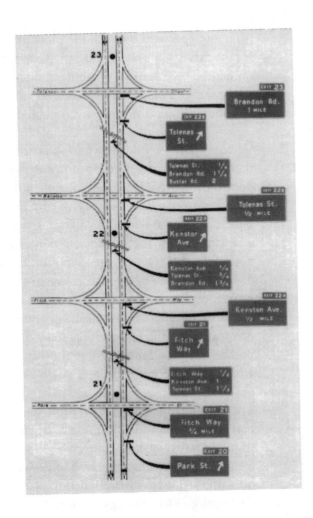

tion information to drivers, guiding traffic through a maze of inter-connected highways and off-ramps (Figure 3.1).

These techniques are useful to remember when designing a large-scale web site. Inadequate visual cues and convoluted pathways through the information space contribute most to that feeling of disorientation while browsing the web, a common experience referred to as being "lost in hyperspace." In such cases, the user usually resorts to the Back button on the browser window and simply backs out of the web site, perhaps never to enter again.

The Web Organizational Framework

The fundamental purpose of an organizational framework for web applications is to provide the user with a clear, obvious structure when traversing the information space. An obvious framework plays a substantial role in the overall usability, efficiency, and usefulness of the web site and is an integral part of the web design process; it is worked on *before* any graphics are produced or HTML pages authored. Rushing into page design without an overall framework is much like contractors attempting to build a house without a blueprint. Without a clear organizational framework, users are potentially confronted with an unusable mess of "spaghetti documents" (Foss 1988), with numerous links to unrelated information. More importantly, a user's goal remains unfulfilled and the navigational mess and unintelligible relationships between web pages will grow tiresome to navigate.

The failure to establish logical relationships between information usually translates into pages with too many unrelated choices confronting the user. Often, the advantages of hypertext linking are misunderstood, interpreted as a means to link *anytime* from *anywhere* to *anything*. Inserting links for the sake of linking is a common trait of the web novice. Links are quickly established without careful planning or forethought, simply because it can be done.

STRUCTURING THE INFORMATION SPACE

Amateurish hyperdocuments are a disaster.
James Martin, *Hyperdocuments and How to Create Them*

Designing a clear organizational framework not only accommodates all information types, project needs, and requirements, but also is flexible enough for continual extension or updating. The benefits of using a clear structure for hypertext is well documented in research papers and conference proceedings. In fact, a lack of structure has been proven to actually inhibit usability and make it difficult for users to find the information they need. The basic conclusion from many researchers in the hypertext community acknowledges the advantages of an explicit structure which adds to usability (Glushko 1989; Foss 1988; Conk 1987). "Our own experience and that of other hypertext designers has shown that usability is enhanced by the use of the explicit structure of documents . . ." (Glushko 1989).

Even when confronted with ambiguity in the ways one could classify elements, a chosen organization structure provides a better solution than none at all. For example, four objects—football, baseball, lemon, orange—can be structured into categories based either on shape or origin—whether manufactured or natural (Ande 1965). Nevertheless, humans tend to think in terms of hierarchy and will attempt to find meaning and organization in everyday life. "The insight for hypermedia is that a hyperbase structured as a set of distinguishable hierarchies will offer navigational and other cognitive benefits that an equally complex system of undifferentiated links does not . . ." (Paranuk 1989).

Indistinct pages which all look alike provide a vague and weak model of the information space for users. One may begin to ask "Where did I come from?" "How did I get here?" or "How do I get back?" Such deliberations, while traversing a web site, are symptoms of an unclear organizational framework. When the structure is obvious, a "sense of place" is also reinforced and communicated to users. The organizational framework defines a precedence and hierarchy of information that communicates recognizable levels of information.

In the design process, navigational pathways to logical groupings of content throughout the framework are defined and tested early in the development stage. Depending on the project goals, content, and nature of the web site, a suitable structure is designed and can be tested through stages of sketches and prototypes. The required user navigation, interaction sequences, and task-flow to fulfill specific goals are verified and tested. Early prototyping prescribed in the design methodology allows for modifications and refinement, before final HTML or graphic production begins.

In terms of usability, clear navigational pathways defined in a structure add much needed *predictability* to the user's flow through the web site. The user can begin to formulate a model of what comes next or where the user has come from. The avenues and pathways through the information space lead to well-defined destinations with clear markings and location cues.

ADDING LINKS TO THE STRUCTURE

The main advantage of hypertext linking is that it supports quick traversal across the information structure to related or needed information. Information may therefore be accessed from multiple locations (or hierarchies) within the organizational framework. This presents a major challenge to the web designer: determining a precedence to provide needed, useful links or functionality, without overloading the page with subordinate functionality and avoiding the disorientation caused by a sudden jump to a different location.

Focusing on the specific user's task and the needed information should always be a determinate to what links and functionality are provided on a web page. Excessive choices clearly inhibits usability and demands a heavy cognitive load for the user in order to figure out what actions correspond to the appropriate controls. Overusing links which are unrelated to the current topic or concept, presents unnecessary diversions to the user and leads to useless trips to irrelevant information. The need for concise wording and brevity when authoring documents to be read on the computer screen correlates with the need to carefully assign hypertext links. The basic concept or thought is focused and direct; the associated information is also direct, clearly related, and useful.

In task-oriented web sites which require extensive user interaction, the primary focus should be on the organization of functionality within the interaction sequence. User tasks are identified and mapped to various interface controls, in order to ensure that system supports the user's task-flow through specific actions. Clear, explicit responses and feedback are also identified and provided.

FIGURE 3.2

A page with a confusing array of form buttons.

FIGURE 3.2

A page with a confusing array of form buttons.

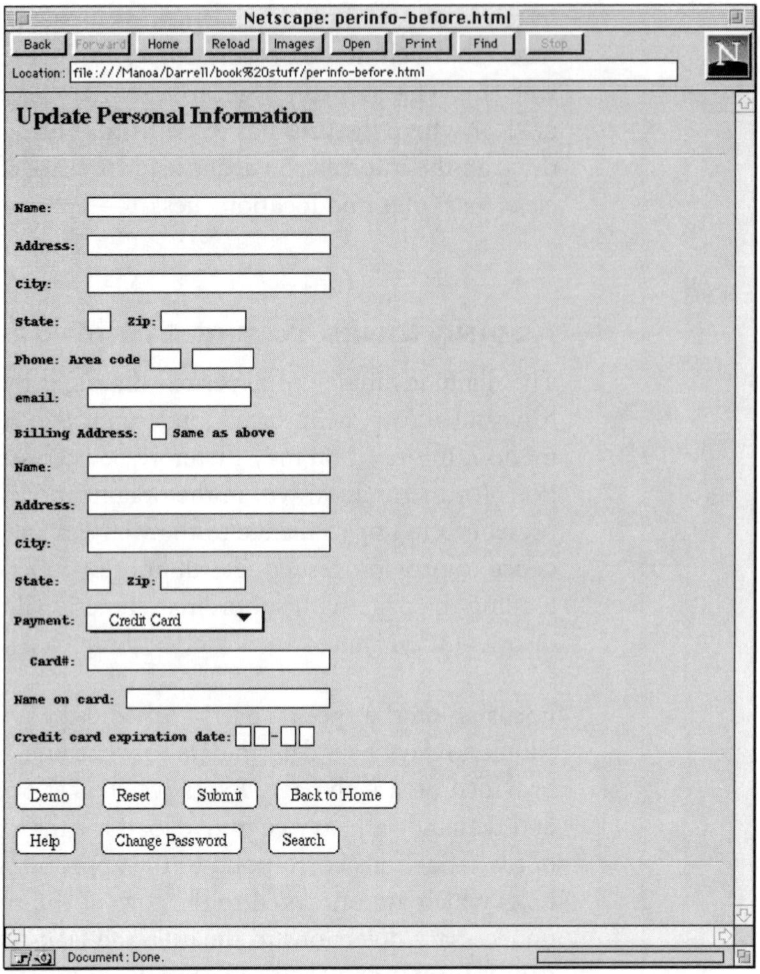

In Figure 3.2, the design of a simple form presents a confusing array of choices for the user near the bottom of the page. There are too many form buttons, most of which are unnecessary and unrelated to the user's current task: filling out then submitting a registration form. An attempt to provide more functionality than is needed (and unrelated to the task) compromises usability. Notice the confusing mixture of buttons, some of which send data to the server based on user input, while other buttons function simply to facilitate navigation and have nothing to do with processing the data in the input fields themselves. For example, the need to initiate a Search while filling out personal information does not make sense, especially when this functionality is reserved only for users who have already registered.

In Figure 3.2, the page buttons are included in a random manner, rather than based on what a user wants to do. The user's primary task is to simply fill-in and submit the form, in order to receive access to a particular service. The buttons in Figure 3.2, however, offer needless functionality within the context of the user's activity.

The redesign of the personal information page is shown in Figure 3.3. The input fields have been grouped and ordered in a logical, top-down format. Bold headings delineate the different groupings of required information. Most importantly, at a higher level, the organizational framework has been reorganized, so the density of buttons is reduced. The single form button is intentional: The primary action of the user is to fill in then submit the form. Navigation to other logical destinations from the form is facilitated through plain hypertext links, explicitly separated from the submit button, below a horizontal rule.

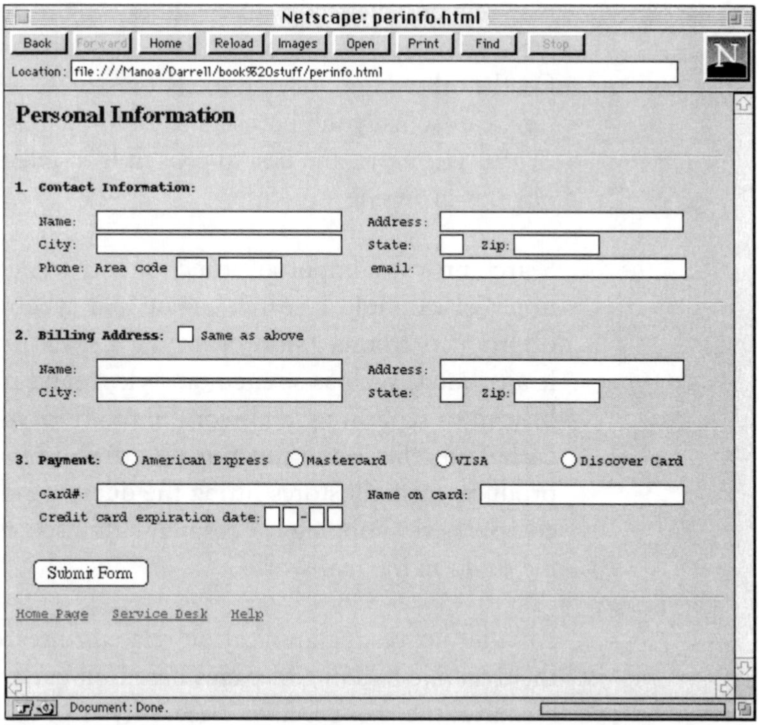

FIGURE 3.3

Redesign, focusing on the primary user task.

Aside from user task analysis, common sense by the web designer is also a factor in determining when to provide a navigation traversal across (or out of) the structure. Again, any link traversal should *always* make sense and be associated with the information. A link should never distract the user from the original thought or concept, but augment or add a measure of utility to the task.

INTEGRATING SEARCH AND PERSONAL PREFERENCES

In large-scale information spaces, search technology complements the organizational framework and should be included in the overall design. Search engine technology provides the necessary means to find documents based on specific user queries, such as date, keywords, or author. It would be inconceivable not to use search for locating a specific research paper in a database containing hundreds of thousands of documents. The main advantage of search technology is that it delivers specific information *to the user*, instead of the user browsing coarse-grained hierarchies to locate it. Although a user in this case may rely on an effective search query engine for document retrieval, the search capability should be an addition to the browsing structure. On the other hand, relying solely on search, without an explicit structure, can actually inhibit users from finding information (Glushko 1989). Therefore, the best approach is to integrate search within an obvious browsing structure.

Search provides important functionality to nearly any web application. For example, a search engine in a cybermall may retrieve a list of products from all stores carrying a specific product, having specific attributes, such as size, color, style, brand name, and price-range. Instead of replicating real-world limitations by forcing users to visit each store, the search functionality does all the leg-work, returning products from all stores fitting the query conditions. In one sense, comparative shopping is possible within seconds, something impossible to do in the real world.

Another interesting application related to search-like functionality is the dynamic building of pages based on personal preferences. In this scenario, the user specifies preferences from a predefined set of crite-

FIGURE 3.4

Selecting areas of interest from a predefined list.

ria supplied from the service provider—for example, general areas of interest in a geographical-natural science on-line magazine (Figure 3.4). Based on user selections, a personal home page is dynamically updated upon entry into the web site, as seen in Figure 3.5.

This feature allows the user to narrow the focus to specific interests, and facilitates direct access to the information fitting the query. The system builds links on the personal page to the information the user finds interesting, which is dispersed throughout the organizational framework. Therefore, the user can access specific areas of interests, rather than having to look for them within the browsing structure.

Such functionality should be planned into the project ahead of time. The development team must understand the technical and functional aspects of the project before implementation begins. Again, the importance of cross-disciplinary collaboration helps in this regard. The organizational framework, or web blueprint, operates as a plan for the development team, mapping out all necessary functionality and information in the web site.

FIGURE 3.5

*The personal page
generated by the
selections made in
Figure 3.4.*

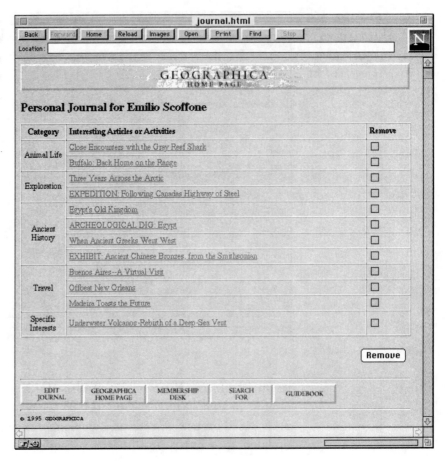

Grouping Content and Activities

Once the project goals and objectives are established, the appropriate content and range of supported activities are evaluated. From this stage, the web development team continues through stages of evaluation and grouping of information into logical, related categories. The steps include the grouping of information, applying hierarchy and precedence among and within each group, and providing the necessary navigation and support for users to flow through the web site.

The example in Figure 3.6 is the listing of content and activities determined for the WorldCupUSA94 web server. The web development team began with a brainstorming session to identify the content which would support the target user (the soccer fan) to find the most important information (scores, schedules, and team information, etc.). All possible content and activities are listed initially, and will be further evaluated individually for relevance and importance.

As each item is further evaluated, certain relationships between information topics begin to group together into related categories. For example, information having to do specifically with the teams or city hosting the event is grouped together. The listing is simplified and reduced to a smaller subset of information by finding relationships common across topics. Throughout the production process, certain developments outside the control of the team may quickly eliminate items from the proposed service structure. For example, various copyright issues may eliminate content from the listing immediately.

FIGURE 3.6

Initial content and activities listed for the WorldCupUSA94 server.

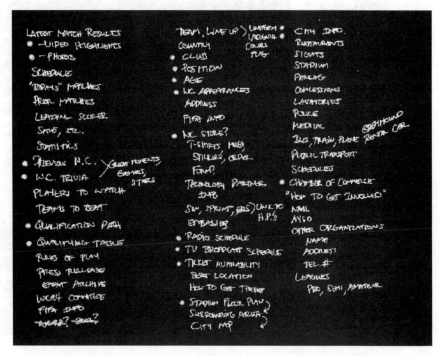

Practical, realistic consideration of the schedule also eliminates certain items which may not be attainable before the event. The main focus is to order elements into groups and subgroups, so related information is logically located together, rather than dispersed randomly throughout the web site.

Five to six general categories of information begin to emerge from the once random listing and can be clearly seen in Figure 3.7. From initial meetings and collaboration of the development team, the information required to begin sketches of the organizational framework is now available.

In the case of a server providing information on a specific sport, the primary user would naturally be a fan of the sport. From this point of view (the soccer fan), the latest daily match results and standings would appear to be the most important information. Therefore, this information is the highest in precedence and importance. All related

FIGURE 3.7
Refined content listing for the World CupUSA94 server.

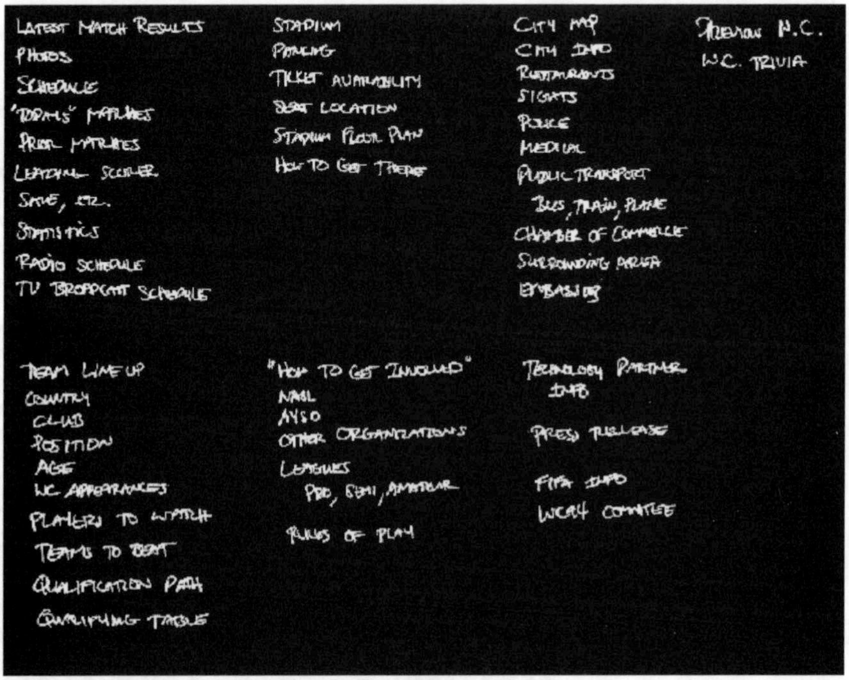

information having to do with match results is therefore grouped into this category. This becomes the first and most prominent grouping identified, *Results and Standings.*

This group also provides some interesting possibilities for web publishing. Posting daily match results and standings during the 26 days of the tournament is a dynamic activity and the service must provide the latest information as soon as it becomes available. That differentiates this group from the others containing static information prepared prior to the event.

The second grouping consists of information having to do with the physical stadium sites for the tournament, a total of nine game site venues located in North America. Related within this category are the schedule for each stadium, floor plan, location and proximity to downtown, transportation to and from, and stadium facts. This information is mainly static and can be prepared well in advance in the production stage prior to the event. This group is relatively subordinate to the information in group one. This second grouping is defined as *Game Sites and Schedules.*

The third group identified is information about the teams participating in the sporting event. Aside from the latest scores and results, the inclusion of team information is relatively important to the fan. This information is also largely static and does not require any dynamic updating. In relation to the primary audience, this information is quite important. In early questionnaires and feedback received via email, requests were made for team photos. Related information for each team, including past record and qualification path, naturally group within this category. This third group is defined as *Participating Teams.*

The fourth group is information about the each of the nine U.S. cities hosting the event. Separate from the stadium information in group two, this information category functions as light-weight travel books about the cities, providing sight-seeing, transportation, hotel and accommodation, and dining information. Since many people from around the world attend this international event, city information seems well suited for tourists planning holidays in these specific cities. The fourth grouping is defined as *Host City Information*.

Finally, the fifth grouping consists mainly of background information about the sport of soccer, the event itself, organizers, technology partners, and sponsors. This group is clearly subordinate to all other information types, but remains complementary to the total web server project. Individuals may be interested in the technology used during the event or perhaps would like to learn the rules of the game of soccer. This information is clearly static, requiring no maintenance during the event. The fifth grouping is defined as *World Cup Information*.

Table 3.1 lists the categories of major information topics for inclusion in the web site. Although subject matter and content differ when designing any web site, the general working methodology demonstrated here is transferable and applicable to any web site project. The process of determining content in relation to user followed by the conscious grouping of information into related categories, paves the way toward the design of an effective organizational framework. These necessary steps are an integral part of the entire design process, and greatly influence later stages in the application of visual design techniques to every page.

The working process includes stages of refinement during which various grouping organizations should be explored. Like any design problem, multiple solutions are possible, but only one (hopefully the most appropriate and optimal for users) can be chosen for final implementation. It is far easier to alter or edit the information structure on paper, rather than on a premature web site, with link dependencies established. In the latter case, the time investment in developing a premature web site is harder to throw out, as the temptation and urge is to cling to whatever design has already been completed in order to save time.

Category descriptions are general, but specific enough to contain the main objectives satisfying user requirements for the needed information. Later steps will break the information down further into smaller, specific units. Opportunities for logical cross-linking and relationships will be identified and documented as the design process continues into the next phase of sketching out the organizational framework structure.

TABLE 3.1 Main Information Groupings for the WorldCup USA 94 Server

Main Groupings	Information Subgroup Descriptions	Type
1. Results and Standings	• Latest match results	Dynamic
	• Current standings	Dynamic
	• Previous match results	Dynamic
	• Statistics	Dynamic
2. Game Sites/Schedules	• Stadium floor plan, seating information	Static
	• Parking information	Static
	• Directions and location	Static
	• Match times and dates at venue	Static
3. Participating Teams	• Team information	Static
	• Team photo	Static
	• Player identification	Static
	• Qualification path	Static
4. Host City Information	• Areas of interest	Static
	• Accommodations	Static
	• Dining and food	Static
	• Map of city, directions to venue	Static
	• Transportation	Static
	• Travel agents	Static
5. WC94 Information	• WC94 background information	Static
	• History book	Static
	• Rules of the game	Static
	• Technology overview	Static

Using Hierarchies to Organize Groups

The concept of hierarchies is familiar to most people, due to their ubiquitous nature in everyday life. Without consciously knowing it, we absorb information in units which are intentionally structured, organized, and ordered into subcomponents. The human eye is able to quickly scan at a higher level and progress further into detail and related information through the use of hierarchies. In complex, information-intensive projects, the need for developing hierarchies is a prerequisite to further understanding.

Using hierarchy in graphic design facilitates better understanding and quick comprehension. The traffic signage in Figure 3.8 uses hierarchy to communicate important information to the driver, within the time duration of a few seconds. The human eye scans the most dominant sign elements, then proceeds to read the smaller units of information. Information has been organized based on precedence into a hierarchy, with visual design techniques used to communicate the importance of each element on the sign. Thus, the dominant element (the numeral) is large, located at the top, and has a distinct color. Next to the numeral is large type indicating the destination for each of the three routes. This level of information would most likely be adequate for most travelers on this particular road. A subordinate level is the

FIGURE 3.8

Road signage relies on hierarchy and precedence to structure information into comprehensible units.

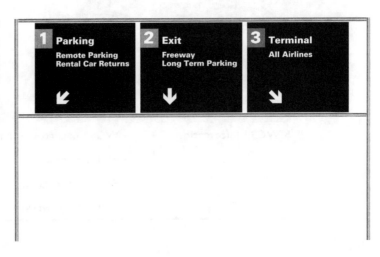

text copy located below, in a smaller size and spatially located below the dominant type identifier. The arrow graphic element is the last element, but still reads clear, due to its unique shape and position. The purposeful organization, scaling, and positioning of elements directs the eye in a top-down path through the information.

Main groupings and subgroups of information in a web site are ordered into a hierarchy based on precedence, significance, and frequency of access. All main groupings must be evaluated in relation to one another, while the content within each category itself is also structured into sublevels of hierarchy and precedence. These are important steps in the design process that will impact the basic layout and design for all pages later in the process. The visual design principles and techniques described later in Chapter 4 are most effective when applied to pages organized by hierarchy and precedence.

The ordering of information into a hierarchy is necessary to facilitate better understanding, but there are practical reasons too. *Everything simply cannot fit on the home page!* It remains doubtful that all information in a web site has the same level of precedence. This can sometimes be a difficult point to communicate to the rest of the development team or client, especially when content is being provided from various other sub-organizations or internal units within the larger, corporate setting. However, practical spatial constraints and a user's reluctance to scroll long documents are reasons enough to develop an effective hierarchy for web page design.

Hierarchy structures should not extend too deep, as shown in Figure 3.9. This forces the user to navigate through too many levels to locate the needed information. Important or frequently accessed information positioned deep within the structure only hampers the usability of the web site. *Remember that the primary goal of a web site is to allow users to fulfill some specific task.* This is accomplished by providing direct access to the needed information supporting the user task.

A symptom of having a structure too deep is web pages which have links leading to further links, leading to further links, and so forth, stair-stepping through too many intermediate pages without provid-

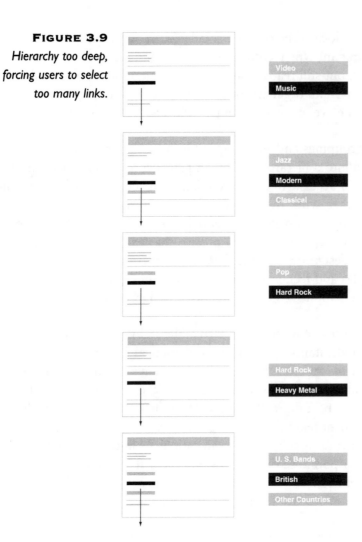

FIGURE 3.9

Hierarchy too deep, forcing users to select too many links.

ing any useful content to the user. The navigation pathway is a narrow, linear one and the user must repeatedly traverse numerous steps down and then back up again. The navigation pathway in Figure 3.9 is too linear and forces the user to traverse through too many meaningless levels. Inadequate grouping earlier in the design stage has produced a structure with too many levels. The user must also travel up and down the hierarchy to access different types of information within the same music category.

Figure 3.10 illustrates a possible alternative, which reorganizes the music grouping so as to better facilitate quicker access to the infor-

FIGURE 3.10
*Hierarchy structure
alternative to Figure 3.9.*

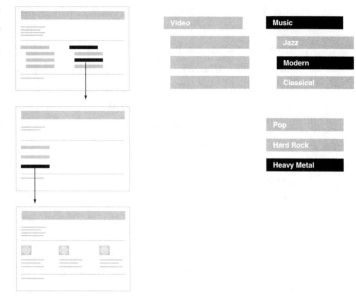

mation while providing better navigation between music subgroups. More choices are provided on the home page. At the second level, the user may quickly choose an alternate subcategory within the Modern music. The international groupings have been eliminated altogether, as they are minor differentiating factors to the people interested in music.

Designing the Organizational Framework

As with any graphic, networks are used in order to discover pertinent groups or to inform others of the groups and structures discovered. It is a good means of displaying structures.

Jacques Bertin, *Graphics and Graphics Information Processing*

Designing an effective organizational framework is mainly a two-step process. First, the information space must be organized and structured into a network-like diagram, indicating obvious hierarchies of major information groups. Second, the interaction flow through the framework for each user task is isolated and exposed, which is visually represented by individual task-flow diagrams. This step is similar to the flow diagrams Computer-based Training (CBT) utilizes for curriculum development. Required user actions to perform every task available in a web site are mapped out and given a diagrammatic visual representation.

These drawings function as early prototypes, testing the structure and architecture of the web site. Most importantly, these drawings communicate functionality and required interaction sequences from the user's point of view to every member of the development team. These visual representations are shared with everyone, especially with the engineering members, providing insight, exposing flaws or technical issues, and opening communication between all interdisciplinary skills involved in the development process.

References to visual metaphors, elements, or graphic style should be deferred until later, so as not to interfere with the primary goal. A clear, effective organizational framework will work with various visual representational approaches; the visual aspect should not convolute or inhibit the important design process at this stage. Keep in mind that a flawed underlying structure will adversely affect usability of a web site, regardless of the visual metaphor or style applied to the presentation layer.

DEVELOPING THE FRAMEWORK

In a hierarchy topology, one node at the top of the structure has no parents, while all others do. Figure 3.11 is one of numerous sketches using hierarchy and precedence to order main information groupings into an organizational framework. At the top of the sketch is the main node (home page), designated in level one, where one enters the information space. (Of course, knowledge of any URL gives users access to *any* page) The directional arrows lead from the initial node to second-level nodes which indicate five major groupings of information. In this sketch, each of these groups correlate with Table 3.1, the content grouping of the World Cup web server. As indicated in the drawing, all second-level groups (or nodes) are bi-directional and can go back up as well as horizontally across to other second-level nodes. Traversing further down the hierarchy sends the user to level three groupings, which actually are comprised of numerous individual sub-nodes, but compressed into a single node in this drawing. Bi-directional navigation is supported to backtrack up the node, as well as traversal across the hierarchy to designated information of relevance. Since nodes have definitive positions in the hierarchy, an abstract sense of distance and depth is implied and will be reinforced in later stages of the design process.

The sketch in Figure 3.11 is a simple example, yet communicates sufficient information early in the design process. Major and subordinate groupings have been given a location in the hierarchy structure

FIGURE 3.11

Organizational framework sketch for the WorldCupUSA94 server.

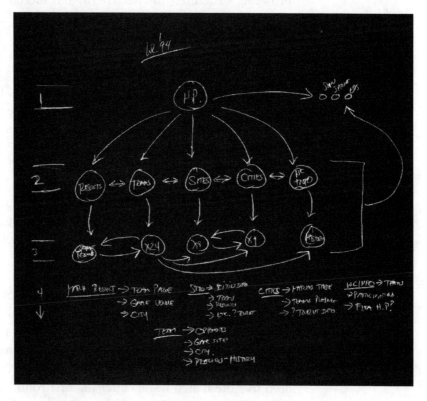

and navigational relationships between major groupings have been defined. The major nodes function much like traffic intersections or hubs, much like the service model for airlines. These major nodes connect the various locations in the web site, providing "avenues," or the means for cross traversal.

Early sketches are rough, simple, and produced quickly. Assigning visual design attributes are consciously avoided for now, in order to concentrate on the organization and structure. Early indications of page elements may begin to appear in later task-flow sketches, after the development of an effective framework structure.

When designing the organizational framework, the priority of information most important to users should ideally be located within two to three levels. Effective grouping and precedence assignment help to simplify the overly complex and make for a more approachable browsing structure. An effective organizational framework communicates the web site content within a glance, just as an effective diagrammatic chart does.

It is up to the web designer to establish and organize the content of a web site into smaller, manageable components. Everything cannot fit onto a single page; therefore, decisions must be made which prioritize the information presentation, based on user need, importance, and frequency of use.

WorldCupUSA94 Framework Example

The major information groups identified in Figure 3.11 are expanded in Figures 3.12 to 3.16. Each second-level category shows the subsequent information accessible from that node, which leads through the hierarchy.

In Figure 3.12, the first grouping, Results and Standings, has been expanded into a more definitive diagram. From this node, the user may access detailed information for up to four matches held a specific day during the tournament. The minimal number of match results posted varies from two to four. Note that the structure anticipates the need to store match results after the first round is complete and provides access to an archive of all previous matches. The smaller circles

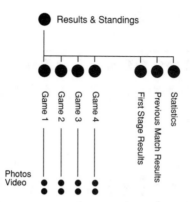

FIGURE 3.12

Group one, Participating teams structure.

in the diagram represent access to additional information found on each of the match summary pages, Game 1, Game 2, and so forth. The user may access photo and video files for each match result. This diagram identifies available information for all match result pages, which ensures consistency and predictability. Users can expect access to photos and video highlights from each game result page.

Figure 3.13 illustrates hierarchy for information in the Games Sites and Schedules grouping. From this node, access to each of the nine city venues is identified, with additional access to the schedule and elimination chart from the major node. From each of the nine city nodes, access is consistent to related information via directional links to Directions, Schedules, and City Information. Each city page has its own unique content for each of these subordinate categories, ordered consistently in the same manner on each of the city pages.

FIGURE 3.13

Group two, Game Sites and Schedules structure.

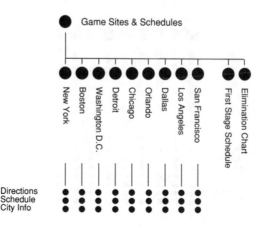

FIGURE 3.14

*Group three,
Participating Teams
structure.*

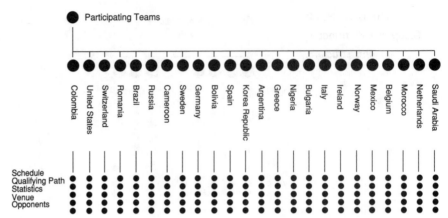

Figure 3.14 is an expanded view of the Participating Teams hierarchy. From this node, access is provided to each of the 24 pages for each country participating in the tournament. All pages share the same position in the hierarchy. A useful navigational requirement identified at this stage is to provide a horizontal, lateral navigation from team node to team node, eliminating the need to traverse up and down the hierarchy. On each of the 24 team pages, the same subordinate content is given. This includes access to Schedules, Qualification Path, Statistics, Opponents, and Venue where each team plays its matches.

Figure 3.15 is an expanded view of the Host City Information. From this node, access to guidebook-type of information for each city host-

FIGURE 3.15

*Group four, Host City
Information structure.*

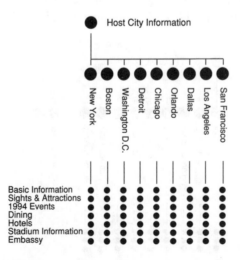

ing the matches is supported. Each of the nine nodes has consistent access to subordinate information groupings. This includes basic city information, sights and attractions, 1994 special events, dining, hotel, stadium proximity, and embassy locale.

Figure 3.16 illustrates the final grouping, World Cup Information. This group is subordinate to the rest, but still provides information relevant to the scope of the entire event. Categories in this group include information about the organization and sponsors of the event, technology background, historical and trivia, and the rules of the sport. Anchors leading from each of these subgroups are lead to unique locations within the structure. The anchors which lead from the technology sponsors would call for links which transfer the user to a location outside the information space.

The diagrams provide an indication of the content necessary for each page and also are early indications of the breadth and scope of work required for actual implementation of the web site. From a random-like listing of content generated during brainstorming sessions with the development team earlier in the process, a clear structure and organization is now emerging.

The diagrams also ensure consistency in available information on all pages within a given node. This implies, and will be illustrated later, consistent positioning on each page for all information within a given node. This avoids links and controls floating around from page to page or, worse yet, forgetting to include a needed component on the page.

FIGURE 3.16

Group five, World Cup Information structure.

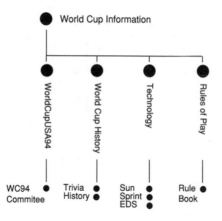

On-line Mall Framework Example

Figure 3.17 is another example of an organization framework, in this case, for an on-line mall. The web site provides virtual storefronts for merchants who wish to rent space on the web site. In order to provide a navigable model for users through potentially hundreds of stores, the browsing structure should be clear and obvious. The major nodes of the information space are identified in four categories, with all storefronts located in this category. Mall services, such as the information desk and special events area, are similar to activities found in a real-world shopping mall. Other global features are the "shopping bag" and "checkout register" which function across all stores. Therefore, in this model, the user may shop through any store, hold products, and check out from a centrally located checkout register.

Obviously, the ordering of merchants into familiar categories provides an easier model for users to locate products. Simply listing all merchants in a long scrolling list would be difficult to selectively scan for specific goods. The grouping of merchants into familiar categories also correlates to common real-world mall directories. Users are therefore familiar with this method of organization.

The expanse and number of products possibly found in a mall infer that a powerful search mechanism is also a prerequisite. This will use the advantages found in the Internet to seek out specific goods from the wide variety of stores and deliver the merchandise to the user.

FIGURE 3.17

Mall-level framework for a cybermall diagram of stores.

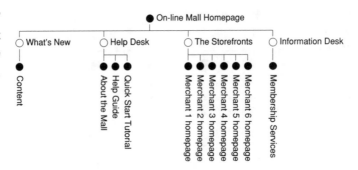

Obviously, the organizational structure differs between a small specialty shop versus a large department store. The challenge then becomes a balancing act between extended functionality for more complex store structures without losing consistency and predictability for users among other stores in the mall. Other issues include the customizing of functionality, navigation, controls, and so forth, which break consistency for uniqueness and differentiation. For example, some merchants may prefer to alter the navigational model or steps in the purchasing process. The rationale for such alterations should be considered in relation to users who must "relearn" the system, if every store changes interface conventions.

An example of the product-level structure is shown in Figure 3.18. At this level, specific interaction sequences are identified and must be accommodated in the information structure. The diagram illustrates how the user selects a merchandise category, proceeds to narrow the view to a specific type, and then "pages" through variations in a product. The horizontal paging activity is synonymous with paging through a real-world print catalog. In a printed catalog, products are presented in a logical, related order, and easily understood. The web equivalent should also support easy navigation between related products in a specific category. The advantages of this structure also avoid up-down traversal to an index page which lists all products. The user navigates through groups and subgroups, drilling down to specific product descriptions, where attribute choices and ordering decisions are made.

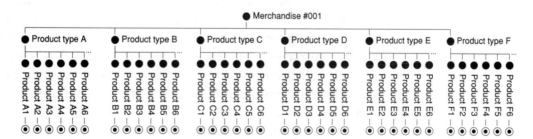

FIGURE 3.18 *Product-level structure.*

The hierarchy organizes the merchandise into groups within a specific category, such as cookware. Subcategory types may be dinnerware, dishes, pots and pans, carving knives, and so forth. Selecting pots and pans may provide another level, into pan types, such as roasting, sauce, steamers, and so forth. At this level, users may browse through variations in a specific category, viewing different brands or styles. When the user finds a product interesting, access is provided to further details and more descriptive data.

Using the concept of progressive disclosure, further product specifications and detailed information are accessed through a subsequent link on each product page. The advantages of structuring the product pages this way are numerous. First and foremost, the density of information on the initial product page remains low, supporting quick browsing through related product "series." There is no need to provide detailed descriptive information to users who may not be interested in seriously purchasing the product in the first place. Second, this technique reduces perceived response time by limiting the amount of graphics and text sent to the client for each page turn. The product pages remain lightweight and sparse, perhaps using small thumbnail product representations, while the product detail pages provides larger viewpoints, variations, or access to video demonstrations. Third, the paging model is familiar to most users, as it resembles the structure when ordering from a print catalog.

The organizational diagrams are simple, clear, and use geometric shapes to represent hierarchies and information groupings. Yet they communicate essential information, and help to previsualize the web site. The focus remains purposefully general and at a high level, avoiding the urge to jump into visual detail or graphic style, which can sometimes diverge attention to surface details and graphic embellishment. Attention is on the continual refinement of an effective, obvious organizational framework for users to complete their tasks.

Design Supporting the User's Task

> *Generally, the organization of functionality should reflect the most efficient sequence of steps to accomplish the most likely or most frequent user goal.*
>
> Deborah J. Mayhew,
> *Principles and Guidelines in Software User Interface Design*

Once the organizational framework is complete, the required interaction for users to complete specific tasks is described, analyzed, sketched out, and verified for directness and simplicity. It may be necessary to later develop a prototype in HTML to fully test the actual interaction and navigation through the organizational framework. The main focus at this stage should be to isolate the specific user task and determine what other information or functionality is important to the user within the context of the particular task. For example, what does a user need to do to subscribe to information, purchase a product, or initiate a financial transaction? The primary objective is to provide the most direct sequence of steps for users to accomplish the task and base the inclusion of controls and functionality on precedence and frequency of use within the task domain.

All possible routes, tasks, and user actions are rapidly sketched, evaluated, and verified through iterative rough drawings. These sketches function as paper-prototypes and are valuable early visual aids for further refinement and exploration. Again, it is much easier to alter the underlying organization and structure of a web site on paper than in actual HTML pages, especially if the development team has already established complex links and dependencies which need to be changed (or thrown out altogether!). The artistic quality of the sketches themselves is irrelevant—it is the rapid visualization of implied interaction sequences that matters most. In fact, it is probably better in early testing to use generic flow diagram representation without any references to page attributes.

While the organizational framework structure provides the higher-level, global "model" of the information space, the task-flow sketches magnify lower-level views of user interaction within a particular node of the structure. The isolated task is exploded, evaluated, and refined. A goal is central in the user's mind and a clear definition of user tasks to attain this goal is described. The design of the web application should then support the user's tasks to attain the goal. This includes support for linking to related information, helpful to users in a particular situation or activity. There are opportunities for hypertext traversal across the framework; these cross links are identified and evaluated for relevancy and usefulness. Determining when and where links are useful is a major challenge to effective web design.

For example, too many buttons and textual links in Figure 3.19 present a bewildering array of choices to the user, who must then determine the appropriate controls after entering the user name and password. The task is a very simple one: to log in. Half of the buttons, however, have nothing to do with the functionality of the form itself, while others operate as navigation links. The ambiguity between the resulting action of "Clear" and "Cancel" in this context is also confusing to the user. The mixed bag of buttons also clutters the page. This single page has usability flaws because the central user task was not recognized and the page was not designed to support it.

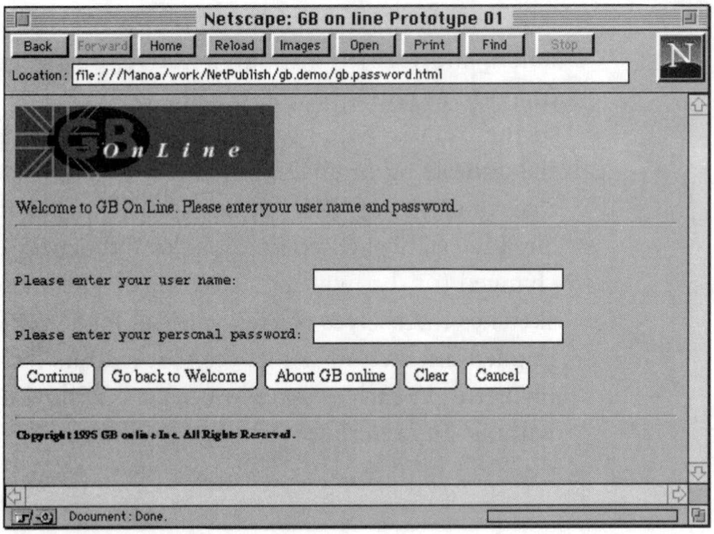

FIGURE 3.19

Confusing array of choices instead of directly supporting the login task for users.

DESCRIBING INTERACTION WITH TASK-FLOW DIAGRAMS

Figures 3.20 and 3.21 are from the World Cup example of isolated task-flow diagrams, which map user actions through the steps required to attain a specific goal. These task-flow diagrams are magnified views into the organizational framework and focus on specific user actions.

In Figure 3.20, two alternate paths to the desired information are provided to users. Since viewing immediate match results has highest precedence from target users' point of view, the score is placed directly on the home page and can be viewed immediately. Selecting a specific result transports the user directly to the specific highlight page for that specific match result. The user may access the same information indirectly, by selecting the Results and Standings second-level page and choosing one of the posted scores.

Similarly, in Figure 3.21, the diagram describes the steps for a user to access game site information. A traversal path requires three sequential steps. In both figures, the needed information is within two to

FIGURE 3.20

Task-flow to access the latest match result.

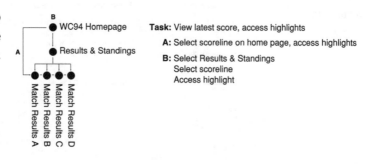

FIGURE 3.21

Task-flow to access game site information.

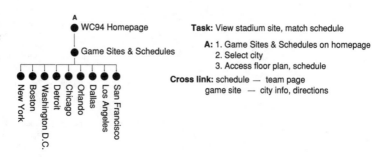

three required user actions. Cross-links to useful, related information are identified and notated on the task-flow diagram. The same approach is repeated for all user interactions across the service structure of the web site. The task-flow diagrams may be in the form of rough sketches; the presentation is insignificant, but the advantages in describing required user actions considerable. Planning ahead avoids haphazard, random-like link assignment to potentially useless information.

Figure 3.22 illustrates a specific task-flow for a user to purchase a product on-line. The organizational structure of the mall (Figure 3.17) uses product pages; detailed product pages with selection attributes; shopping bag for temporarily storing products during a session; checkout register to authorize the purchase transaction; and receipt generation. The user's task is examined for efficiency, directness, and intuitive actions; the user flow through the structure is verified for directness and clarity; and relevancy is checked for all related cross-links and general navigation. The task-flow diagram describes the interaction which layered on the product-level structure.

FIGURE 3.22

Task-flow to purchase a product.

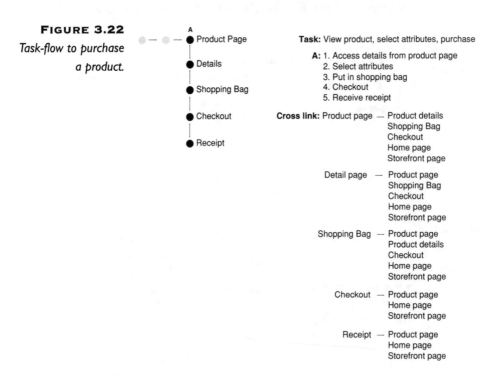

The sketch in Figure 3.23 illustrates a more complex interaction sequence. The task-flow diagram visualizes the various user-interaction scenarios for subscribing to published documents under access control for a publishing web site. This model uses the notion of "member" (a registered user who has agreed to pay a monthly fee) versus "guest" (unregistered). A flat fee is charged to users upon submission of the registration form, at which time the user enjoys full access to all nodes of the structure. Guests, on the other hand, are given access to "abstracts" or preview information of the publications. The previews are seen by both members and guests. Guests must somehow be routed to the "registration desk" if full access is later desired, beyond the preview stage.

An interesting trait unique to the web is for users to know the Universal Resource Locator, or URL (the address which references the HTML document) to a given document under access control. Therefore, interaction sequences must be planned ahead of time for "Guest" users who may traverse to a URL under access control. This situation should not be confrontational or jarring to the user. Concise, clear wording describing the options available should be included in the form of a notifying page or equivalent. Allowing the user to at least browse a subset of the information will probably support a more forgiving attitude from users. This also provides a notion to users of the breadth and scope of the information before purchasing the service, much like browsing a book before actually buying it. Access control applied to the free and open nature of the web contrasts greatly with the controlled, constrained manner a user enters a fixed CD-ROM product, which forces a user through a single entry way.

In the sketch in Figure 3.23, the left column of rectangles represents a guest traversing through the web site, browsing through the free area and viewing abstracts. At some point, however, the guest may "hit" an area under access control, and must graciously be informed of the current status. Options to join and be sent to the registration desk should be provided, along with the choice to continue browsing the free areas. The "Member Entrance" allows users who have already registered direct access to all information, once the correct login and password are provided.

FIGURE 3.23 *Task-flow through information under access control for a publishing web site.*

Another tricky situation is when registered members browse the web site, but fail to initially log in. The server, therefore, has no knowledge of their member status, and they are treated as guests. If custom functionality such as personal preference pages are implemented, the user will not be served any of this special functionality, until officially logged into the system. The registered users must have easy access to the login functionality or they will most likely set a hotlist or book mark to their preference pages, which will automatically call the access control CGI.

A much simpler model is to allow an "all-or-nothing" approach to the web site. In this case, the user must register to gain access or no further interaction is supported. Although simpler to implement, the main trade-off is that users do not receive any direct, tangible proof of why they should subscribe. The user is forced to register (and may or may not have to pay a fee) before viewing anything. This is quite a different model from what consumers are accustomed to—"try before you buy" attitude found in book stores. The benefit is the availability of user information visiting the web site, providing accurate demographics and statistics.

Trial offers with a prescribed time limit for access may also be implemented. Users are familiar with the notion of a trial offer; the advantages, of course, are that users get to "test drive" before actually purchasing the product. A "timestamp" which gives free access to the entire information space for a prescribed duration, can be assigned to the user upon registration. Many on-line services, such as America Online, offer free 30-day trials in order to entice users and increase membership to the service. After 30 days, the service will charge a user the appropriate fee for continued service.

Each of these various scenarios, when implemented on the web, is potentially confusing and complex to the user. Task-flow diagrams help to test and verify the required interaction sequences before production begins, when it becomes too late or impossible to alter a flawed design.

TUNING TASK-FLOW DIAGRAMS INTO "PAPER-PROTOTYPES"

The task-flow diagrams provide interaction mappings for further refinement through "paper-prototype" sketching. These rapid visualizations resemble computer-based training (CBT) flow diagrams and function much the same way: to test program logic and structure. Sketches help to visualize the user's flow through the structure and access to information or services, providing another verification step in the design process. The sketches explore routes users will take when accessing specific information, along with the sequences necessary to perform all tasks in order to fulfill a particular goal.

These sketches also begin to previsualize the actual pages, as detail is added. The formal character of the pages starts to emerge from these sketches and work may proceed to budget or estimate media and contract costs. The detail furnishes realism to the prototyping stage, but the final graphic language or metaphor is still open for exploration and refinement.

As the organizational framework provides the higher-level, overall view of the web site, these sketches indicate specific interaction and visual detail for each node in the structure. Sketches, as in Figure 3.24, now use page representations instead of abstract, geometric

FIGURE 3.24

Adding detail, verifying task-flow through the structure.

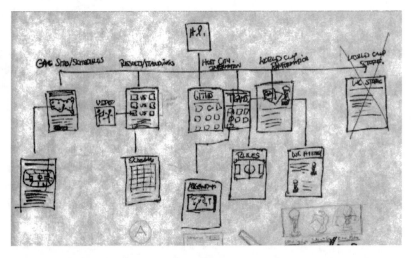

shapes. The sketches further refine the interaction sequences for users to navigate the structure. This will help to determine the necessary navigational controls included on pages.

The sketches in Figure 3.25 show added levels of detail in the page sketches. The geometric circles used in the framework and task-flow diagrams are now HTML page sketches. Specific tasks are drawn: The interaction sequence to access stadium information, for example, is tested on the left side of the drawing. Page information identified in the earlier framework diagrams and content table is now indicated on the pages. Paths are drawn in the page sketches, for example, which suggest the user task-flow to attain the match score, an important user task within the context of the WorldCupUSA94 server. This information was largely provided earlier in the process. Previous planning and steps in the design process gradually shape the form of the web site.

In Figure 3.25, two alternate paths to access match highlights are indicated. From the top node or home page (A), the user may directly access the highlights (C) via selection of the score posted on the home page, or by indirectly navigating to the second-level Results and Standing (B) home page. The design supports direct access to specific highlights or indirect access where other information, such as the standings table, can also be viewed. In either case, the frequency of use and precedence of this information require access within a minimal sequence of user actions.

Useful cross-links identified in earlier task-flow diagrams are sketched with the addition of visual detail in Figure 3.26. The second-level Game Sites and Schedules (A) home page supports access to the stadium information (B) from a direct selection. The second-level Participating Teams (C) home page supports access to specific team information (D). A useful cross-link from each of the 24 team pages (D) should link to the stadium where each team will pay a particular match. Likewise, the match schedule posted on each stadium page (B) should link to the specific team home page (D). Identifying useful, relevant cross-links before page production begins ensures that all pages in a certain node provide a consistent set of cross-links.

More importantly, the sketches describing cross-links are carefully considered and discussed, rather than a situation occurring in which links are randomly assigned by a singular individual on the development team.

Aside from further refining and visualizing the task-flow diagrams created earlier in the design process, these sketches also indicate general visual requirements for the later stages of graphic design production by identifying design elements early. In Figure 3.26, the sketches indicate stadium floor plans and a map of the U.S. continent. The map will provide a useful visual method for accessing stadium venues by allowing the user to click on a particular site. Work can begin in locating these existing assets or initiate estimates for contract illustration.

Practical schedule and resource considerations, along with copyright issues, are considered during the paper-prototyping stage. In the multimedia and visual design business, production schedules (and budgets) are usually defined at the outset. Budget and resource allocation must be determined well in advance; early visualization sketches can provide insight as to required resources (illustrators, artists, CGI scriptors, etc.) needed for customized functionality for the web site.

FIGURE 3.25
Paper-prototype sketches for Results and Standings (group 1).

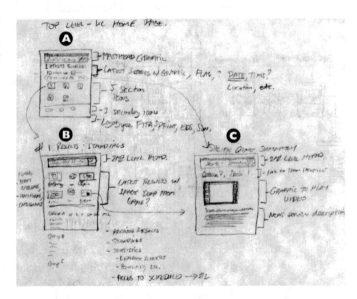

FIGURE 3.26

Paper-prototype sketches for Game Sites (grouping 2) and Participating Teams (grouping 3).

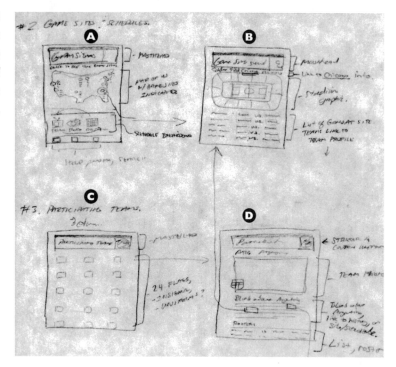

The earlier these requirements are exposed, the greater the chances that the development team will have to execute the designs to meet the project budget and schedule.

Further refinement in the publishing service provider example is illustrated in Figure 3.27. Added detail to the pages communicates realism and provides a better indication of specific user interaction with the system—in this case, entering as guest versus member.

The guest pathway (A) supports the user access to unprotected nodes of the browsing structure. Information which describes the user status is provided (A-1), and an opportunity to register to become a member (C) via a fill-in form. In this sketch, the guest user has a separate browsing structure which is somehow differentiated from the member pages (A-2), perhaps with a corner banner or other undefined visual distinction. When entering as guest, access is always provided to the membership desk (C). Members (B-1) enter via the login page (B-1) and then enjoy full access to all information (B-2). Full functionality to features such as search, member services, account information, personal preferences, and so forth, is now available on all subsequent pages for members.

Guests who may use the URL for a page under access control will be sent to the membership desk and given the opportunity to apply for membership. Registering as a member does not necessarily mean a fee is charged, as many web sites use the registration data to send update information or for demographic statistical purposes.

Sketches quickly test design variations without having to spend time developing actual HTML pages. The sketches in Figure 3.28 are alternate models for access control. The translation of task-flow diagrams into paper-prototypes gives the development team tangible, visual data to evaluate and further develop the design. Simply rushing content onto the web while neglecting the steps outlined in this chapter will most likely produce a web site below the expectations of your development team and audience.

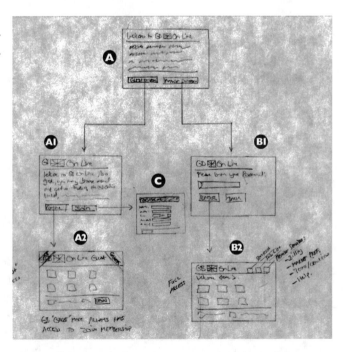

FIGURE 3.27
*Paper-prototype of
one variation of
access control.*

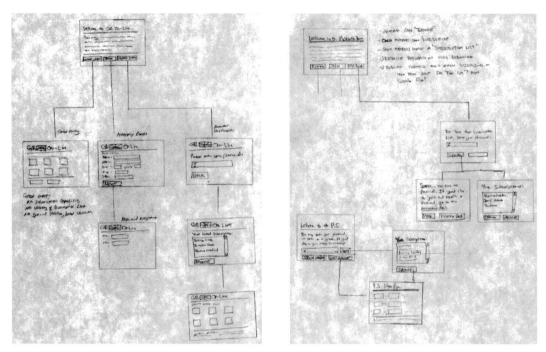

FIGURE 3.28 *Rapid sketches exploring alternative models for handling access control.*

HTML PROTOTYPES

At this stage in the design process, a clear structure should be nearly finalized for implementation, along with descriptions of all user interaction. The many paper-prototype sketches now provide the direction for actual HTML page authoring.

Translating these sketches into HTML pages or a working prototype of the web site is fast and does not require much effort. A prototype allows actual user interaction and testing. In the best circumstances, the prototype evolves into the finished web site through the addition of all graphic elements. Later, the pages are accessed on-line by the rest of the development team and perhaps a variety of users, with comments and feedback given on the current design direction.

This process is effective *if* the prototype is initially lightweight and flexible. An overly detailed prototype, with meticulous graphics and substantial time investment by artists or contractors, may not be advantageous in the long run. Comments from users may require rewording of page terminology or reevaluation of the underlying structure, and the time spent on making the pages graphic and exact is wasted. The graphic ornamentation may also hide serious problems in the interface instead of allowing the user to focus on basic usability concerns. A more serious danger, however, is to cling to the initial prototype, because of the time, effort, and possible financial investment, even if flaws are later exposed.

When developing an HTML prototype, attention should focus on the interaction cycles required to access information or perform an action and to test the navigation pathways through the information space, as shown in Figure 3.29. Initially, text-only pages function well, as the underlying organizational framework is quickly mapped out. Textual links functioning as navigation controls and textual heads clearly identify each page. These are the first basic elements on the pages.

Prototyping in HTML is a fairly simple, quick process. Chunks of HTML are rapidly copied and pasted into new document files, mak-

FIGURE 3.29

Basic initial prototype pages without graphic detail, focusing on navigation and interaction.

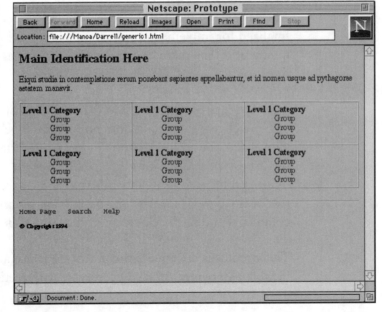

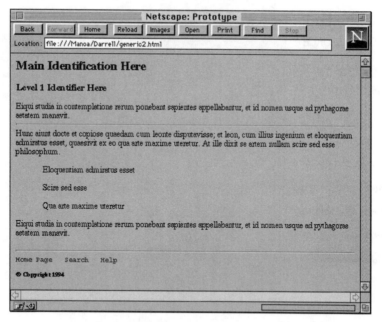

ing it easy to reuse existing HTML tag constructs (Figure 3.30). Basic pages are similar to templates in a page layout program and are customized specifically to project needs. The unintuitive authoring of HTML documents in a text editor is fairly straightforward and easily mastered within an hour. As direct manipulation tools become available, HTML authoring should even be easier for the novice. Be aware, however, that many HTML conversion programs and authoring tools do not support all the advanced functionality found in all browsers. This is particularly the case with Netscape Navigator, which seems to remain a step ahead of the authoring tools in supporting its features.

The WebFORCE™ software environment by Silicon Graphics, Inc. is an example of current web authoring tools available for the Internet (Figure 3.31).

There are many free resources on the web which offer valuable information for HTML novices. An extensive listing of HTML resources, style guides, tutorials, and so forth, can be found on the Netscape home pages at http://home.netscape.com/assist/net_sites/index.html.

FIGURE 3.31

The WebFORCE

software environment,

including WebMagic™

Author 1.0,

MovieMaster™,

and enhanced digital

media tools. (Image

courtesy of Jonathan

Herbert Computer

Illustration, NYC.)

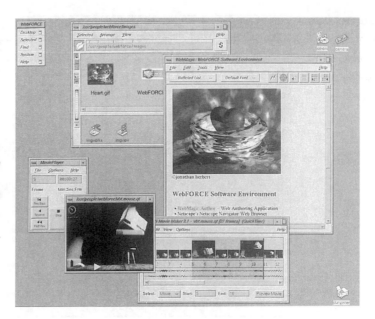

These pages also provide helpful information concerning Netscape extensions and capabilities in the latest 2.0 version of Navigator.

The working prototype (or actual project) is distributed on a network, so other members on the development team (along with the client) can view the design remotely while development is in progress. Most importantly, the design prototype is in the medium of its final delivery and can be tested on multiple platforms with different connection configurations. This is especially important throughout the entire design process, as graphics and CGIs (Common Gateway Interfaces) or Java applets are incorporated into the web site, adding full functionality. Designing web prototypes in authoring tools not originally designed for web authoring can lead to false evaluation feedback and, in turn, set unrealistic expectations. For example, erratic response time and overhead of graphic image loading cannot be reproduced and accurately tested with a non-HTML prototype. Nor can the prototype be viewed on multiple platforms, a requirement for large-scale web site production. This fact may later hinder the production process, if extensive reworking or modification is required by adopting a design built and viewed under artificial circumstances. For the time investment in scripting and producing a prototype in these other software products, actual HTML pages could have been built and tested in the final medium and viewed in a distributed environment.

Most importantly, these non-HTML prototypes cannot be handed off directly to engineering for actual implementation. It remains critical, as the design continues to evolve to the presentation layer, that the *user interface translates directly to code without alteration in implementation.* By working in HTML from the very initial prototyping stages, the integrity of the design is better ensured. The engineering team uses the original HTML pages *from the designer* and then writes the necessary code for implementation.

The Organizational Framework Reveals Page "Types"

A definition of various page "types" required for the web site helps in the upcoming visual design and production stages. Certain page types need common or shared functionality; this is noted so as to ensure consistency across all pages. The page designer and development team will then have a better sense of the overall page system needed for effective implementation. The pages are designed within a coordinated, cohesive design system, rather than in an ad hoc manner. A by-product of this process is to remove the guesswork out of determining which element belongs on what page. Every information type, control, and anchor on every page is accounted for. Clarity to all members on the development team is ensured. This is especially useful if the development team is large, distributed, and utilizes the assistance of contractors. The page design *specifications* are blueprints for the construction of every page in the system.

The granularity of the page specification is dependent on time and the working arrangement for the specific project. In large-scale web site design, the advantages are clear when the development team is

FIGURE 3.32

*Sample page types for
store on the web.*

Home Page

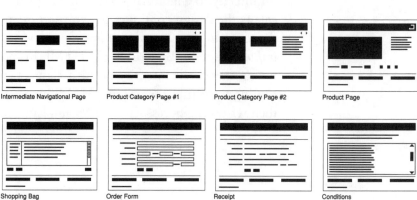

Intermediate Navigational Page   Product Category Page #1   Product Category Page #2   Product Page

Shopping Bag   Order Form   Receipt   Conditions

large or location of team members distributed. Since large-scale web
production is mainly a collaborative, cross-disciplinary activity, the
design specification clearly communicates the design to all members.

Each known page type is identified, along with its functionality, contents, controls, and cross-links. Quick line drawing or sketches may
suffice; even textual descriptions can communicate the basic design
to everyone on the development team. Figure 3.32 summarizes the
various page types for a particular storefront within the cybermall
example.

The following sections briefly describe the necessary pages for common web sites and the possible requirements for these pages.

HOME PAGE

The home page is the main entrance into the web site and can
impress users, generating interest and curiosity or, if poorly designed,
cause indifference or even repel users. If first impressions count, the

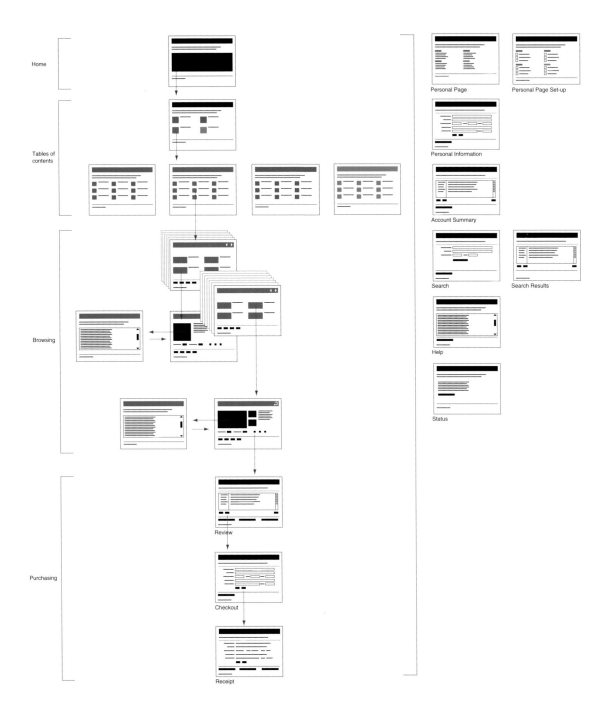

COLOR PLATE 1: *Page types supporting various operations within a Web site are identified. This aids in visualizing the organization of the proposed Web structure before HTML authoring is begun. For example, pages that are considered global (available anywhere from any page) are identified on the right, with the service structure pages on the left. The specific task-flow in this drawing illustrates the browsing activity through final product purchase. Usability, efficiency, and navigational issues are emphasized at this stage, and not the visual presentation or graphic style.*

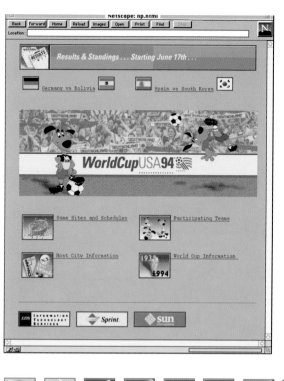

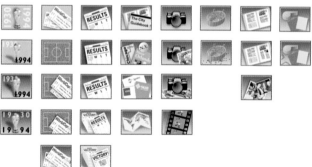

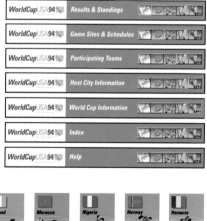

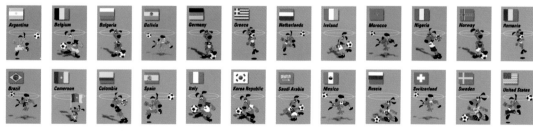

COLOR PLATE 2: *Large-scale commercial Web sites benefit from establishing a visual design program, which ensures cohesiveness and consistency. The WorldCupUSA94 Web server, designed and implemented for the soccer world championships by Sun Microsystems, Inc., illustrates an extensive visual language program, related to the marketing efforts of the event. The many visual elements combine to form an identity system on-line, synonymous to comprehensive design programs created for other major sporting events, such as the Olympics. (Copyright Reserved FIFA and En-Linea. WorldCupUSA94 logo © WorldCupUSA.)*

Windows95

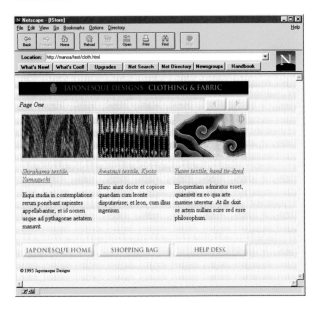

Silicon Graphics

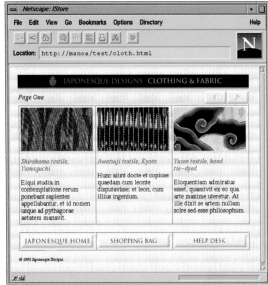

Sun SparcStation 20

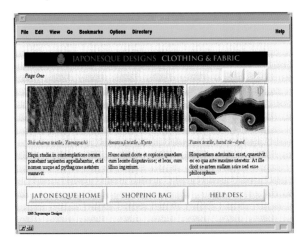

Macintosh

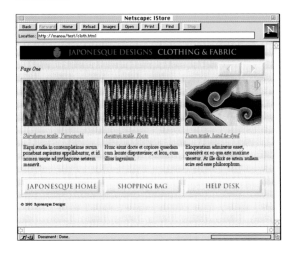

COLOR PLATE 3: *It is always worthwhile to test pages on various computer platforms, and with different connection speeds. This is especially the case when using textured background patterns. The tatami matting background visually reproduces well across platforms, insuring readability and reasonable viewing for users. Minor variations across platforms includes size differences in default text styles (alters line breaks and column depth), rendering of table borders, and variations in user configuration of the browser controls and menus.*

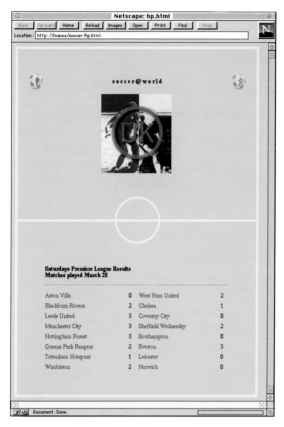
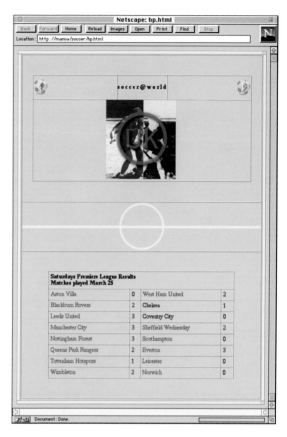

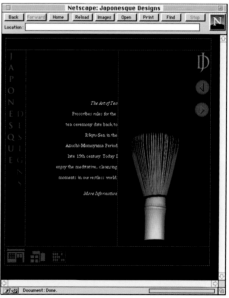

COLOR PLATE 4: *Both of these page designs use HTML tables to position text and graphics in the browser pane. Pages displaying table borders (right) help to verify alignment and spatial arrangement during design. The soccer field example uses a table to contain the outer border graphics of the field, and nested tables for positioning internal page contents. The Asian store example uses a single table with various alignment tags for positioning elements within each table cell.*

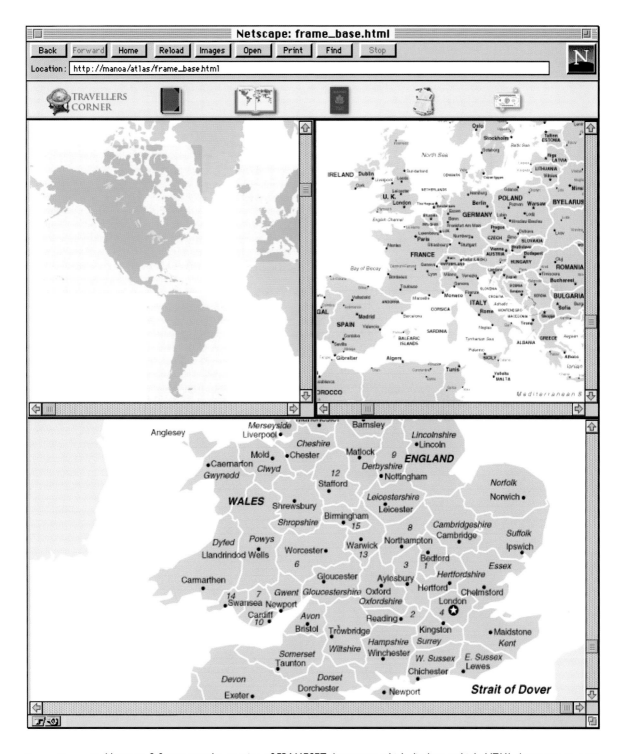

COLOR PLATE 5: *Netscape 2.0 supports the creation of FRAMESET documents, which displays multiple HTML documents in a single browser window. Each frame is assigned a unique name, which can then be referenced by other frames through hypertext linking. The contents of frames can include elements such as images, background textures or colors, Java applets, etc. The atlas allows a user to browse through world, region, and country levels in the hierarchy.*

COLOR PLATE 6: *S.P.Q.R. by CyberSites, Inc. allows the user to explore 4th century Rome in a mystery and learning adventure. The images are beautifully rendered, demonstrating the strong architectural-3D CAD background of the designers. Similar to the popular Myst™ CD-ROM game, S.P.Q.R. is an example of the future richness in presentation of web applications. (Copyright © 1995 CyberSites, Inc. All Rights Reserved. http://pathfinder.com/twep/rome)*

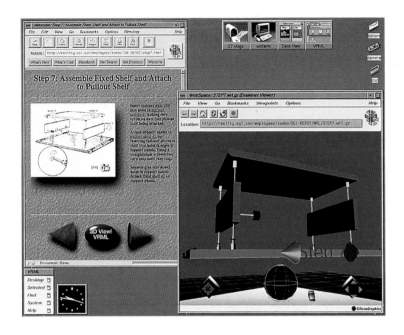

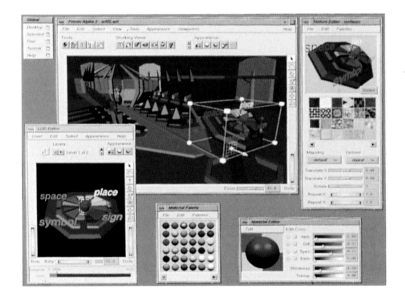

Color Plate 7: *Using VRML (Virtual Reality Modeling Language), immersive, 3D multi-user virtual worlds are possible. Browsers supporting VRML include WebSpace™ Navigator (top), and for creating virtual space, WebSpace™ Author (bottom). Both of these tools are from Silicon Graphics, Inc., and are indications of the desire to provide easy-to-use tools for designers and artists. (Images courtesy of Silicon Graphics, Inc. http://www.sgi.com)*

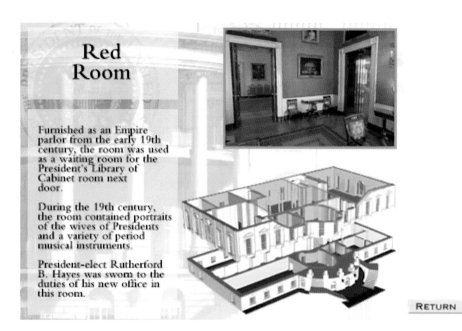

Red Room

Furnished as an Empire parlor from the early 19th century, the room was used as a waiting room for the President's Library of Cabinet room next door.

During the 19th century, the room contained portraits of the wives of Presidents and a variety of period musical instruments.

President-elect Rutherford B. Hayes was sworn to the duties of his new office in this room.

RETURN

COLOR PLATE 8: *Apple's QuickTime® VR allows Macintosh® and Windows™ users to explore spatial interactions without any special add-on hardware. There are two techniques available in QuickTime VR: object movies, allowing the user to examine objects interactively, and panoramic movies, enabling users to explore spaces (as shown above). The panoramic movie technique uses a 360-degree panoramic photographic (or illustrated) view, and supports "hot spots" within the 360-degree scene. A user may launch a variety of media, including text, images, video, audio, and another QuickTime VR scene. (Copyright © 1995 Apple Computer. All Rights Reserved. http://www.apple.com)*

home page largely determines whether the user will enter the site or continue surfing the web.

Minimal information required on a home page should include identification of what the web site provides to the user and who the publisher is. There should be a clear indication of the content within the site, so the user can determine its relevancy. Essential navigation controls to further information are provided. Access to help pages and/or profile information about the web publisher should also be included.

Commercial applications may allocate advertising space, company logotypes, or sponsored links to other web servers. For very large-scale information spaces, immediate access to a search query page is necessary to provide an alternative to browsing. Subordinate information, which should include a copyright tag, should also be considered.

INTERMEDIATE NAVIGATIONAL PAGES

Topic categories are placed on intermediate navigational pages, which may not provide actual content, but function primarily as avenues for users on the way to the information. Careful topic organization and groupings allow these pages to function as intersections for users. Intermediate navigation sequences take users from the large and general to the specific in a minimal number of steps.

USER LOGIN PAGE

If access control is implemented, especially for a fee-based web site, a login page is required. Minimal elements should include identification elements, labels and fields for user input, and a submit button to initiate verification. Users without access should have the means to acquire access through accessing the registration procedure. During the stage of structuring the information space, decisions as to the scope of free versus paid access should be determined. For example, web sites may decide to allow "Guest Entry" for a limited or indefinite time period. Additional pages which clearly explain the usage policy are included.

USER REGISTRATION PAGES

User registration pages are required for web sites limiting access. Within this category, access may require a charge or be free. Free web sites may still elect to require or optionally ask users to enter registration information. The reasons may include marketing, statistical, or simply to communicate via email to the registered user. Registration forms should include the basic required information in a printed form, including name, address, phone, mailing, billing and shipping address, credit card number, and expiration date.

Optional fields to capture user occupation, income, interest, hobbies, and so forth can be accessed through a link to generate pages tailored to individual users. Customized home pages or preference pages are easily generated from this information. This information may also be useful for demographic or marketing purposes. The registration pages may be a component of the "Membership Desk" area of related functionality, which supports modification of user information and account review activity.

Typical registration forms may be viewed by some as rather cold and impersonal; clearly, their inclusion in a web site prohibiting access is, at the moment, a new experience in the open world of the web. Information may be acquired through informal questioning throughout the browsing experience, eliminating the user from direct confrontation with a wall of form input fields. Clever wording, staging, and timing of the message can transform the registration experience into an unobtrusive side trip.

PERSONAL HOME PAGES

Personal home pages extend the customizing of the web into personal information management systems. The user is able to choose from predefined choices set up by the service provider; these later become the criteria for which information is presented for the user. Information located throughout the service provider's information space is brought to the user, and posted on their personal page. The implications are powerful, as the user does not have to manually browse or search through the structure to find needed information. Update intervals are dependent on the nature of the service provided, but can range from daily (news services, financial) to monthly (certain publications and subscriptions). Related functionality includes the ability for the service provider to send targeted information to the user, based on personal preferences.

SEARCH QUERY AND RESULTS

Search becomes a necessity in large-scale web sites and complements the browsing structure. Depending on the needs of the project, the search capability may span the web site or several web sites, and may utilize authentication and security. This limits access to certain documents, such as proprietary information or confidential data. The search features are defined by the nature of the information published, but generally include Boolean, proximity, dictionary, and thesauruses.

An example of search engine technology is Verity's Topic® Information Server, which uses agents to help users search for information across the Internet. The product has forms-based support for customizing the types of searches, layout of the results, and other search parameters. More information can be found at http://www.verity.com.

HELP PAGES

It is a good idea to include help pages in a web site, especially if there exists a high degree of interaction with the system. Of course, ideally, the system should be easy enough to use so that no help is required. However, in commercial applications supporting secure financial transactions, the user may require additional help before completing a transaction in order to fully understand the implications.

A central help system should be accessible, but also there should be context-sensitive help which points into the central help system depending on the context of the user activity. For example, a user in the middle of ordering a product would select the help button and link directly to the page discussing product ordering.

CONTENT PAGES

The range of content found on the web is truly varied, with the latitude for expression wide. However, basic page elements should always include an identification element to inform the users where they are in the web site. Navigation back to intersections or intermediate navigational pages should be provided, and perhaps a link to the very top of the structure, the home page. Content pages may be layered using progressive disclosure to provide additional detail in a certain category or topic. These pages and their requirements should also be identified, based on the nature of the service provided.

TERMS AND CONDITIONS

Most commercial services must legally post the terms and conditions of their service somewhere in their web site. Users who register may view some of these screens during the registration process. This information is clearly subordinate and only included for legal reasons.

Developing Design Specification

Sketches and prototypes are materials which are used as material for a design specification for the web site. The specification is a requirement for the development team and organization establishing the web site. Items specified include the organizational framework, page types, cross-links, and descriptions of user interaction. The specification does not necessarily define visual attributes or presentation style, but focuses on the requirements for implementation.

This information is invaluable to all members of the development team. Engineers are able to understand in a tangible manner the model of the web site. Artists and designers can begin to visualize all elements required to support functionality. The organization or client can review the document, approve the direction, and sign off for development and implementation.

FIGURE 3.33
Design specification diagram describing navigation.

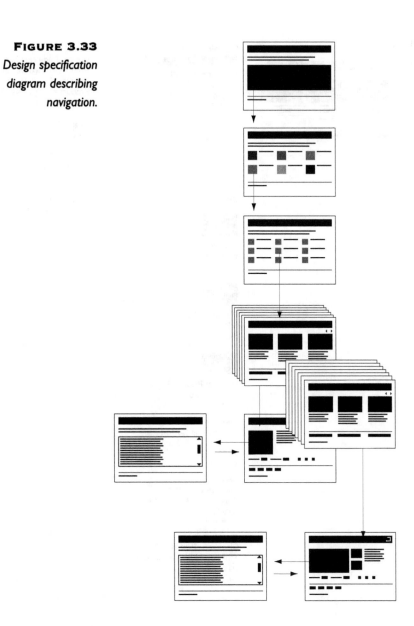

Figure 3.33 is an example of a diagram from a specification document which describes navigation through product pages in an on-line store. Figure 3.34 is a detailed specification for product pages. All elements, controls, and text are identified. All pages have a similar specification page.

FIGURE 3.34

Page specification for the product page in the on-line store.

Product Category Page

Graphic Elements:

Head Identification
w572 x h34
Trajan 12pt R G B Spacing=2
4-bit .GIF

Previous Button
w34x h34
3-bit .GIF

Next Button
w34x h34
3-bit .GIF

Product Photo #1
w180 x h120
5-bit .GIF

Product Photo #2
w180 x h120
5-bit .GIF

Product Photo #3
w180 x h120
5-bit .GIF

Home Page Button
Trajan 12pt R G B Spacing=0
w180 x 34
4-bit .GIF

Shopping Button
Trajan 12pt R G B Spacing=0
w180 x 34
4-bit .GIF

Checkout Register Button
Trajan 12pt R G B Spacing=0
w180 x 34
4-bit .GIF

Text:
Current Page Number
Product #1 Text Description
Product #2 Text Description
Product #3 Text Description
Copyright Tag

Cross-links:
Previous Product Page
Next Product Page
Product #1 Details
Product #2 Details
Product #3 Details
Home Page
Shopping Bag
Checkout Register

In summary, the *organizational framework* functions as a blueprint for the web site, providing an obvious structure of the information space for the user. Using the techniques of *grouping* and *hierarchy*, the framework emerges with major nodes and traversal pathways identified. An indication of user task-flow through the information space and useful cross-links are identified with *task-flow diagrams*. The diagrams are refined further by sketching *paper-prototypes* which describe the user's actions performing specific tasks. The paper-prototypes are used as blueprints for *HTML prototypes* which initially test and verify the structure, but later will evolve into the web pages during the production stage. The *design specification* summarizes all these steps into documents for the development team and organization establishing the web site.

Interest cannot be created by multiplying various elements into a busy design. By dispersing points of interest, we only create confusion by conflicting effects that, in the end, give no impression at all.

Paul-Jacques Grillo,
Form, Function, and Design

4

APPLYING VISUAL DESIGN FOR THE WEB

Visual design techniques are helpful to transform the organizational framework from a blueprint into a functional, navigable information space for users. It is essential that the design reflects the organizational structure in an obvious way, communicating a tangible model of the information space to users. This is the job of the web designer(s), who assembles all the various elements—text, images, drawings, video, audio files, and so forth, and determines the arrangement, relationships, and formal visual quality of each page, while ensuring that every element fits into a cohesive, overall design.

The language of graphics is powerful, and requires skill and experience for effective application in any medium, including the design of web pages. In web applications, good visual design facilitates good communication, allowing users to access the needed information quickly and perform the required tasks in the most efficient manner. Aside from these paramount concerns, good visual design should add a level of aesthetic appeal, attractiveness, and a perception of quality and attention to detail to the web presentation.

Design across Disciplines

In large-scale commercial sites, the visual design application may relate to a larger, enterprise-wide communications strategy. In this case, it is important to regard the web site as an integral part of the whole, not designed within an isolated vacuum. Coordination is likely a necessity across the company and will most likely include establishing working relationships and communication between otherwise autonomous departments or subsidiaries. Indeed, the advent of the web has spurred the need for communication between groups of individuals who would perhaps normally never interact with one another.

This working scenario has an impact on the web design process and the method in which to handle communications for large organizations or corporations. The plan may be one of coordination and cohesiveness, with established guidelines and standards for how design elements appear, reflecting the appropriate character of the organization. Another approach taken may support separate operating units having a distinct, unique presentation visually unrelated to one another and focused more on the qualities, products, or nature of business within each unit. The distancing between subunits may be a purposeful strategy. In either case, the final visual design form is most contingent on the nature of the content and the organization publishing it.

More and more organizations and businesses consider their web presence a serious, integral marketing and communications component, and have, or are in the process of establishing, dedicated, cross-disciplinary teams to establish and maintain their web sites. In the development team, the contribution of the visual or user interface designer to humanize the web site is critical, since the end user sees only the web pages and *not* the underlying engineering architecture or database schema. Though implementing a large-scale web site requires engineering expertise and technical know-how, the pages themselves provide the controls for user interaction with the system. Technical jargon specific to the organization implementing the web site (for example, banker's lingo for a home banking system), should remain hidden from users. This is especially important if the home user or mass consumer market is the primary target audience.

Aside from focusing on the interaction design of web production, a major activity up to this stage in the design process has been the organization and structuring of content. Publishers, information designers, multimedia designers, and graphic designers perform this activity on a daily basis, under the demands of definitive budgets, technical constraints, and real-world time schedules. This experience adds positively to the collective effort of the web development team.

The visual design direction chosen determines the style and communicates meaning and metaphor of the web site to the user. The opportunities for expression in web publishing are great and as varied, for example, as the hundreds of magazines found on newsstands.

The presentation character, even among magazines which share the same subject category, is tremendously varied. A single generic formula solution or recipe would seem limiting and confining.

The same opportunities for expression and creativity exist for web publishing, as in print publishing. For example, a rock-n-roll band's home page would naturally provide an energetic, progressive layout as opposed to the stability and reputable look for an investment bank home page. A game site may purposefully inhibit navigation by forcing users to play through successive layers of dialogs, quizzes, and interaction, while it is essential for a research site to provide direct access to text-oriented research documents via a powerful search query. Financial on-line services require high user interaction, using task-oriented, form-based interfaces, while implementing access control, security, and encryption. Contrast this with a shareware site, which is free, open, and totally unrestrained. From web sites supporting activities such as chat or VRML experiences, to viewing static information in a document repository, the variations in design, page layout, and presentation style for the particular web application are limitless. Matching the overall visual language and page structure appropriately to the information presented is the primary goal when applying visual design to the web.

In the development team, competent visual design skills are needed. Every element on every page type identified requires design decisions which shape the entire character and presentation of the web site. Variations in the formal and stylistic dimension are endless, but the chosen direction should at least remain compatible with the project goals and character of the organization publishing the web site.

Designing a web site requires initial considerations concerning presentation choices which impact the final outcome of the project. The many limitations and constraints discussed in Chapter 2 will undoubtedly impact the design decisions which, for example, impact the size or quantities of graphic imagery. Refer to the organizational framework sketches and/or HTML prototypes, which should furnish an indication of major page types, screen elements, and necessary text and navigation controls. The framework structure defines the general types of pages needed to handle information in an obvious, organized approach, while task-flow diagrams describe interaction sequences users perform to achieve specific goals. This identifies mappings of user action to specific controls on the web page, such as in form-based pages requiring input for further processing; navigation pages supporting intermediate traversal through the information space; content pages; search query pages; and so forth. Once information and required user tasks on pages have been described, the elements are arranged into an effective composition which facilitates quick comprehension, efficiency, and aesthetic appeal.

A web space should be designed to accommodate all information types and activities requiring support by implementing a page design system, which is based on all the steps outlined earlier in this book. A page design system satisfies the entire spectrum of activities and information presented in a web site.

Finally, the overall visual language and presentation style determines the signature of the information space, adding aesthetic appeal for users. The final web presentation should be cohesive, interesting, easy to navigate, and most importantly, satisfy user goals and expectations.

Visually Reflect the Organizational Framework

The primary goal at this stage in the design process is to communicate the organizational framework structure to the user (Figure 4.1). As discussed earlier in Chapter 3, the problem of users when lost in hyperspace is usually a symptom of an unclear, maze-like structure or web pages that all look the same without any emphasis to communicate a hierarchy to the user. The focus and attention in designing an organizational framework are precisely intended to alleviate this dilemma. The web space, synonymous with a building, must now be constructed from the blueprint plan.

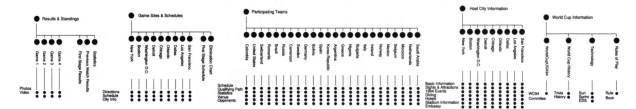

FIGURE 4.1 *Overall diagram of the WorldCupUSA94 web site structure.*

ESTABLISHING VISUAL RELATIONSHIPS

Various information groups have been identified and assigned levels of precedence within a hierarchy. Visual design techniques are applied to these groups, now communicating a *visual* precedence to the user. Page elements are organized into hierarchies visually communicating and reflecting levels of importance, based on user needs and frequency of access. When designed well, users are able to scan rapidly across the web page, with the most important information visually salient, providing the necessary cues to access further information or perform the required user interaction. The visual designer manipulates scale, position, color, and texture communicating meaning through the arrangement and chosen attributes of screen elements.

Well-designed pages display the information clearly to the user, rather than forcing the user to search for it on an overly crowded page. Wild, random variations in size, shape, color, and positioning of essential page elements (such as navigation controls) *within the same hierarchical level* disrupts a user's ability to perceive logical relationships within the structure. In Figure 4.2, the left image uses hierarchy and precedence to order the page elements in a clear, top-down task flow: Fill in information, make a selection, press the Submit or Reset button. Globally available navigation controls are designed as a cohesive set at the bottom of the page, visually differentiated from form buttons for local functionality. In the right example, all buttons are in the same level of the hierarchy, mixed within an ad hoc arrangement, presenting a confusing and difficult set of choices. Unneeded navigation controls are interspersed with form buttons required to process the input data.

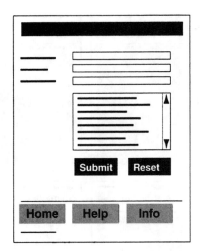

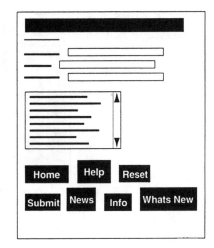

Controls which apply to specific tasks within the local context should visually appear distinct and be spatially separated from global controls. These sets of controls reside in different hierarchical levels and should therefore assume differentiated visual attributes. Mixing the two groups together in an ad hoc manner presents a confusing array of choices to users, as the control ordering and positioning constantly fluctuate from page to page. The user can no longer predict to find the necessary control in the exact same position on each page or with the same visual look. Well-designed web pages add predictability for users, so as to lessen the time spent in relearning the required interaction for each page.

PROVIDING CONTEXTUAL INFORMATION

In applying visual design to web pages, the overall objective includes providing critical identification and contextual information for users. Users should always know where they are within the web site, so as not to become confused or lost. By simply providing obvious location cues, the usefulness of the web site is immediately increased.

Various visual design techniques and metaphors borrowed from the real world help to establish a user's sense of place. For example, daily newspapers use sectional identifiers and typographic cues to inform readers where certain information is located, as shown in

FIGURE 4.3
*Newspaper sectional
heads and
layout system.*

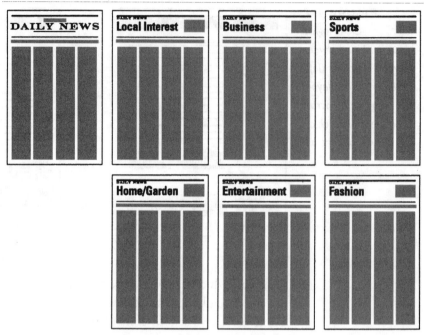

Figure 4.3. Familiar general categories, such as sports, business, or local interest, have corresponding sectional banners, always located at the top of the page. Since everyone has at one time or another read a newspaper, the organizational model and identification technique are familiar to most people.

Real-world shopping malls have storefronts with signage, directories at the mall and store level, and departments within each store. Stores categorize merchandise into familiar groupings and provide signs or maps to shoppers to help them locate their product. These landmarks located throughout the mall provide important visual cues, identifying relative position within the mall and indicating navigable pathways to reach a specific store. Web sites require the same type of organizational signage for the users as they traverse through the web site.

A major feature of the web—the sheer abundance of information—can contribute to information overload. Aside from identifying pages, overview diagrams or maps provide information in the global context, while showing local detail within a specific area. Interesting research in this field includes computer-generated generalized "fish-eye" views (Furnas 1986; Sarkar and Brown 1992) which are attempts to provide local detail and global context in the same computer display. The effect is similar to a camera's wide-angle lens. However, the view relies on quick dynamic updating and can also display unnatural distortion.

Effective overviews are possible in HTML using Netscape frames. This feature allows multiple areas within the browser pane to display separate documents. Each window within the browser may contain views ranging from the coarse-grained to fine detail. For example, Figure 4.4 illustrates the frame's functionality in a campus directory. The top-level window provides the overview for the entire campus. The area is partitioned into subsections, which are then selected and

FIGURE 4.4

A possible implementation of Netscape frames using multiple windows to locate information while preserving context.

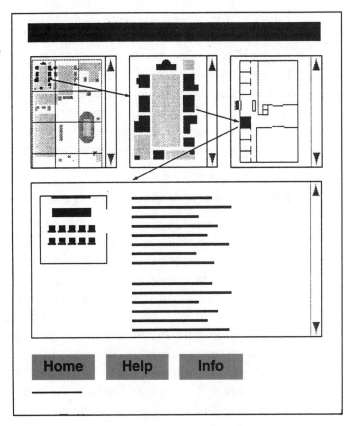

displayed in the top-middle window. At this stage, the user may select a specific building, once having the additional information provided in the view. The next level provides building-specific information. Finally, the specifics of the room itself, perhaps indicating equipment and operational hours, are provided in the last view.

Throughout the navigation, the context is preserved in the subsequent windows. Selecting a different structure in the top-most view may update information in subsequent views.

Contextual overview information need not be graphical. Even HTML text clearly identifying the page or current state within the interaction sequence adds valuable contextual information. A comprehensive index is extremely useful for viewing the entire contents of a web site, while providing direct access to information.

It should be noted that information "agents" and personal preference capability for information retrieval may help to alleviate the more pervasive problem of information overload. Such technology functions similar to persistent queries, constantly filtering for user-specified information. For example, a personal preference page may allow a user to select choices from predefined areas of interest, which then filters newsfeeds, loading only those articles which fit user-defined categories. Such pages should also be designed well in advance, so that the appropriate information is formatted into the design framework.

DESIGNING A VISUAL SYSTEM FOR PAGES

For large-scale web sites accessing huge information databases, designing a comprehensive page design system has many advantages. The HTML pages are completed by the web page designer, then passed on to the engineering team. Engineering then implements the underlying functionality, adding the necessary code, CGIs, perl scripts, Java applets, and so forth, to pull the required information out of the database and format the pages to the exact specification from the web page designer. The integrity of the original design is maintained through the direct adoption of the designer's original HTML pages. These pages function like templates which display the information to the end user in a predefined manner, consistent with the total visual language of the web site. The alternatives to this approach are either to allow engineers to design the pages as code is developed or hand-build each page, which may number in the hundreds of thousands for large database sites.

The major advantage of designing a systematic visual program for web pages is that this approach eliminates the ambiguity of design specifics, such as the scale or positioning of page elements. Questions regarding "what buttons go where and in what order" are already answered and described in the design specification completed earlier. Work now focuses on producing well-designed pages which support user tasks, while refining the user interaction through sketches and prototypes.

A page design system also adds to a user's perception of quality associated with the publisher of the web site. This perception is an important factor for recognition and differentiation with the competitive marketplace, as many more businesses and organizations establish web sites. A cohesive, clear organization and elegant navigation model communicate an attention to detail, thoughtfulness, and planning, which are a good reflection on the organization publishing the web site.

SIMPLICITY AND CONSISTENCY— THE GOLDEN RULES

> *The real truth is that everybody is afraid of honest simplicity, because it hides nothing.*
> Paul-Jacques Grillo, *Form, Function, and Design*

Consider simplicity and directness as a central, overall objective to help ensure clarity and understanding. The page designs should enable, and not get in the way, of the user through the required task-flow sequences. Needed controls and functionality are given recognizable visual form and positioned in a conspicuous, consistent location on every page. Indiscriminate clutter, purposeless graphics, and confusing jargon hinder users from perceiving their immediate task. More importantly, the primary message and its significance, may be obscured or misunderstood. Remember that on the web, less is more (and is faster to download).

Any design system is ineffectual when applied inconsistently. The regularity and predictability established among web pages becomes disrupted. Keep page designs consistent. Navigation buttons that change location or inconsistent wording compromises predictability and obviousness in the web interface. Adhering to a simple, consistent design will always benefit users.

Visual Design for Page Elements

Changes in size, contrast, texture, and relative position imply a visual hierarchy, or order of relative importance, which should echo the hierarchy of the writing.

Suzanne West, *Working with Style*

The hierarchy and precedence of the organizational framework is visually communicated by carefully controlling the scale, color, and positioning of all elements on HTML pages. Each page type identified in the framework and task-flow diagrams is designed within a cohesive, overall page design system. Information included on each page should be prioritized and given a particular visual attribute which communicates its relative importance to the user. Various design presentation alternatives and metaphors are explored by completing quick thumbnail sketches.

It should be noted that the visual design of the presentation layer for web pages may differ greatly, depending on the content and nature of the organization. However, the underlying organizational framework and functionality described in the task-flow diagrams remain constant and will determine page functionality, regardless of graphic style. A well-designed organizational framework with well-described user interaction sequences will translate into nearly any graphic representation, while a faulty structure cannot be saved, no matter how beautiful the graphics may be.

ORDERING PAGE ELEMENTS

Basic information and design elements include an obvious indication of the nature of the content, who is the owner or publisher, and controls for users' access to further information. An effective web page keeps the visual interference from too many graphics or wordy copy to a minimal. The page should be focused, clear, and simple. Content regarded important to users should be located in an obvious position on the page and given visual attributes which facilitate quick recognition. Relative size, position, and color of page elements purposefully lead the eye through information; the effect should facilitate understanding and quick comprehension, rather than disruption or obstruction. Visual designers employ an intuitive visual vocabulary to help communicate the intended message. Skill is used to control and manipulate the scale, color, position, texture, and so forth, of formal elements. These components together provide the means for users to effectively absorb the page information.

Sketching is important at this stage as in the earlier development of the organizational framework. Quickly jumping to the initial idea or clinging to preconceived notions without fully exploring alternatives limits and constrains the design.

SKETCHING ALTERNATIVE LAYOUTS

Figure 4.5 is a sketch of the home page for the WorldCupUSA94 web site. In this direction, a stadium is chosen as the dominant metaphor for the home page presentation. Positioned at the top of the page are the official WC94 identification mark and copy, which clearly identify this as the official World Cup web site. Below this information is the stadium graphic, which will be tagged as an ISMAP having defined hotspot regions. Below the stadium graphic is an area designated to hold the posting of the latest scores and results, with the subordinate information at the very bottom of the page.

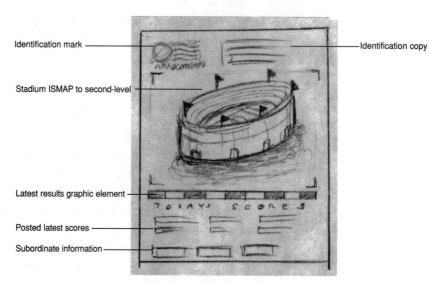

Identification mark

Stadium ISMAP to second-level

Latest results graphic element

Posted latest scores

Subordinate information

Identification copy

FIGURE 4.5 *World Cup home page sketch using a stadium metaphor for accessing further information.*

Since the latest game scores are highest in priority, the design in Figure 4.5 does not give enough emphasis to this information. The scores are positioned below the stadium graphic and could be hidden in cases where users have smaller display resolutions. Reordering the page contents will later shift the posted scores to a higher position on the page, providing greater emphasis and visual precedence.

This design sketch also uses a large graphic ISMAP, which can receive coordinate values from where the user makes a selection. It is helpful to provide clear, obvious clues to where the hotspot regions are within an ISMAP graphic element. Without obvious hotspots, users frequently click repeatedly in random locations within the graphic. The stadium sketch in Figure 4.5 is an interesting visual element, but requires more visual indication of where to make selections.

Since posting immediate game results remains the highest priority of this web site, the direction shown in Figure 4.6 raises the precedence of the match results to the top of the page. A graphic element delineates this area for dynamic posting of match results. In the middle of the page, another ISMAP graphic provides access to the second-level categories. The subordinate information is placed at the very bottom of the page, again reflecting its lower precedence.

The sketch in Figure 4.6 is taken a step further and a page mockup is quickly completed, as shown in Figure 4.7. Note the clear distinction between designated areas on the page to hold specific information types. At the top of the page, an area is allocated for posting the latest game scores. The space accommodates posting two to four match results a day, providing a daily dynamic character to the home page. An identification banner, displaying the official logotype and visually consistent with the WorldCupUSA identity program, distinguishes this site from unofficial World Cup sites on the web. Access to team, game site, host city, and World Cup background information is via the ISMAP graphic.

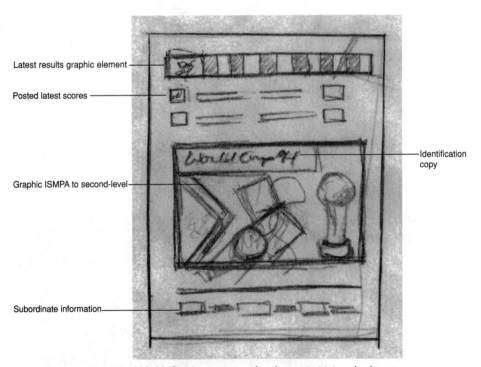

FIGURE 4.6 *World Cup home page sketch, reprioritizing the latest score information to a higher position on the page.*

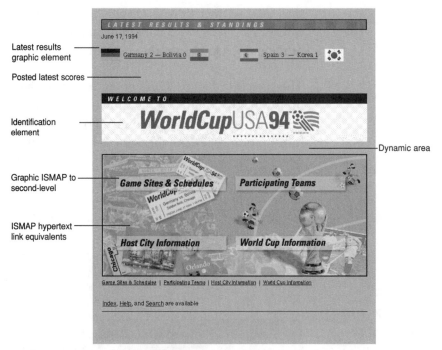

Latest results
graphic element

Posted latest scores

Identification
element

Dynamic area

Graphic ISMAP to
second-level

ISMAP hypertext
link equivalents

FIGURE 4.7 *Sketch in Figure 4.6 is mocked-up in a paint program. (WorldCupUSA94 logotype Copyright © En-Linea. All Rights Reserved.)*

Figure 4.8 is a close-up of the graphic ISMAP. The graphic indicates where a user should position the pointer with obvious textual labels on the underlying graphic. ISMAPS should provide obvious hotspot "affordances" (or cues) for users, so they will know where to click.

FIGURE 4.8
ISMAP graphic for home page sketch in Figure 4.7. (Copyright Reserved FIFA and En-Linea. WorldCupUSA94 logo © WorldCupUSA.)

The lack of visual distinction between elements which may or may not function as clickable items is a common error seen in web sites using ISMAPS. The user must repeatedly reposition the pointer and click the mouse to invoke an action.

The coordinate information from the user's mouse action causes the server to launch a CGI program which determines what URL (or page) to serve to the user. In terms of system performance, using an ISMAP requires an extra program execution on the server, which can be an issue if the site is expected to have a large number of simultaneous "hits." Since this was the case for the World Cup home page, more sketches explored alternative layouts without implementing an ISMAP.

Remember also that the larger the graphic ISMAP, the longer the loading period for users. This can be especially annoying for home users connected with 14.4 or 28.8 modems. Since many home users with modems do not choose to load the images in exchange for better response times, hypertext link equivalents should be provided whenever an ISMAP is included. If users choose not to load images, and do not have hypertext link equivalents, they will be stranded and unable to access any further information in the web site.

A third directional sketch for the World Cup home page is shown in Figure 4.9. The large ISMAP graphic has been substituted with an array of four graphic buttons, with hypertext equivalent links for accessing second-level categories. The graphic buttons offer obvious, clear definitions of the second-level information groupings, while providing hypertext link equivalents in close proximity to the graphic button. This is necessary so full functionality is provided to users who defer image loading. The rest of the sketch is similar in arrangement and order as seen in the previous example.

The sketch in Figure 4.9 is applied to actual page design mock-ups and final design implementation, as seen in Figure 4.10. The page has been divided into sections to hold the required information. Highest precedence is given to dynamic posting of game scores, positioned at the very top of the page. The colorful graphic banner elements designate the top of this area, providing final game scores immediately when viewing the home page. Selecting the hypertext

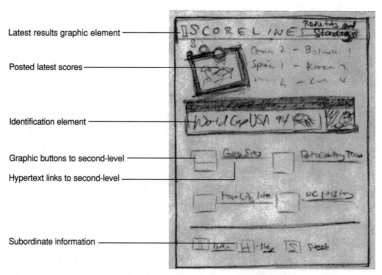

Latest results graphic element

Posted latest scores

Identification element

Graphic buttons to second-level

Hypertext links to second-level

Subordinate information

FIGURE 4.9 *Third World Cup home page sketch, displaying buttons instead of an ISMAP.*

will serve the user the appropriate highlight page for that specific game. The identification elements function much like a newspaper banner, which clearly identifies the web site as the official World Cup server for the event. Below this identification element is an array of graphic buttons which provide access to the second-level categories. Subordinate information about the technology partners is located at the very bottom of the page.

Throughout the home page design process, the sketches explored various presentation arrangements for the information. Intentional decisions were made in the positioning, scaling, and color choices that communicate the level of precedence in the information. The page remains focused and free of extraneous information or elements which have nothing to do with the event.

A general design goal is to provide a hypertext link for all graphics functioning as links on the web page. This is important when users defer image loading or view the page with a text-only browser, such as Lynx. Also, alt tags are useful to provide a brief description of the graphic for text-only browsers.

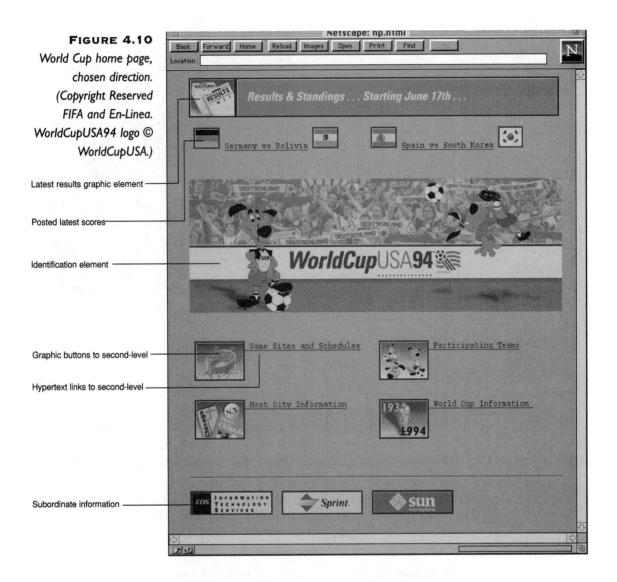

FIGURE 4.10

*World Cup home page,
chosen direction.
(Copyright Reserved
FIFA and En-Linea.
WorldCupUSA94 logo ©
WorldCupUSA.)*

Latest results graphic element

Posted latest scores

Identification element

Graphic buttons to second-level

Hypertext links to second-level

Subordinate information

```
<IMG ALT="WorldCupUSA94" SRC="banner.gif">
```

In this example, a user who does not load images will read "World-CupUSA94" on the display. Note that an alt tag for a link will continue to function as a link.

The visual style of the World Cup pages was to communicate the color and carnival atmosphere of the sporting event. The identification element was composed of various composited graphic elements,

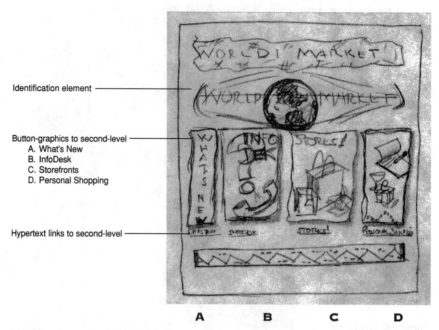

Identification element ⎯⎯⎯⎯⎯⎯

Button-graphics to second-level ⎯⎯
  A. What's New
  B. InfoDesk
  C. Storefronts
  D. Personal Shopping

Hypertext links to second-level ⎯⎯

A   **B**   **C**   **D**

FIGURE 4.11 *A cybermall sketch.*

with eight different versions displayed at random intervals throughout the tournament. The colorful bars at the top of the home page were updated daily, using a perl script written by the webmaster, which would display the appropriate banner for that particular day. This added a sense of dynamic newness to the pages, in contrast to static, fixed pages, which seemed somewhat lifeless for such an exciting, colorful sporting event.

Similarly, Figure 4.11 is a sketch ordering page elements for an online mall. Basic page elements in the sketch include a main identification graphic, with four major second-level categories, each represented by a separate graphic element. Below each graphic is a hypertext link equivalent.

The secondary categories are communicated by separate, unique graphic representations and textual labels:

What's New (A)—for the latest specials or openings at the "World Market"

InfoDesk (B)—for user help, questions, registration, and general customer services

Storefronts (C)—the directory to all stores in the cybermall

Personal Shopping (D)—a personal preference page generated by user selections on a variety of predefined query choices.

In Figure 4.12, a sketch of the home page orders the information into an alternative presentational. The Storefronts category is now assigned a dominant spatial precedence to allow users direct access to merchants. Since activities, such as user registration, will probably not be as frequent as users requiring access to the stores, the priority shifts the InfoDesk, What's New, and Personal Shopping categories into a vertical bar located on the left side of the home page sketch.

The advantage of the design in Figure 4.12 is providing direct access to storefronts from the home page. However, issues for using an ISMAP mall plan include scalability for future stores and lack of hypertext equivalents. What happens when a dozen new stores are added to the mall? How does such a graphic scale? Maintenance is also an issue with any home page displaying large ISMAP graphics.

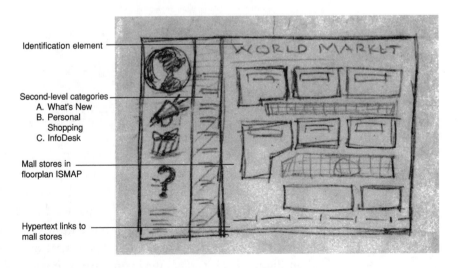

FIGURE 4.12 *Alternate home page sketch for the cybermall.*

FIGURE 4.13
*Large graphic ISMAP
(top) and text-only ver-
sion (bottom) available
for user with slower con-
nection speed.*

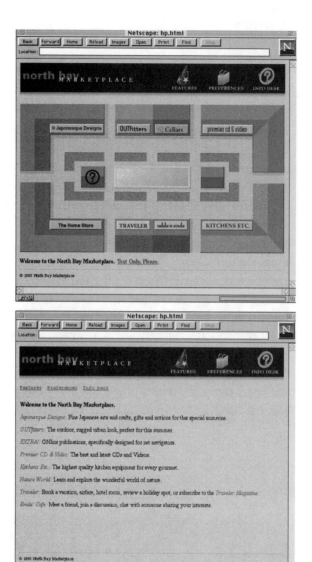

Any future changes or alterations mean the entire graphic must be
regenerated and inserted. Also, provision for hypertext link equivalents must still be included when using an ISMAP and are included
below the floorplan graphic. If image loading is canceled, the user is
unable to select a merchant from the nonexistent floorplan. Note
that the perspective chosen for representation, as seen in the top page
in Figure 4.13, is somewhat unnatural to users. People normally

walk through a mall; they rarely fly over one. The vantage point from directly above, though interesting at first, is an unfamiliar one. Note the inclusion of a text-only link, which will display the bottom image in Figure 4.13. HTML text is substituted for those with slow connection speed. The main title bar graphic is still included since cached in local memory after the first download.

As these examples illustrate, content is not simply thrown on pages in careless order, with disregard to relevancy and importance for each separate element to the user. Purposeful arrangement and ordering of page elements structure the page into partitions containing specific functionality or categories of information. Intentional sizing and positioning of elements communicate a precedence and grouping of information. Also included are identification elements, to be discussed next, providing contextual information for the user.

Graphic or Textual Elements for Identification

Many examples in the real world offer techniques which can be applied to web pages for providing identification. As illustrated earlier, a common daily newspaper uses clear sectional heads for Sports, Business, Classified, and so forth. Information is organized into these general categories; banners located at the top of each page identify the section. Most people are very familiar with this metaphor; using sectional heads is one approach of identifying the major information groups within the organizational framework.

Controlling the background of the web browser, when used effectively, can also add important contextual location information. However, there exist numerous considerations when using backgrounds, such as the possible cross-platform color inconsistencies and degradation of page legibility. Backgrounds should add positively to a web page, relate to the visual language of the web site, and not be indiscriminately applied simply as busy surface effects.

GRAPHIC AND TEXTUAL BANNERS

An example of using graphics as sectional banners is illustrated in Figure 4.14. These elements designate the second-level World Cup home pages. Each of the five major categories, along with index and help, receives a banner positioned consistently at the top of the page, providing clear textual identification for the section. Every page in the web site falls within one of these categories and therefore receives an appropriate banner assignment. This identifies the second-level groups on all pages in the web site.

The banner graphic is subdivided into sections providing either identification information or functional navigation controls. The left area specifies a region for placing the official World Cup logotype. This "brands" the site as the official World Cup web site. Positioned in the middle, within the blue bar, is text which identifies each second-level category. The text is set in the designated official font for the World Cup, Univers italics. Positioned right is an array of miniature icons for navigation to each of the second-level pages from anywhere within the web site.

FIGURE 4.14
World Cup second-level banners for identification. (Copyright Reserved FIFA and En-Linea. WorldCupUSA94 logo © WorldCupUSA.)

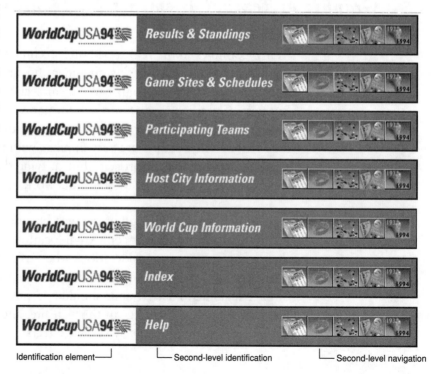

Identification element ⎦   ⎣ Second-level identification   ⎣ Second-level navigation

The small postage-stamp size reproduction of the home page icons within each banner provides instant access to the home pages for each of the five major second-level categories. This eliminates the required round trip for users to traverse up to the home page and back to the selected second-level page. Since these home pages are major "intersections," functioning as intermediate navigational "hubs," the user is within a single action from full access to all intermediate navigational pages within the web site. This design supports early task-flow sketches which described this functionality.

The major function of the banner is to identify the pages for the user. Users who jump wildly across the framework structure will subsequently always know where they are within the web site. The users will also be able to navigate to the second-level nodes from any page. These second-level nodes are the major arteries or intersections, where users access further information. Direct access to these nodes is clearly beneficial. Figure 4.15 is an example of a second-level page using the identification head, positioned at the top of the page.

From a visual design perspective, the banner graphics not only complement the graphic treatment and style for the web site, but also fit in with the identity program for the sporting event itself. Conscious design decisions are made that ensure a visual consistency with the entire scope of the event, so as to function as a part of the whole communications design strategy. Consistent color palette, typography, and graphic elements applied to all aspects of the web site add consistency and cohesiveness to the presentation.

Figure 4.16 is another example of identification banners within an on-line store. These banners function again like newspaper sectional mastheads, identifying areas within the web site.

Department identification is included within the graphic element. The user (or shopper) who browses the web site will always know the department currently within by reading this element, which is always positioned at the top of the page. In cases where images are not loaded or text browsers are used for viewing, the alt tag reflects the exact syntax of the identification information.

```
<IMG SRC="head_edible.gif" ALT="Edible Gifts">
```

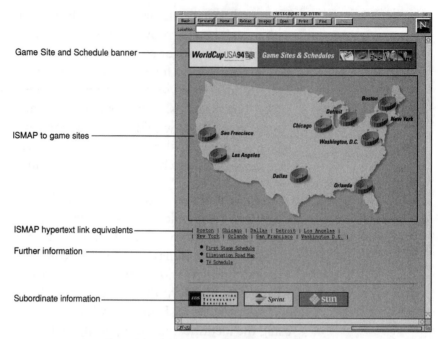

Game Site and Schedule banner

ISMAP to game sites

ISMAP hypertext link equivalents

Further information

Subordinate information

FIGURE 4.15 *Second-level home page with identification banner.*
(Copyright Reserved FIFA and En-Linea. WorldCupUSA94 logo © WorldCupUSA.)

Every page will receive a banner, consistently positioned at the top of the page.

The graphic banner element also functions as a guide for horizontal width of the web page. For example, the on-line mall must accommodate users with 640 x 480 screen resolution, the common notebook display. This determines that, ideally, page elements must not exceed 572 pixels horizontally or the width of the banner. The banner can function as a recommended width for users to size their windows.

Identification does not infer the need to always include a graphic banner. Text identification information on pages provides the same needed information to users. Text works just as well as the graphic banners, as long as the spatial positioning and size are visually salient. In Figure 4.17, text identifies each page, much like labels in dialogs of a typical application software product. The pages requiring user input must be clearly marked.

FIGURE 4.16

*Identification banners
for an on-line store.*

Whether browsing through an on-line store or hierarchies of research information, the presence of identification cues for the user is helpful (and well appreciated).

BACKGROUNDS FOR CONTEXTUAL INFORMATION

Netscape provides the capability to alter the background of the browser pane by either specifying a solid hexadecimal numeral or

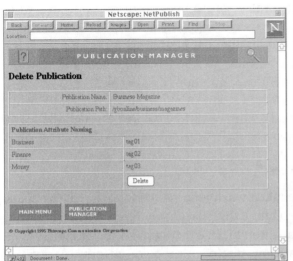

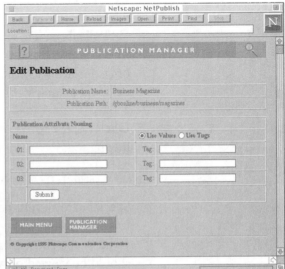

FIGURE 4.17 *Textual identification for pages in a web-based publishing application.*

tiling a graphic image. Altering the background of the browser window can add much needed contextual information for users and can create added interest and appeal to a web page. However, text or images over altered backgrounds can be problematic. Too much color, contrast, or saturation may inhibit readability or cause unnecessary eye strain for the user. Bear in mind that it's already more difficult to read text on a computer display than print on a page. Also, unpredictable results can occur when viewing backgrounds on different displays and platforms. The best advice for using backgrounds is to test the effect on as many different computer platforms as possible.

Specifying Solid Background Colors

There are basically two methods of controlling the background in Netscape. The first method uses a hexadecimal number which represents a solid color. This numeral is then entered in the beginning of the HTML document in the following format.

```
<BODY BGCOLOR="rrggbb">My Document</BODY>
```

The "rrggbb" represents a red-green-blue triplet which fills the background with the solid color. The hexadecimal format is not exactly the color specification language of visual designers, but most paint or image processing conversion programs handle this format. It is worthwhile to work out pleasing swatches, as seen in Figure 4.18, which avoid the oversaturated, garish hues normally associated with CRT displays. These colors were originally developed on a Macintosh computer and tested on different platforms. Most, not all, colors translate well, though again, the best insurance is to view the color on as many different configurations as possible.

Likewise, the foreground text may also be colored through the following tag:

```
<BODY TEXT="rrggbb">My Document</BODY>
```

Special care should be taken when altering the foreground text color. It is much safer to keep text either black or white, depending on the value of the chosen background. In either case, the color chosen should be viewed on various platforms for color integrity. A hexadecimal color which appears fine on a Macintosh may appear com-

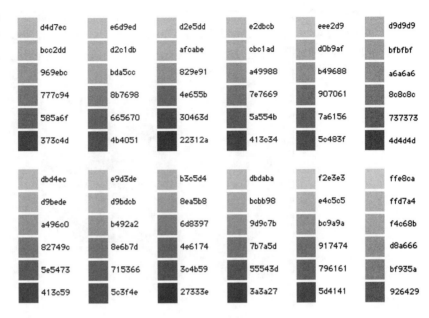

pletely different on a Windows PC or UNIX system. The only real way to ensure page legibility and expected color consistency is to view the page on as many platforms as possible.

Figure 4.19 is an example of a page which uses the body background tag to change the background to a grass-green color, simulating the background of a soccer field. A low-saturated green hue (afcabe) is defined in the <BODY BGCOLOR> tag, with the text remaining black. The page is tested across platforms, and reproduces the intended effect well. See also Color Plate 4.

The colored background differentiates the soccer pages from other sport pages within the Web site. Different page backgrounds for hockey, basketball, football, road racing, and so forth, would add uniqueness and interest to the Web site. These pages function as the initial presentation for each specific sport.

Specifying Images as Background Textures

Netscape supports the capability to tile the background of the browser by referencing an image file. The image may be a solid

FIGURE 4.19

*Changing the
background to a
solid color.*

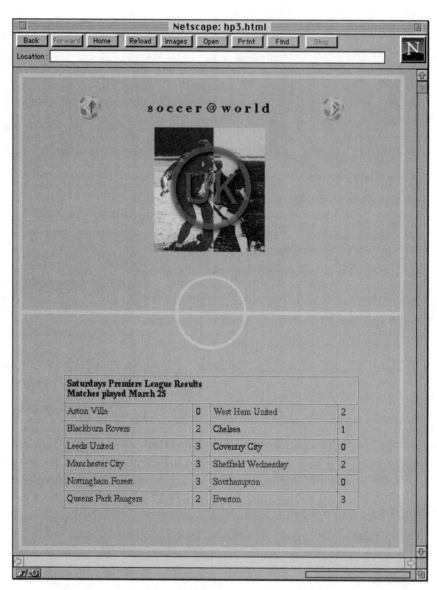

color, texture, or a continuous tone photograph, or line art. Since the swatch is an editable graphic element, the possible effects include limitless textures and patterns. This can, however, be problematic if color contrast is too high or texture too busy. The subtle interaction of colors between the foreground image and background texture may also alter the visual quality of images. Care should be taken to test pages using backgrounds on multiple platforms.

The <BODY BACKGROUND> tag, which specifies an image file in either GIF, XBM, or JPEG format, is tiled repeatedly, filling the background of the browser. The image can be any size and will repeat regardless of size chosen. In terms of response time and performance, however, backgrounds are loaded like any other graphic element. Therefore, the larger the image size, the longer it takes to initially download the image, then decode the page.

Figure 4.20 is a texture swatch for a Virtual Aquarium page. In this case, the aquarium is part of a much larger information space, with many activities, exhibits, and information, containing geography, earth science, and nature content. The use of the background pattern clearly helps users define their location within the web site. It also provides interest and added visual appeal, especially within the intended audience, which includes young children and high school students.

```
<BODY BACKGROUND= "water.gif">Virtual Aquarium</BODY>
```

The water graphic has a fairly random pattern to begin with, which works well for generating a seamless tiled visual effect (Figure 4.21). In general, the more random the pattern, the better the tiling, creating an overall solid fill without discernible borders. Graphics with subtle variations in value or gradations create perceptible hard edges where the graphic elements align adjacent to each other. Therefore, the pattern created appears obviously tiled to the user. This somewhat cheapens the effect, resembling more wallpaper or a vinyl flooring rather than enhancing the message.

FIGURE 4.20

A graphic image for a background.

FIGURE 4.21

Virtual Aquarium
page using a
background texture.

The graphic file in Figure 4.22 effectively functions as a background texture resembling Japanese tatami matting for an Asian arts and crafts store. The regularity in the small graphic replicates well, visually blending into an overall continuous pattern. The color is neutral and unsaturated; when placed on the page in Figure 4.23, it adds a level of elegance to the store, which communicates the nature of the merchandise. The background fails to interfere with the overlying page elements, but functions instead in a complementary manner. The textured effect reproduces well across platforms, as also seen in Color Plate 3.

FIGURE 4.22

A graphic file for replicating a tatami (Japanese matting) background.

Again, the background differentiates this store from others in the virtual mall. If there are numerous merchants, distinguishing one store from another becomes a priority, from the point of view of usability, as well as for marketing motives. No matter how large the virtual mall may be, the users will always be provided with important contextual information as to their current location.

FIGURE 4.23

A store using a background pattern for differentiation.

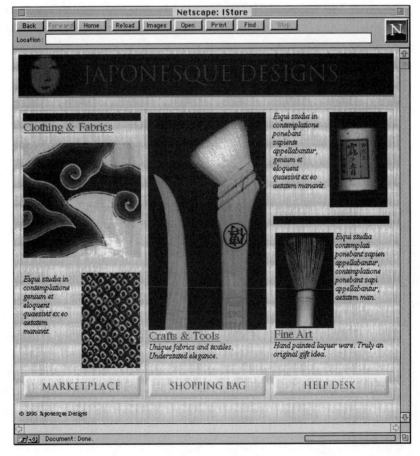

The overiding concern when using backgrounds is to make sure the pattern or color does not conflict or inhibit readability or cause visual interference. Allowing time in the development schedule for testing the effect on multiple platforms is the best way to avoid unexpected results.

It is also wise to make sure your audience has a browser which can take advantage of the background functionality. Non-Netscape browsers simply ignore these tags and display a page in the regular default background color.

Consistency for Identification Elements

As with any design system, consistency counts. Visual design reinforces the hierarchy, but only when consistently applied. Haphazard ordering and careless placement of essential identification elements destroys the logical relationships in a clear organization and hierarchy. The result is confusion and bewilderment, as the perceptual cues do not reinforce the ordering of the same information between pages.

Designing Pages for the Web

The grid, then, is the discipline that frees one from the time-consuming burden of making certain decisions (dimensions, proportions) without which fruitful and creative work is extremely difficult.

Paul Rand, A Designer's Art

Early work by artists of the Dutch de Stijl movement in the 1920s explored effective methods of subdividing two-dimensional spaces. Work by artists like Piet Mondrian and Theo Van Doesberg explored spatial relationships and structure, highly influencing the coming modern movenment of design, which ultimately shaped the early history and tradition of modern graphic design. Some of the principles applied from graphic design, especially the use of grid-based layout, are helpful and translate well onto the web.

GRID-BASED DESIGN PROGRAMS

Grids in graphic design function much like proportion regulators, determining the placement, position, and scale of all elements and their spatial relationships on the page. The grid *program* anticipates an unknown number of items by establishing a system of proportions and spatial positioning across an entire project. The basis of typographic grids in graphic design is columns and interval spacing between each column. This provides rhythm and regularity to the page and throughout the entire printed application. When used by a graphic designer, the grid becomes part of the design process, while maintaining flexibility to add interest and vary page compositions. The grid also contributes to ease of maintenance when distributed as templates across an organization, such as in newspaper or publication design.

For large-scale, information-intensive graphic design, the grid continues to fulfill an important role in the working process neccessary to manage complex and vast quantities of information. Without an effective grid structure, for example, a flight timetable or daily newspaper (Figure 4.24) would be nearly impossible to read. Aside from organizing and structuring the complex, grid systems also streamline maintenance by allowing the designer to focus more on the overall design, rather than on the measurement details, which have already been worked out in the initial design system.

In most commercial page layout programs like Framemaker™ or QuarkXPress™, generic templates remove guesswork for design

FIGURE 4.24
Common newspaper grid for organizing and structuring information.

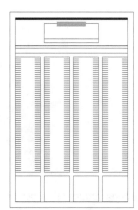
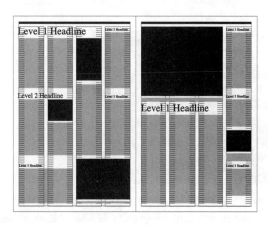

novices by providing adequate, predefined grid systems. Such templates are beneficial, with immediate results in little time and effort, especially for non-designers. Reasonable results are possible for anyone without the designer's expertise or training. These generic templates can easily be extended or modified into custom solutions when appropriate, offering the starting point for unlimited variations and unique applications.

In multimedia applications, grid-based design systems also provide benefits and immediate improvements to the overall organization of the screen. In Figure 4.25, the redesign sketches for a multimedia kiosk for Sun Microsystems, Inc. illustrate the dramatic improvement when regularity and structure are added to the project. The two screens in the before example (A) illustrate an unclear organization and information hierarchy. From a visual design perspective, the screens appear as if they are from two separate applications. The

(A) Before   **(B) After**

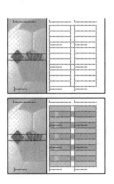

FIGURE 4.25 *Multimedia kiosk redesign sketches illustrating spatial relationships and underlying grid-based structure. (Copyright © 1995 Sun Microsystems, Inc. All Rights Reserved.)*

designs lack cohesiveness and desperately need alignment and a visual hierarchy. The redesigns (B) use an underlying grid structure providing a tighter, cleaner presentation, while maintaining cohesiveness between all screens in the project.

USING HTML TABLES AND FRAMES IN NETSCAPE

The implementation of tables in HTML 3.0 clearly delivers the needed capability to publish well-organized page designs and supports flexible control in an otherwise unstructured environment. However, unlike fixed-dimension grids based on typographic size in the traditional print arena, web tables are dynamic, flexible, accommodate change, and define cell areas rather than type and leading. Typographic grids in graphic design are precise and exact and determine the placement of all page elements within a fixed page size. HTML tables are much more general in their approach to layout, which reflects the inherent architecture to accommodate cross-platform viewing.

When designing tables, it's important to remember that users frequently alter the aspect ratio of the browser window, which may cause a dramatic reflow of page contents. User preferences may also change type style or size, or defer image loading, which can also dramatically alter the spatial relationships between carefully placed page elements. Text copy reflows within the table column, repositioning images and changing the overall look of the page. Text and images are not positioned in fixed locations by the designer, as in traditional print or multimedia design. Such flexibility for web page design calls for a different approach by the designer, furnishing the best solution for a given page type and its unique requirements, while providing enough openness to adjust to variations in font size or browser resizing.

In some cases, the designer is able to fix the size of the web page by using exact pixel dimesions for the width and height of the underlying table. When used this way, the table does not resize when the user changes the aspect ratio of the browser window. The table locks the layout; however, remember that platform differences in available fonts and user preference settings still alter the content position in the table, though not the table itself. Page elements may reposition and text lines break differently, although the table remains fixed in size.

Generally, the same advantages when using grids for print are present for designing web pages. Production details, such as image sizing and positioning of elements, are worked out ahead of time, freeing the designer to spend valuable time refining the interaction and overall user model. An overall table-based program determines general sizes for screen elements, which is then used to format the various page types. A design specification is developed, built on the table-based program, and functions as a guide for design implementation for all pages in a web site. This approach is especially helpful when designing large-scale web sites with a cross-disciplinary development team. The consistency and integrity of the original design is maintained, as the page specifications are passed along to all members of the development team.

For database-intensive web sites, the design of table-based templates is an essential step towards the generation of dynamically updated pages, generated from databases. Design layouts are worked out and specified by the web designer and later prototyped in HTML to test interaction and navigation. The HTML prototype pages are refined; when ready, they are later accessed by the engineering team members for actual implementation, adding necessary CGI programming or Java applets to create a full-featured web application. These pages are the interfaces to large-scale databases, as the visual appearance of the output is specified by the original HTML template. In a large-scale web site, page elements may be stored in an RDBMS containing hundreds of thousands of graphics or documents. Manually authoring each page would be an impossible task.

In this process, the visual designer assumes a new role in the large-scale web production team, designing comprehensive, table-based page systems. This arrangement is quite advantageous for designers, for the opportunities for controlling the page design throughout the web site are great. The direct implementation of HTML pages originating from the visual designer ensures that the design does not degrade or alter through the engineering implementation process. Designers who are able to master the simple constructs of HTML are in an influential position to directly affect the entire user presentation of the web project.

There are various HTML editors on the market, but most leave something to be desired when attempting to lay out an effective HTML page design. First, not all editors support HTML 3.0 (including tables and Netscape frames), let alone the many extensions unique to Netscape Navigator. Since Netscape offers the highest degree of control in terms of page design and layout, an editor which does not support these extensions compromises the logic in designing for Netscape to begin with. Secondly, many tools edit HTML, and *not* the actual page design, by direct manipulation. True WYSIWYG authoring tools are needed (and soon available), not HTML editors. Most of these HTML editors are cumbersome to use and may actually require more time to lay out a well designed page than when using a text editor, especially when the author must constantly hand tweak the HTML for specific needs. And finally, HTML is not that difficult to learn. The sheer number of web sites today (including personal home pages) infers that HTML can't be difficult to learn. Documents are written by the novice within half an hour. Once written, the page formats can be duplicated, reused, and extended for any application or need.

Page layout programs have conversion programs which take existing files and convert them to HTML. As with editors and authoring tools, however, most programs are in a catch-up phase with browser features, so it is best to verify if specific functionality is supported.

PAGE DESIGN EXAMPLES USING NETSCAPE TABLES

> *Like the architect's plan, the grid system employed by the graphic designer provides for an orderly and harmonious distribution of miscellaneous graphic material. It is a system of proportions based on a module, the standard of which is derived from the material itself. It is a discipline imposed by the designer.*
>
> Paul Rand, *A Designer's Art*

When developing a web-based page design system, consider the needs and requirements of the information being presented. The visual design of the page depends on the nature of the content. For example, a research site may publish text-oriented documents without images or photography, requiring minimal formatting. In contrast, an on-line catalog for a merchant may have a variety of products, services, and available levels of interaction for users, requiring different page layouts supporting the entire range of services.

Visual design in HTML differs from traditional print, or even CD-ROM multimedia production, mainly because the users are able to redesign certain aspects of the pages themselves. The capacity to lock-in exacting design specifications in print or CD-ROM production is exchanged for flexibility, fluidity, and some degree of user modification of the web page. Designing for HTML means shaping pages towards a more general formatting direction, rather than delivering precision and rigorous exactness.

Viewing web pages across platforms also reveals differences in how the final design appears to users. The apparent conflict between layout control and cross-platform viewing is an inherent characteristic of HTML. Flexibility should be designed into the pages, taking into account the dynamic visual quality found in web pages.

Basic Page Layouts

As in graphic and multimedia design, rough sketches are helpful to previsualize layout and spatial partitioning of the page. Rapid thumbnails explore various page arrangements and layouts, indicating size, scale, and positioning of essential page elements, as illustrated in Figure 4.26. Spatial partitions holding essential page elements, such as identification graphics and navigation controls, and textual copy are worked out, ordered, and positioned on pages. Copyfitting, type size, leading, and so forth, are meaningless for web pages. Areas holding content are determined instead of precise, measurable specifications.

An overall, table-based page design program is implemented to format all page types within the web site. Consistent positioning of identification elements and content is assigned for all pages.

FIGURE 4.26

Sketching content areas which fit into a table-based design program.

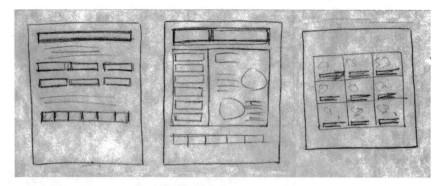

In these home page sketch examples for a prototype of an on-line nature and science magazine, a general page size is determined and rough indications of the underlying table-based structure are determined. An effort is made to fit page content within the boundaries of the table. A decision to minimalize user scrolling suggests the breakdown of content into smaller units, which fit within the table on each page of the web site. Various subdivisions of the page hold the different groupings of information or functionality. Areas for identification, navigation controls, and content are identified and ordered on the page.

Figure 4.27 is the HTML page. The home page design identifies three major areas:

1. The identification element, located at the top of the page

2. The main table structure which holds the page content

3. An array of controls for navigation and access to specific functionality.

Instead of using icons or buttons representing general categories of information, this home page example presents the content of the current issue in a table format, reflecting the metaphor of a magazine. All content within the table changes after a defined time period, providing user access to an entire new issue. This keeps the presentation fresh and changing, with new stories and activities. The page functions like a dynamic magazine table of contents, rather than a typical home-page reflecting static groupings of information.

The table-based program is applied to all page types identified in the web site, including the following pages: user login and password verification; subscription choices; membership services, including account summary and ability to cancel services; personal preference page; personal preference setup page; notices and verification; and search. Each of these service pages is formatted using the same underlying table-based program, which provides continuity and cohesiveness among all service pages. These pages provide functionality, such as filling out the registration form, or provide feedback and status information to users while navigating the web site. The actual story content may have a completely different visual appearance or table layout, based on the unique qualities of the information.

Since the magazine charges an access fee, pages must be provided for user login and password verification (Figure 4.28). All or a subset of the web site may remain under access control. In either case, the user must be provided with the necessary pages to input user name and password. Note that the form controls in HTML are unique to the platform. Unfortunately, for the moment, the form buttons cannot be substituted by a more visually compatible image, and the platform-dependent controls depart from the visual cohesiveness and continuity of the page.

Pages should be provided to users to inform them of their actions and current state while navigating the web site. Confirmation pages are necessary, for example, when the user has input the incorrect password or when an unregistered user attempts to access content requiring a fee (Figure 4.29). The current action or state is communicated to the user in the area designated for identification text information. This provides the user with immediate feedback. Subsequent explanatory copy is included between the horizontal rules, with the appropriate navigation controls specific to the user's context.

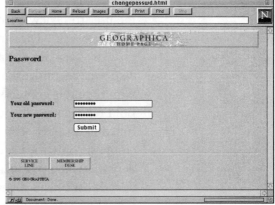

FIGURE 4.28 *User login and password pages.*

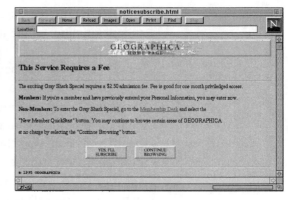

FIGURE 4.29 *Error and state notification pages.*

Web sites vary in degrees of interaction and, in some circumstances, provide as much interaction as shrink-wrapped software applications. The advent of secure commercial transactions and support for richer multimedia datatypes now delivers the capability for developing complete, highly interactive web applications, rich in functionality. Full-featured software applications use floating dialogs and notices for immediate feedback when a user completes an action. As in good software user interface design, essential feedback is necessary and needs to be designed into web applications as well.

The ability to charge and control access requires pages which allow the user to review current billing charges or cancel services, as shown in Figure 4.30. These pages are formatted within the table-based program and remain visually consistent with the other service pages. The page identification is clearly positioned at the top of the page, with the table contents below, followed by the navigation controls. Bold type is used throughout the web pages for heads only, so as to function as an effective coding mechanism. This reserves the visual emphasis only for heading information. The currently available six definitions for type heads are more than enough for visually coding text. Most of the pages shown use, at the most, three to four type sizes. Overuse of type sizes, bold, and italics adds confusion when

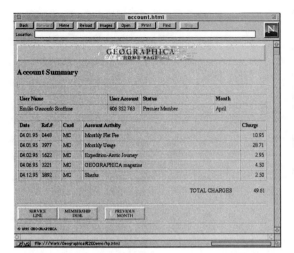

FIGURE 4.30 *Account summary and service cancellation pages.*

the application does not mirror warranted importance or needed emphasis.

Although the initial layout of an HTML table requires a moderate amount of effort, the finished page is easily cut and pasted into a new document, altered for specific functionality, and saved under a new name. Reusing HTML tables eliminates redundant effort.

As in good graphic design, alignment in forms is critical for legibility. Tables can format the text into structured layouts, which display columns of tabular data for increasing readability for users. Prior to the table, the use of <PRE> or fixed-width font spacing, was the only method for alignment of elements. Using the <PRE> tag is synonymous with attempting to align text when using a typewriter. Repeated hits of the space-bar between irregular columns must compensate for different word lengths, a laborious, time-consuming task.

Support for implementating user-definable preferences (referred to as "Personal Journal" in the examples) is also accommodated in the service pages (Figure 4.31). Users should access and edit their own personal preferences. The edit personal preference page allows the user to choose topics of interest from a predefined set of subject cate-

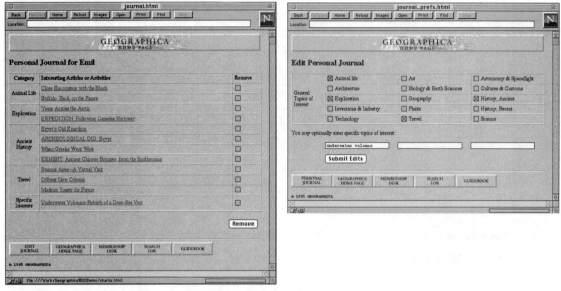

FIGURE 4.31 *Personal journal and edit personal journal pages.*

gories. Specific areas of interest may be input into the three textual fields provided on the page. As information is published by the service, articles which fit within the user personal preference appear on the personal page. The user accesses the information directly, rather than browsing the hierarchy.

The pages have the defined identification graphic, including the clear textual identication. The tables enclose the choices and nonexclusive checkbox controls allowing for more than one choice are included within the table. The action button follows the logical flow through the task in a top-down fashion, very much the flow in forms design. At the bottom of the pages are the global navigation controls.

Web sites may require full-featured customer service areas to allow users to input and edit personal information, password, user name, change billing options, and so forth (Figure 4.32). The functionality supported is very similar to that found in other on-line service providers currently on the Internet. Any site implementing secure transactions will require the user to input billing information and provide a password and user name for authentication and access.

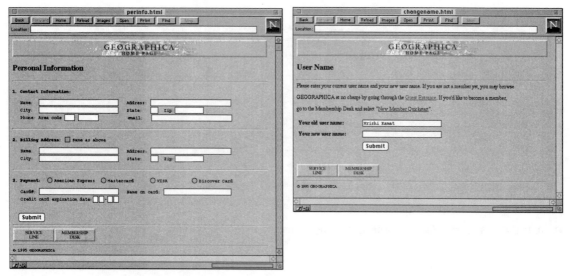

FIGURE 4.32 *Personal information page and editing the user name.*

Pages should provide the ability to alter or update this information.

The pages containing actual content in the web site vary their appearance and presentation, depending on the specific subject matter activity. For example, the Virtual Aquarium (Figure 4.21) has a dramatically different visual presentation, which visually correlates with its subject matter, differentiating itself from the design of the service pages. This helps to add liveliness and unexpectedness to content pages. A clear visual difference between the service pages and actual content pages reflects the intentional structuring and organization of the web space.

Figure 4.33 shows sketches for another table-based design program—in this case, for an on-line store selling fine Asian arts and crafts.

The initial design sketch (left) began with a three-column, table-based design program for the store home page. This initial design used the table as an explicit structuring guide for areas of the page, controlling the scale and position of all images and text. Modular sizes for images were chosen which best reproduced the product, but also added regularity and repetition to the page, establishing a pleas-

FIGURE 4.33 *Sketch for an on-line store using a three-column table system.*

ing rhythm. Pragmatic reasons for choosing modular sizes for images include easy image processing and speeding downloading. This will be discussed later in this chapter.

Sketches (middle) and (right) are product-level pages and show layout variation for text and image. Note the inclusion of arrow buttons for paging through a series of information within a given product category. This would support the user paging through a particular product category, such as sake cups or textiles. A system of head identification elements was designed to communicate the section of the store.

The home page in Figure 4.34 shows a three-column table, with each column width set to 180 pixels. The absolute pixel width dimension locks each column width, though expansion is vertically accommodated. The images are scaled to fit within the table, based on predefined sizes. Various alignment settings allow text to be positioned on the right or left of the images, with the black bars echoing the main identification element located at the top of the page. The background is generated from a small swatch of the tatami pattern, which replicates well with no visible borders. The navigation buttons located at the bottom of the page are designed to visually appear consistent with the entire flavor of the page, without separating into their own visual layer.

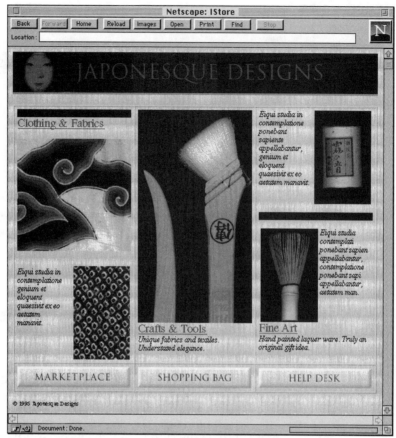

In Figure 4.35, the same table-based program is used for all product pages in a given area of the store—in this case, a page showing three swatches of textiles. Every product page in the web site has an identification head, followed by the three-column table which encloses the product image and a brief textual description. A separate table encloses the navigational controls which are on all pages throughout the web site. In cases where a series of related products are available, buttons provide a paging capability for the user to flip through, much like in a real-world catalog.

The explicit table structure blends well with the notion of tatami matting, remaining visually consistent with the usual linear borders found on the actual matting. Various values control the border thickness and bevel dimensionality, though in most cases, a border of one or two

pixel thickness suffices. Table borders exceeding two pixels appear visually heavy and introduce a lattice-like pattern within the page.

Figure 4.36 is the shopping bag page. The on-line store supports saving products from various departments within the store in the shopping bag. These products remain persistent for a determined length of time and the user may inspect the contents of the shopping bag at any moment during the shopping experience.

The page is visually consistent with the rest of the page design system. The identification head is followed by the table, which formats the product information in a readable, easy-to-understand manner. The product name is a link which returns the user to the product description page. Functionality includes editing the quantity and removing any product in the list. Below the table is an array of form buttons which initiate the available actions. Note that the visual disparity between these form buttons and the custom-designed navigational buttons. Unfortunately, the form buttons are platform-

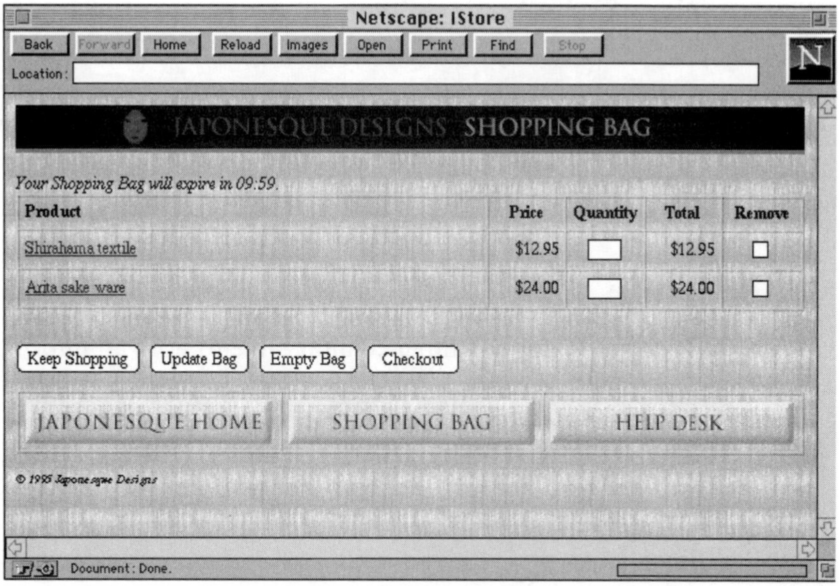

FIGURE 4.36

*Shopping bag page
from the store.*

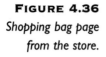

dependent and cannot be altered by substituting a custom-designed graphic file.

Asymmetrical Page Designs

As the previous examples have shown, tables also are useful for developing regularity and adding structure to specific page layouts. The repetition of regular units and logical simplicity in symmetrical designs provides an adequate solution for organizing most pages. For certain needs, the use of tables adds much needed explicit structure to page layouts, especially for input forms or the display of tabular data.

In some cases, however, the use of explicit structure may be too heavy-handed and cause interference or remain inconsistent with the visual presentation desired in the web page layout. Tables are also used by implicitly controlling the page layout and positioning of elements *without* showing the border. Asymmetrical page designs are easily accomplished using HTML tables, adding variety and interest to the web's otherwise static, totally symmetrical web page. The dynamic compositional effect of assymmetry adds activity and interest to pages. With a little creativity, special effects and unusual page designs are also possible.

The sketches in Figure 4.37 are for the previous example of an on-line Asian arts and crafts store. However, in this example, the use of asymmetrical page layouts corresponds nicely with the aesthetic of Asian art. Such designs would be impossible in HTML without using tables and the attribute values which control the positioning of page elements within the defined columns. Rough thumbnail sketches imply a three-column table to hold all information for various pages. The home page (left) provides the identification element, sized photography, and control buttons for access to needed functionality. The basic underlying table definition is repeated for intermediate navigational pages (middle) and product pages (right).

Figure 4.38 is an example of the page design. (See also Color Plate 4.) The various elements are positioned within a three-column table. The spatial relationships controlled by the various alignment attribute values and discussed in Chapter 5. As in the other examples, the table definition uses exact absolute pixel dimensions for the table width, which locks the page layout, regardless of when the user resizes the browser window. However, the ample empty space surrounding elements accommodates expansion if the user selects a larger font size. The page is given a solid black background through a hexadecimal value.

FIGURE 4.37 *Sketches for asymmetrical page layouts.*

FIGURE 4.38

Asymmetrical page layout using tables with no border.

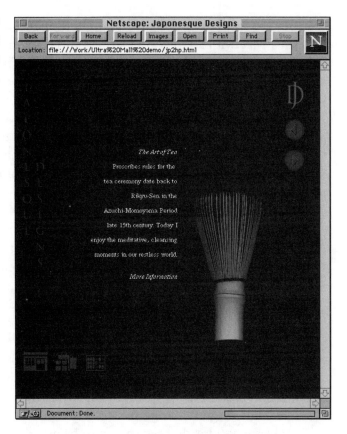

Page identification is provided, along with previous and next paging buttons. The product occupies the third column, with the descriptive text located to the left in a separate column. At the very bottom of the page, in the lower left-hand corner, are the navigational buttons to other departments within the store space. The choice of colors intentionally places the navigational controls in a separate visual layer from the product photography and accompanying text. This is an intentional design decision, in order to establish a visual precedence among page elements. The navigational buttons repeat on all pages and are therefore subdued so as not to interfere with the overall balance of the page.

Every page element has an alignment attribute associated with it, except for the text. By default, elements without an alignment tag are vertically centered in the middle of the column. The effect works well for the text in this design, but also anticipates users who may view this page with a larger font size. In this case, the text would simply occupy more space than currently displayed. The ample amount of empty space above and below the text ensures that there is room to grow or accommodate unknown user-type style and size preferences.

When designing pages with tables, it is helpful to see the table outline by setting the border attribute to at least one pixel width. This provides an important and useful visual reference during the design process and helps to verify the positioning and placement of elements during the edit-reload authoring cycle. Figure 4.39 is an example of the page with the border set to one pixel width. The table is set to a fixed width dimension, functioning much like traditional print-oriented grids, guiding the placement and alignment of page elements. This approach is similar to working in a page layout program. Designers frequently toggle the view of the underlying grid, which aids in verifying spatial positioning during the design process. Once the design is complete, the border attribute is set to zero, hiding the table borders from view. The HTML table definitions and alignment tags used in these examples are explained in Chapter 5.

Custom Page Arrangements

Tables have already been shown to be useful for controlling alignment and spatial positioning of page elements. HTML tables, along with some creative forethought and design, can provide interesting page designs which rival the presentation characteristics commonly found in CD-ROM multimedia projects, while still utilizing HTML text. The advantages of providing HTML text include the ability to edit or update content (at the expense of complete typographic control across platforms). This is still a better solution for web pages, instead of designing large, full-screen bit-mapped graphics, containing bit-map text. This latter approach is common in CD-ROM-based multimedia products, which use full-screen, hand-tuned bit-map pages. Text is generally fixed and noneditable, directly composited into the background layer. This approach is inapropriate for web page designs. Huge, full-screen images cause prolonged load time, especially for home users, and demands an entire new page update when editing is necessary.

FIGURE 4.39
*Visible table borders
during layout help in
page alignment and
positioning of elements.*

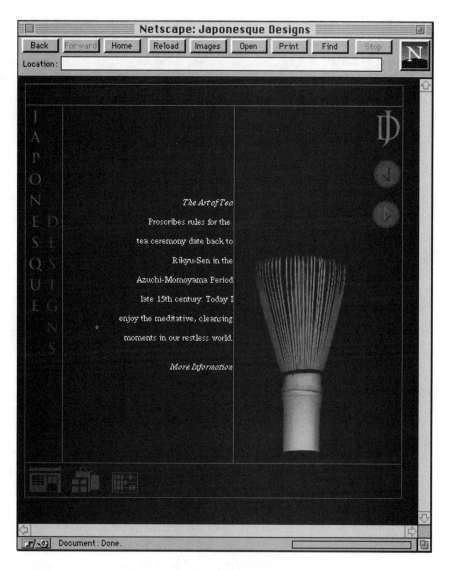

Figure 4.40 is an example of a virtual book, which uses nested tables for the positioning of all graphic elements. In this application, the Expedition Journal visually differs from other pages in the web space, providing the user with obvious and visually interesting contextual information. The icons located in a row at the bottom of the page are links to other travel document pages, allowing the user to view related information during the virtual expedition. Each of these

FIGURE 4.40

Tables can be used for exact positioning of graphical elements. In this case, edges of the book are separate graphic files, placed within a nested table. The table borders are hidden from view, completing the illusion of a book.

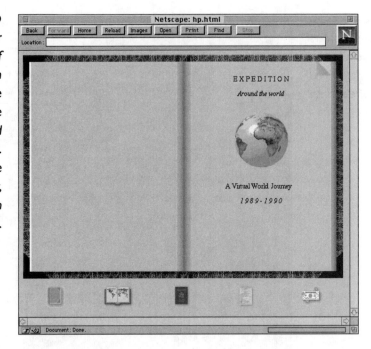

documents uses a similar table-based layout for the illusion of the particular document.

Such a special design application for web pages is effective and works within expectations *if* the amount of content is limited, controlled, and known ahead of time. The page content must be carefully monitored in this case or the illusion is destroyed. Whenever there is HTML text within the table, ample empty space should be present to accommodate variation in font size. When using absolute pixel dimensions for table columns, the table remains locked and will not resize if the user chooses a large font. The type will extend beyond the table border and actually flow outside the perimeter of the table. Examples of table effects are seen in the visual design workshop section in Chapter 5.

The table functions as an invisible layout tool for positioning of page elements without an obvious explicit structure. An outer table contains the edges of the book, using the alignment tag. Within the book, another table controls the placement for all graphics on the book pages, including the HTML text. The alternate approach is to image process one large graphic file for each page, which would demand a long load-time for the graphic and also use ISMAP functionality. By hiding the table borders, the illusion of a continuous image surface is quite convincing. Figures 4.41 and 4.42 are other pages in the design.

Note that the background has been changed to a solid neutral color <BODY BGCOLOR="eee2d9">. This color choice simulates paper well; the blending of images into this background during the image processing stage helps to achieve the book illusion. To view the actual HTML tags for this layout, see Chapter 5.

This technique provides interesting possibilities for added contextual information to users. For example, in this application, the various document icons at the bottom of the screen lead to pages which are

FIGURE 4.41

Pages in an HTML virtual book.

also designed in the same manner, using HTML tables to produce books for the user to page through. This graphic treatment lends itself well to travel material, since most people are familiar with various travel documents in the real-world.

Standard Sizes for Elements

When developing table-based layouts, the images for placement within the tables are formatted into predefined standard sizes. Designing standard units for images and graphic elements has many advantages for web page layouts.

First, developing modular sizes for screen components eliminates unnecessary size variation. Visual designers use scale and contrasts to communicate meaning to the viewer, connotating precedence and hierarchy. Important elements are given larger size dimensions than

FIGURE 4.42

Pages in an HTML virtual book.

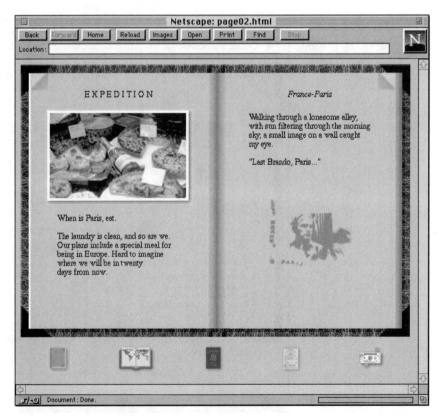

FIGURE 4.43

Modular sizes for elements (left) establish perceptual levels in the visual hierarchy versus a more haphazard approach (right), exhibiting wild scale variations for page elements.

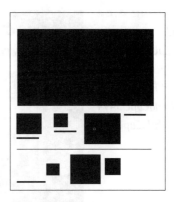
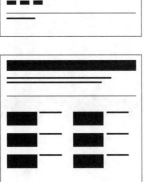
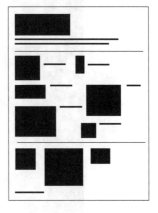

subordinate ones. This produces a visual layer for the user, who can perceive groups of elements based on scale and spatial relationships. An array of icons or thumbnail images within the same hierarchy grouping should therefore share the same scale dimensions. Haphazard or careless sizing of page elements disrupts the visual hierarchy and ordering of information on the web page. Also, from a visual design standpoint, the page appears sloppy and reflects a lack of attention to detail and design. Figure 4.43 illustrates the differences in approach.

A second advantage when using standard units is the ease in maintenance. Web sites are not static entities. As opposed to a book which, once printed, is finished, a web site is an evolving entity, constantly reinventing itself and adapting to advances in technology and public taste. Standard dimensions shared with members of the development

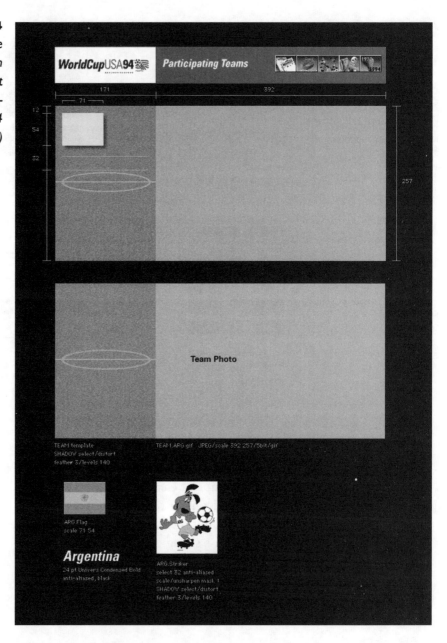

team ensure consistency and results within expectations. Questions pertaining to sizing are eliminated when alterations or modifications are required at a later date. Images from contract artists or designers fit neatly within the design format when dimensions are shared with members of the production staff.

In Figures 4.44 and 4.45, the dimensions for graphic elements for the World Cup home pages are worked into a design specification. Each of the 24 teams participating in the tournament has a home page, which includes a team photo and other information. In Figure 4.44, the major graphic elements are specified and sized accordingly. There

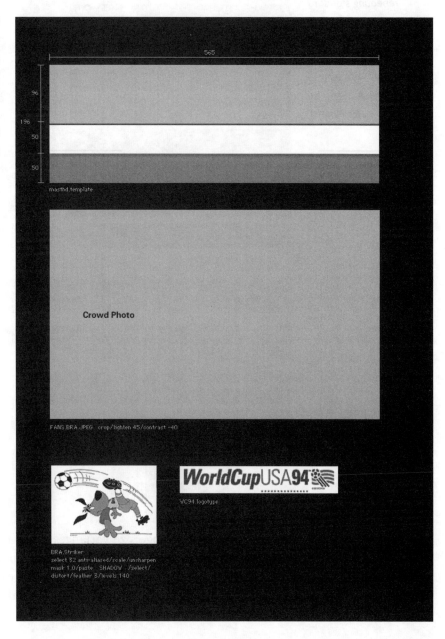

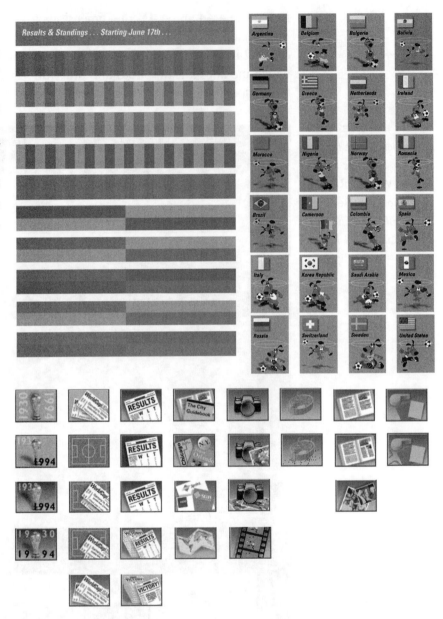

is little reason for strange size variances in the team photos. This may also be perceived as emphasizing a certain team over another. The page elements are sized and relationships established between elements, including the banner heads located above the team photo. Image processing steps are also notated, useful for later reference.

Figures 4.45 shows the same approach to the design of the home page banner. Standard units for graphic elements establish visual relationships between the pieces which add up to the presentation. Reusing common dimensions removed the guesswork from sizing decisions for related elements. All page elements fit into the design system, like pieces in a Lego building, which provides a cohesive, well-integrated presentation. (See also Color Plate 2.)

FIGURE 4.47

Various graphic elements for an on-line store, sharing standard dimensions for functionally related components.

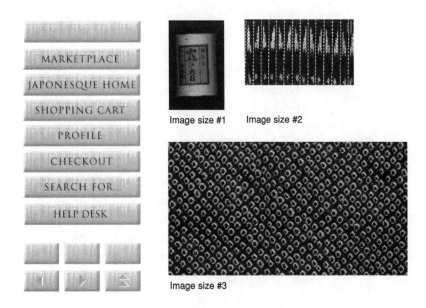

Standard units for graphic elements help tremendously when a large quantity of images must be processed. Standard sizes support batch procesing of images with special tools, such as Equilibrium's De Babelizer™. This cross-platform image processing tool processes hundreds of images by executing a series image processing and file format operations, resizing, reducing colors, and saving each image in GIF or JPEG format.

When a comprehensive table-based layout system is designed, the choice of standard sizes for graphic elements adds visual benefits as well. The pages appear visually cohesive, with elements better integrated, contributing to a wholeness in the presentation. Figure 4.46 illustrates a variety of graphic elements, all designed within predefined standard sizes for ease in implementation and production.

A more pragmatic reason for using standard sizes for graphic elements is that the image dimensions, if included in the image HTML tag, can actually speed up screen decoding (rendering) by the Netscape Navigator browser. This is done by providing the correct height and width values in the <IMG SRC> HTML tag.

```
<IMG height=32 width=100 SRC="button.gif">
```

When the size dimensions are provided, the browser does not have to figure out the "bounding box" which contains the graphic before displaying the image. This information is given in the tag; thus, the image is displayed faster. The height and width values should always be included, since the user should receive all possible benefits enabling quicker page decoding.

From an HTML authoring perspective, using standard units is advantageous in that the entire tag can be duplicated without reediting the image size values. Common sizes for icons, for example, do not require laborious retyping of different height and width values. Only the image name differs. Obviously, strange, meaningless size variations for images require more laborious HTML editing, if the height and width options are used.

Hopefully, WYSIWYG authoring tools will largely eliminate the worry about HTML details. For now, however, a basic understanding of these constructs can only help the web design.

Similarly, Figure 4.47 show common components in an on-line store. The identification elements share the same size, and therefore have similar HTML tag constructs. The same approach is taken with the buttons. Dimensions are also worked out for product photography in small and large sizes. This allows using a batch image processing tool for uniform scaling to common dimensions. Obviously, this is extremely handy if the store has thousands of products.

Design Supporting Navigation

A well-defined organizational framework is the determinant factor for effective navigation through the web site. A well-defined structure, as described in Chapter 3, provides the user with an obvious, clear model of the information space. Visual design and layout should therefore reinforce this structure; obvious visual elements, controls, and cues help the user traverse through the hierarchy of information. When appropriate, cross-links are provided to related information which adds a benefit to the given user task for that particular moment. The cross-link may traverse the structure, but the user should always know the current position by noticing visual identification or contextual information. Aside from navigating a browsing structure, search interfaces, personal preferences, indexes, and help systems aid in navigation for users in large-scale web sites.

NAVIGATION TO MAJOR NODES AND INTERSECTIONS IN A HIERARCHY

A hierarchy has a root node, which has no others located above it. This is likely to be the entryway into the web site or the home page. Subsequent nodes further down the hierarchy have ancestors and the navigation assumes a path up and down the tree. The various levels at which a node resides are contained within an abstract notion of depth. Therefore, levels are implied in the hierarchy.

From a visual design perspective, nodes sharing a common parent also should share some common visual traits, while nodes in separate trees appear visually differentiated. Visual design defines a graphic language for relationships among the hierarchy. This makes the structure visually salient, thus aiding navigation.

Hierarchies have sub-nodes, or intermediate navigational pages, which may or may not provide content, but function more as second- or third-level home pages along the path toward the needed information. It is useful to allow all sub-nodes direct access to their intermediate navigational pages. For example, in Figure 4.48, all pages in level three should have direct access back to the Business/Finance page located in level two. Access to the top node of the hierarchy would also be needed, to allow users to select a different category in level two, such as Food/Home. Visual controls for navigation to the intermediate page must be provided when a user traverses down the hierarchy, to avoid forcing the user to make circular round trips.

There may be navigational controls which are accessible globally from any page in the web site. For example, our Asian arts and

FIGURE 4.48

In this service structure, the user traverses through four levels of the hierarchy, and may return to the major intermediate navigational pages directly.

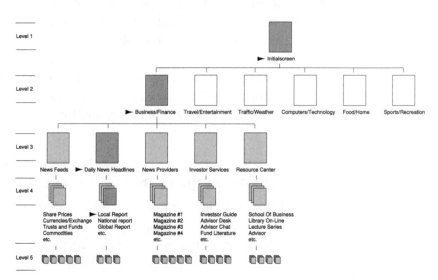

crafts on-line store has a Shopping Bag and Checkout model, with pages providing the respective functionality to review all possible purchases and actually purchase the product. These activities may be accessed by the user at any time, from anywhere within the web site, so navigation to this functionality must be provided on all pages. The visual design chosen is graphic buttons, which remain visually consistent with the background pattern and are positioned toward the bottom of every page in the store.

Figure 4.49 shows the positioning of three global navigational buttons, which the user may access from any product page within the on-line store. The array of buttons is consistently located at the bottom of the page. Care has been taken to attempt to fit all product pages within the 640 x 480 resolution.

RING STRUCTURE FOR SERIES OR RELATED INFORMATION

Note the inclusion of previous and next buttons in the top right corner of the page in Figure 4.49. The purpose of this control is to allow the user to page through a series of related information, much like the natural behavior when flipping through a print catalog. This

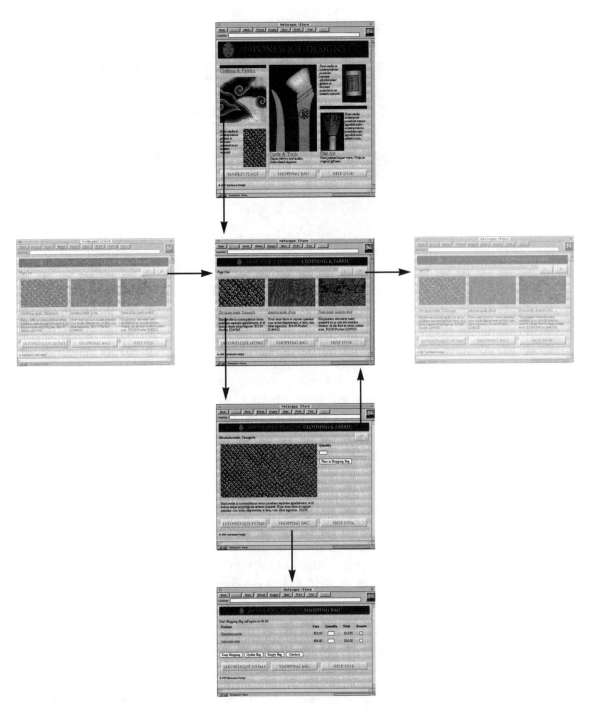

FIGURE 4.50 *Navigation path through an on-line store. See also Color Plate 1.*

is also a common functionality in many CD-ROM-based multimedia titles. In this example, any product in the the store is grouped with related products; the user may choose to browse through related products of interest. The user-flow is illustrated in Figure 4.50.

The user traverses through related products in the browse path. When the user is interested in a particular product or desires more detailed descriptive information, the user can access the product detail page. At this stage, the user may select attributes, place the product in the Shopping Bag, or return to browsing through the related products. Access to the home (in this case functioning as the main table of contents), Shopping Bag, and Checkout pages is provided throughout all pages in the web site; these buttons are consistently located at the bottom of each page.

The visual presentation supporting navigation need not be limited by the examples given. Certainly, the richer presentation functionality, including VRML (Virtual Reality Modeling Language), Sun Microsystems' Java language, Apple Computer's QuickTimeVR, and advances in greater bandwidth offer opportunities for exploring new methods of navigation for users. Netscape 2.0 Frameset documents also provide the opportunity to design effective navigational structures by revealing multiple views of the Web site hierarchy. As functionlity increases, opportunities to support rich interaction and dynamic feedback will be possible. This opens the door to web applications rich in graphics interaction and experiences for users.

*Design formatting stan-
dards and follow them
consistently in all
screens within a system.
The related screens in a
system should always
have standard types of
information located in
the same part of the
screen.*

Deborah J. Mayhew, *Principles and
Guidelines in Software User Interface Design*

5

VISUAL DESIGN
WORKSHOP

Netscape Extensions to HTML

Netscape introduced a set of extensions which rapidly set the layout and presentation capabilites of the Netscape Navigator browser apart from others. The familiar tagline "for best veiwing, use Netscape" has become a common recommendation on many web sites. A large reason for the popularity of this browser is due to its superior graphics and layout capabilities, which are what publishers and content authors wish.

Remember, however, that all browsers do not support the advanced layout capabilties of Netscape Navigator. It is always best to test your designs across browsers if dependencies exist. Some of the features in Netscape, such as tables, are a proposed feature of HTML 3.0 and will (hopefully) mean eventual support for tables across browsers.

Note also that early HTML editors or authoring packages do not yet support tables or the functionality specific to Netscape. Editors and authoring software seem to be in a phase of catch-up with browser functionality. Therefore, an understanding of HTML is probably the most direct and effective method to fully exploit the advanced capabilties found in Netscape 2.0 today.

This chapter assumes the reader is familiar with HTML, and has prior experience in authoring HTML documents. The following examples will provide an added depth in understanding the basic HTML constructs for most novice users.

This section will not cover every Netscape HTML extension, but only those that are directly useful and particularly applicable for supporting good design and layout. The complete list of extensions is avaliable at http://home.netscape.com/assist/net_sites/index.html.

NETSCAPE EXTENSIONS

The most useful set of extensions is associated with images. The image tag has a variety of values for alignment. From a visual design

FIGURE 5.1

Image and text in
HTML 2.0.

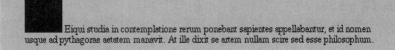

standpoint, the ALIGN=left and ALIGN=right are extremely useful for layout. These two tags support "stacking" text either flush left or right, adjacent to an image. The horizontal dimension of a page can now be used, partitioned into areas holding content toward the right margin. Figure 5.1 is an example of images and text prior to the Netscape extensions.

The same image and text, with the ALIGN=left option added to the tag, stack the type flush left of the image, as shown in Figure 5.2.

```
<IMG SRC="square.gif" ALIGN=left> Eiqui studia in contemplatione rerum
ponebant sapientes appellabantur, et id nomen usque ad pythagorae
aetatem manavit. At ille dixit se artem nullam scire sed esse
philosophum.<BR CLEAR=left>
```

Also note the addition of the BR CLEAR=left option. The BR tag normally just inserts a line break in text. The addition of the CLEAR option controls where the text break is and continues text after this tag below the image, against the left-hand margin. The BR CLEAR=left has been placed after the first sentence, with the result illustrated in Figure 5.3.

```
<IMG SRC="square.gif" ALIGN=left> Eiqui studia in contemplatione rerum
ponebant sapientes appellabantur, et id nomen usque ad pythagorae
aetatem manavit.<BR CLEAR=left>At ille dixit se artem nullam scire
sed esse philosophum.
```

Image alignment set to the right positions the image to the right margin of the browser window, with the text positioned to the left. The BR CLEAR option functions in the same manner, as shown in Figure 5.4.

FIGURE 5.2

Alignment options added
to the image tag.

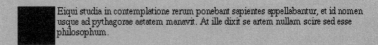

FIGURE 5.3

*Continuing text with the
break option.*

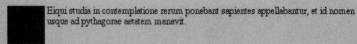

```
<IMG SRC="square.gif" ALIGN=right> Eiqui studia in contemplatione
rerum ponebant sapientes appellabantur, et id nomen usque ad pythago-
rae aetatem manavit.<BR CLEAR=right>At ille dixit se artem nullam
scire sed esse philosophum.
```

Other image alignment tags are useful for short captions or labels next to the image. The ALIGN=top aligns the image with the highest line item, while ALIGN=texttop aligns the image with the cap height, as shown in Figure 5.5.

```
<IMG SRC="square.gif" ALIGN=top HSPACE=4>This text is
align=top.<BR CLEAR=top>
```

FIGURE 5.4

*Image alignment option
set to right.*

Another tag, HSPACE, stands for the horizontal space which is added around an image, so the text does not butt up against the image. Note, however, that this tag also adds a four-pixel space on the left-hand side of the image. This is apparent if another image is placed directly above, with no HSPACE option, as shown in Figure 5.6. VSPACE is also an available option and has the same effect on the top and bottom perimeter of the image.

The ALIGN=middle centers the text baseline horizontally with the image. The text, however, doesn't appear optically centered in rela-

FIGURE 5.5

*Image alignment top
and texttop options.*

FIGURE 5.6

*The HSPACE
(and VSPACE) add a
specified pixel space
between image and text,
but do so on both sides
of the image.*

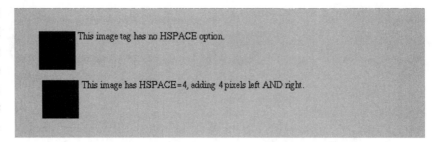

tion to the image. The ALIGN=absmiddle, or align to the absolute middle, provides an optically better solution, attempting to align the X-height, or visually strong height of the lowercase text, with the image, (Figure 5.7).

```
<IMG SRC="square.gif" ALIGN=middle HSPACE=4>This image is
align=middle.<P>
<IMG SRC="square.gif" ALIGN=absmiddle HSPACE=4>This image is
align=absmiddle.<P>
```

Finally, the ALIGN=bottom aligns the text baseline horizontally with the bottom edge of the graphic image, as seen in Figure 5.8.

```
<IMG SRC="square.gif" ALIGN=bottom HSPACE=4>This image is
align=bottom.<P>
```

Netscape adds the WIDTH and HEIGHT values to the image tag, which can speed up loading and display of the page. This tag should always be used, as any gain in speed is important for users. As mentioned earlier in this book, the design of standard units supports easy HTML maintenance for classes of images types, reducing the need to change these tags for arbitrary size variations. Here is the format of the tag:

```
<IMG WIDTH=48 HEIGHT= 48 SRC="square.gif">
```

FIGURE 5.7

*Image alignment middle
and absmiddle options.*

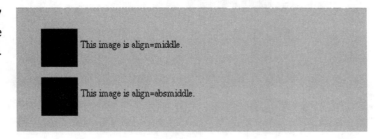

FIGURE 5.8

Image alignment set
to bottom.

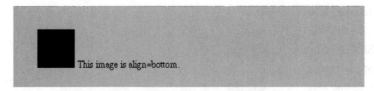

Altering the WIDTH and HEIGHT values will scale the image, as shown in the examples in Figure 5.9. Note that there may be distortion; image scaling done in an image processing program, like Adobe Photoshop, will yield better results.

```
<IMG WIDTH=48 HEIGHT= 48 SRC="square.gif">
<P>
<IMG WIDTH=96 HEIGHT= 24 SRC="square.gif">
<P>
<IMG WIDTH=24 HEIGHT= 96 SRC="square.gif">
```

When images function as hypertext links or ISMAPS, the graphic exhibits a two-pixel border around the image. With irregular-shaped images using a transparent background, or subtle graphic imagery, the effect is heavy-handed and just plain ugly. Netscape allows authors to turn this border off for images by using BORDER=value. Since these images function as links, hypertext equivalents should also be provided, though not shown in the example. Figure 5.10 shows the transparent image with and without the border.

```
<A HREF="fish.html"><IMG SRC="fish.gif"></A>
<A HREF="fish.html"><IMG BORDER=0 SRC="fish.gif"></A>
```

FIGURE 5.9

Using the WIDTH and
HEIGHT values to resize
(and distort) images.

FIGURE 5.10

*Image with border and
set to BORDER=0.*

The <HR> horizontal rule element has additional controls which include setting the thickness and width. When used with the width option in tables (discussed later), the consistency in alignment of the horizontal rule with tables allows for a tighter, cohesive visual appearance. Less useful is the width value, which allows authors to specify overly heavy, "slab-like" rules in documents.

The first addition is the SIZE=value option. This controls the thickness of the rule, as shown in Figure 5.11.

```
<HR><!-default rule->
 <P>
<HR SIZE=1> <!-one-pixel line->
 <P>
<HR SIZE=2> <!-same as default rule->
 <P>
<HR SIZE=4>
 <P>
<HR SIZE=8>
```

The size can be as large as one would like. Note that the default rule is equivalent to SIZE=2. Generally, the default works well for most needs.

An option is available to remove the dimensionality with the NOSHADE option. The same horizontal rules in Figure 5.11 are shown with the NOSHADE option in Figure 5.12.

```
<HR NOSHADE>    <!-default rule->
 <P>
<HR SIZE=1 NOSHADE> <!-one-pixel line->
 <P>
<HR SIZE=2 NOSHADE> <!-same as default rule->
 <P>
<HR SIZE=4 NOSHADE>
 <P>
<HR SIZE=8 NOSHADE>
```

Width of the rule is defined either in a percentage of the current browser window width or by providing absolute pixels. A percentage

FIGURE 5.11

Horizontal rule thickness options.

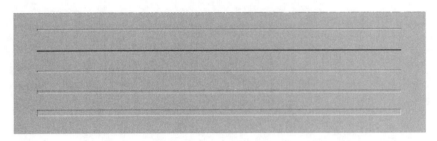

rule lengthens or shortens as the user changes the aspect ratio of the browser window. With absolute pixels, the rule is fixed regardless. The default alignment is to center the rule. Figure 5.13 is an example.

```
<HR WIDTH=80%>
<P>
<HR WIDTH=100>
```

Horizontal rules are aligned left, center (default), or right. A rule without any WIDTH=value will span across the width of the entire browser window and therefore negate the alignment options. The same rules in Figure 5.13 are shown with alignment left and right in Figure 5.14.

```
<HR WIDTH=80% ALIGN=left>
<HR WIDTH=100 ALIGN=left>
<HR WIDTH=80% ALIGN=right>
<HR WIDTH=100 ALIGN=right>
```

Another useful positioning tag in Netscape is the <CENTER> tag. Text, images, and even tables can be centered using this tag. Figure 5.15 is an example.

```
<CENTER>This text is centered.
<P>
<HR WIDTH=200>
<P>
<IMG SRC="square.gif"></CENTER>
```

FIGURE 5.12

Horizontal rules with the NOSHADE option.

FIGURE 5.13

Horizontal rules given a percent and absolute width.

Notice that any element within the <CENTER> container is affected until the </ CENTER> cancels the effect.

Finally, Netscape allows the HTML author to change text size with the <FONT SIZE=value> tag. However, since fonts are largely dependent on the platform and preferences chosen by users, the use of this tag may be impractical. Besides, many web sites exhibit an

FIGURE 5.14

Horizontal rule alignment left and right.

excess of font variations. It would be better to concentrate on using two to three fonts at the most for web pages. An example of this command is given in Figure 5.16.

```
<FONT SIZE=1>This is fontsize 1</FONT SIZE><P>
<FONT SIZE=2>This is fontsize 2</FONT SIZE><P>
<FONT SIZE=3>This is fontsize 3</FONT SIZE><P>
<FONT SIZE=4>This is fontsize 4</FONT SIZE><P>
<FONT SIZE=5>This is fontsize 5</FONT SIZE><P>
<FONT SIZE=6>This is fontsize 6</FONT SIZE><P>
<FONT SIZE=7>This is fontsize 7</FONT SIZE>
```

FIGURE 5.15

Using the <CENTER> tag.

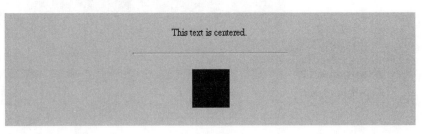

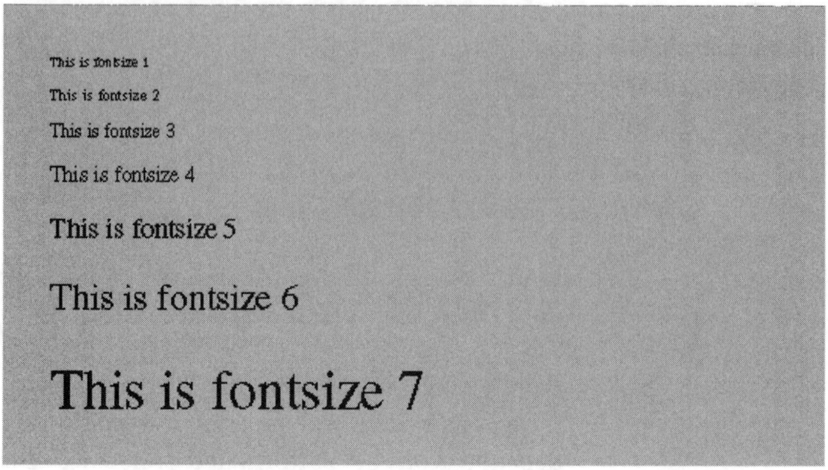

This is fontsize 1

This is fontsize 2

This is fontsize 3

This is fontsize 4

This is fontsize 5

This is fontsize 6

This is fontsize 7

I generally avoid using this tag, and instead, use the default text for all body copy, assigning header specifications as needed. For example, in Figure 5.17, three visually different fonts are used for most applications.

```
<H2>This is a head</H2>
<P>
<STRONG>Subhead here</STRONG><BR>
Eiqui studia in contemplatione rerum ponebant sapientes appellabantur,
et id nomen usque ad pythagorae aetatem manavit.
```

Finally, a useful extension is the copyright tag, shown in Figure 5.18.

```
&copy Copyright Me
```

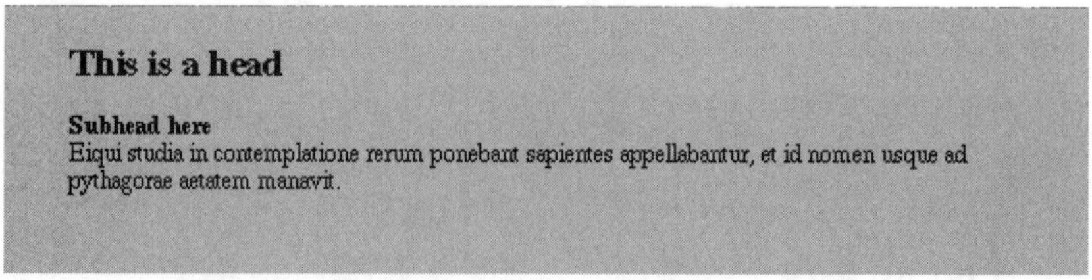

This is a head

Subhead here
Eiqui studia in contemplatione rerum ponebant sapientes appellabantur, et id nomen usque ad pythagorae aetatem manavit.

© Copyright Me

Designing with Tables in Netscape

Netscape Navigator was the first browser to support tables. Tables are easy to learn and offer the needed control for positioning elements on the web page. By mastering a few HTML constructs, your pages will benefit greatly from the added spatial control and layout appearance for web pages. Note that these table tags and attributes work with Netscape Navigator and may not appear as illustrated with other browsers. Also, emphasis is on HTML tags which are *useful* for designing visually pleasing pages, so again, all HTML tags are not discussed. This section is not meant to be an exhaustive HTML reference manual or style guide, but to illustrate, through numerous examples, the HTML constructs in Netscape tables which are useful for manipulating spatial positioning and arrangement of page elements. For more HTML information, see http://home.netscape.com/assist/net_sites/index.html.

USEFUL TABLE TAGS FOR DESIGNING HTML PAGES

The main wrapper for all other table definitions is the <TABLE> </TABLE> tags. These tags begin and end all other tags and page elements positioned in the table. Tables may contain form elements and graphics, along with text, and can be nested for complex layouts. Here is a simple table definition in HTML and how it appears, as shown in Figure 5.19:

```
<TABLE BORDER=1>
   <TR>
       <TD>This is cell #1</TD>
       <TD>This is cell #2</TD>
       <TD>This is cell #3</TD>
   </TR>
</TABLE>
```

Notice how the <TABLE> tags enclose the entire definition. An optional value defining the table border may be used and is included within the table tag. If no value for the border is given, the table will display no borders.

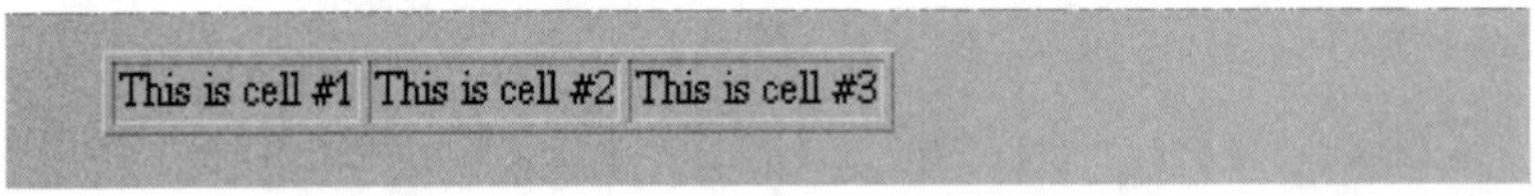

FIGURE 5.19

A simple table.

The <TR></TR> stands for table row. Each row in a table has a sep-arate <TR> tag. For example, to add another row to the table in Fig-ure 5.19, simply copy the table row definition and paste it after the </TR> tag, which would result in Figure 5.20.

```
<TABLE BORDER=1>
   <TR>              <!-This is Row #1->
      <TD>This is cell #1</TD>
      <TD>This is cell #2</TD>
      <TD>This is cell #3</TD>
   </TR>
   <TR>              <!-This is Row #2->
      <TD>This is cell #4</TD>
      <TD>This is cell #5</TD>
      <TD>This is cell #6</TD>
   </TR>
</TABLE>
```

Comments are added in HTML by the <!—comment here—> tag. Comments are useful for annotating your HTML and should be used to add clarity, especially when multiple authors contribute to the web site.

The <TD></TD> stands for table data. Table data lives in "cells" which appear in a table row. (Visual designers may think of columns instead of cells, which may provide an easier model to understand, but the term cells will be used here.) Like a traditional graphic design grid, the number of cells per row may vary, as columns vary in a page layout program. A table row with fewer cells will simply add "padding," or blank cells, as shown in Figure 5.21.

```
<TABLE BORDER=1>
   <TR>              <!-This is Row #1, 3 cells->
      <TD>This is cell #1</TD>
      <TD>This is cell #2</TD>
      <TD>This is cell #3</TD>
   </TR>
   <TR>              <!-This is Row #2, 2 cells->
      <TD>This is cell #4</TD>
      <TD>This is cell #5</TD>
   </TR>
</TABLE>
```

FIGURE 5.20

Table with two rows, three cells.

This is cell #1 | This is cell #2 | This is cell #3
This is cell #4 | This is cell #5 | This is cell #6

When table cells are uneven, as in Figure 5.21, the dimensional padding in the extra cell may be removed by inserting a <BR> tag into the table cell definition, as illustrated in Figure 5.22.

 stands for break, and is used to force a line break in text. Text, images, or form controls are placed within the cell; it is in this tag that alignment attributes support positioning and arrangement for effective, interesting page layouts. Alignment options will be discussed later.

FIGURE 5.21

Table with unequal cells in rows.

This is cell #1 | This is cell #2 | This is cell #3
This is cell #4 | This is cell #5

The ROWSPAN attribute controls how many rows a cell can vertically span in the table. This is useful, for example, to position labels next to image arrays or groups of related information, as in Figure 5.23:

```
<TABLE BORDER=1>
   <TR>
      <TD ROWSPAN=2>Heading Here</TD>
      <TD>This is cell #1</TD>
      <TD>This is cell #2</TD>
   </TR>
   <TR>
      <TD>This is cell #3</TD>
      <TD>This is cell #4</TD>
   </TR>
</TABLE>
```

The <TH></TH> stands for table head. The only difference between using the table head versus the table data tag is that text is automat-

FIGURE 5.22

Adding <BR> to remove the extra cell "padding."

This is cell #1 | This is cell #2 | This is cell #3
This is cell #4 | This is cell #5

FIGURE 5.23

*Example using
ROWSPAN.*

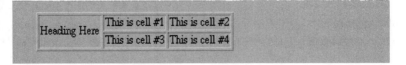

ically set to bold for emphasis and centered by default. The same effect is accomplished by including the <STRONG></STRONG> tags before and after the text. In order to effectively use a table heading, the COLSPAN or column span attribute is used, as seen in Figure 5.24.

```
<TABLE BORDER=1>
  <TR>
        <TH COLSPAN=3>Table Heading</TH>
  </TR>
  <TR>              <!—This is Row #1—>
      <TD>This is cell #1</TD>
      <TD>This is cell #2</TD>
      <TD>This is cell #3</TD>
  </TR>
  <TR>              <!—This is Row #2—>
      <TD>This is cell #4</TD>
      <TD>This is cell #5</TD>
      <TD>This is cell #6</TD>
</TR>
</TABLE>
```

The COLSPAN attribute is useful for complex forms which have various input fields and controls, demanding cells which span across different column widths. If COLSPAN is not used, the heading would appear as in Figure 5.25.

The <CAPTION></CAPTION> provides a caption positioned either above or below the table, outside the border. The caption tag is placed inside the <TABLE> tag, but remains outside the <TR> and <TD> tags. Captions are positioned horizontally centered in relation to the table, and cannot be positioned flush left or right, as seen in Figure 5.26.

FIGURE 5.24

*Example using
COLSPAN.*

Table Heading		
This is cell #1	This is cell #2	This is cell #3
This is cell #4	This is cell #5	This is cell #6

Table Heading		
This is cell #1	This is cell #2	This is cell #3
This is cell #4	This is cell #5	This is cell #6

FIGURE 5.25
Table without using COLSPAN, showing extra "padding" in the top row.

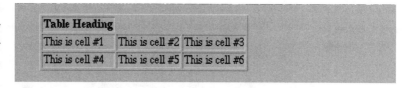

```
<TABLE BORDER=1>
   <TR>
      <TH COLSPAN=3>Table Heading</TH>
   </TH>
   <TR>            <!-This is Row #1->
      <TD>This is cell #1</TD>
      <TD>This is cell #2</TD>
      <TD>This is cell #3</TD>
   </TR>
   <TR>            <!-This is Row #2->
      <TD>This is cell #4</TD>
      <TD>This is cell #5</TD>
      <TD>This is cell #6</TD>
   </TR>
  <CAPTION ALIGN=bottom>This is the caption</CAPTION>
</TABLE>
```

The <TABLE> tag has a variety of attributes which control the visual appearance and behavior of the table, directly influencing the presentation of the web page. Three such attributes are border, cellspacing, and cellpadding.

The border attribute controls the thickness of the table border. In Figure 5.27, the tables illustrate various border settings. Setting borders values higher than two creates an exaggerated, over-dimensional visual effect. In most cases, the table border does not require such heavy treatment. The default value is no BORDER=0.

```
<TABLE BORDER=1>
<TABLE BORDER=2>
<TABLE BORDER=4>
```

The CELLSPACING attribute controls the space between cells in the table. This visually adds thickness to the border, as shown in Figure 5.28.

Table Heading		
This is cell #1	This is cell #2	This is cell #3
This is cell #4	This is cell #5	This is cell #6

FIGURE 5.26
Example using the <CAPTION> tag.

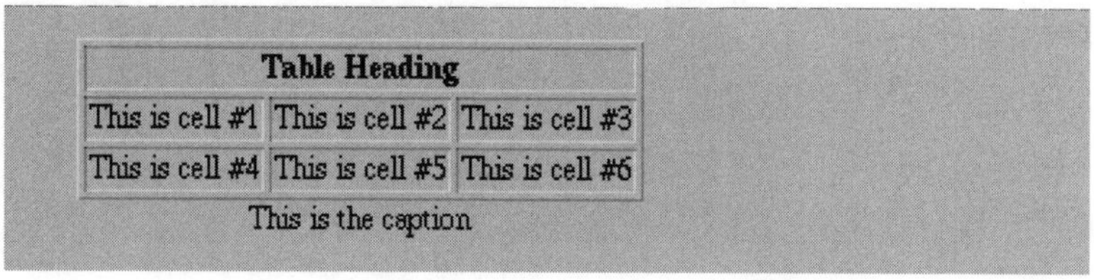

FIGURE 5.27

Borders set to one, two, and four.

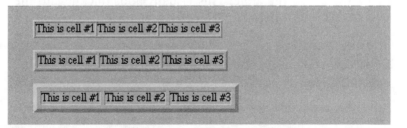

```
<TABLE BORDER=1 CELLSPACING=1>
<TABLE BORDER=2 CELLSPACING=2>
<TABLE BORDER=4 CELLSPACING=4>
```

As seen from the examples, the border attribute controls the thickness of the angled border, much like a picture frame, while cellspacing adds thickness or width to the flat area inside the perimeter of the angled border. This is illustrated in the close-up in Figure 5.29.

CELLPADDING controls the amount of space surrounding the cell contents. This is an important command when table borders are explicitly shown. When set to zero or not defined, the table contents tend to "hug" the contents, as shown in the top table in Figure 5.30. Adding values to the CELLSPACING attribute provides much needed space for the text to visually appear "uncrowded" within the cell. The default value is CELLPADDING=1.

```
<TABLE BORDER=1 CELLPADDING=0>
<TABLE BORDER=1 CELLPADDING=2>
<TABLE BORDER=1 CELLPADDING=4>
```

There are two different methods to control the size of tables; these values can be applied in different levels of the table definition. Table widths may be set by absolute pixel dimensions or percentage of the current document width. Both of these methods have different advantages and behaviors.

FIGURE 5.28

CELLSPACING attribute set to one, two (default), and four.

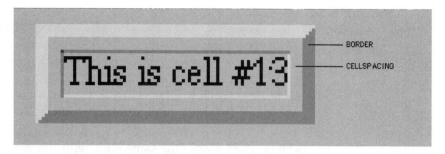

When a table does not have any width value, the table will size to the width of its contents. In Figure 5.31, the table tag does not have a width value. Note that each cell width is determined by the text in the cell; the entire table will rescale to fit into the browser window, when sized by the user.

```
<TABLE BORDER=1 CELLSPACING=0 CELLPADDING=2>
   <TR>
       <TD>This is cell #1</TD>
       <TD>This is cell #2, a longer line.</TD>
       <TD>This is cell #3</TD>
   </TR>
</TABLE>
```

In Figure 5.32, a WIDTH attribute is provided in absolute pixels. The entire width of the table is set to 300 pixels. The table width is fixed and will not alter as the browser window is sized by the user. In effect, the table width is "locked." Added space is seen in the second column, in order to stretch the table out to 300 pixels.

Figure 5.33 shows the same table as in Figure 5.32, but with various amounts of text in each cell. Note how the table holds its 300 pixel width, while growing vertically. This accommodates variances in font sizes between platforms, such as users who view pages with the huge

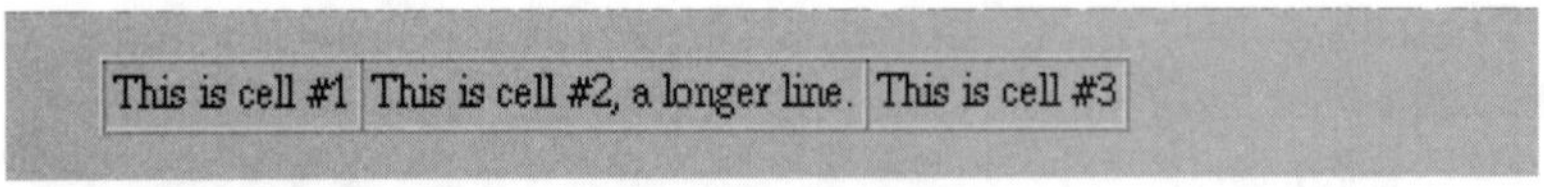

FIGURE 5.31

Table with no WIDTH
attribute value.

This is cell #1 | This is cell #2, a longer line. | This is cell #3

font size chosen in their Netscape preference setting. Note that each table cell, however, has a different width, based on the amount of text.

Figure 5.34 shows the same table with the width set to 100 percent. A setting of 100 percent means the table will occupy 100 percent of the width of the browser window, as altered by the user. Therefore, the table will resize as the user changes the aspect ratio of the browser window. This will cause the reflow of cell contents.

The same table as in Figure 5.34 is shown in Figure 5.35, after the browser window has been sized smaller.

FIGURE 5.32

Table WIDTH set to
300 pixels.

This is cell #1 | This is cell #2, a longer line. | This is cell #3

For more control, the table WIDTH attribute may be used in the individual cell definition tags. This allows size control of each of the individual cell columns, which add up to the entire table width. Again, the values may be in absolute pixel or percentage.

Figure 5.36 is a table with each cell width set to 100 pixels. Note that cells containing less text have the copy vertically centered in the cell. Alignment options, discussed later, allow changing this.

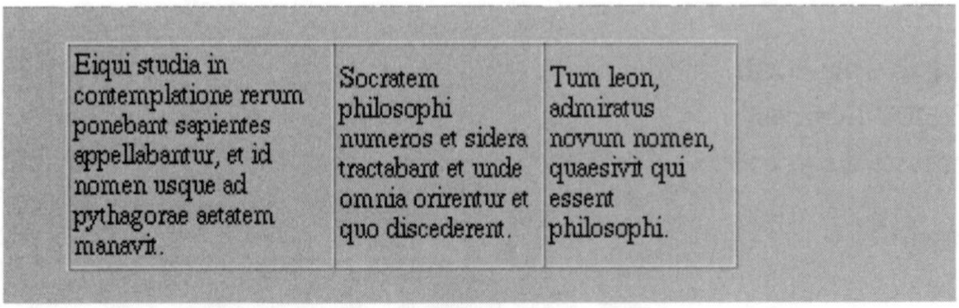

FIGURE 5.33

Table WIDTH set to
300 pixels.

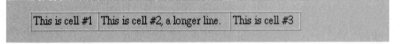

| Eiqui studia in contemplatione rerum ponebant sapientes appellabantur, et id nomen usque ad pythagorae aetatem manavit. | Socratem philosophi numeros et sidera tractabant et unde omnia orirentur et quo discederent. | Tum leon, admiratus novum nomen, quaesivit qui essent philosophi. |

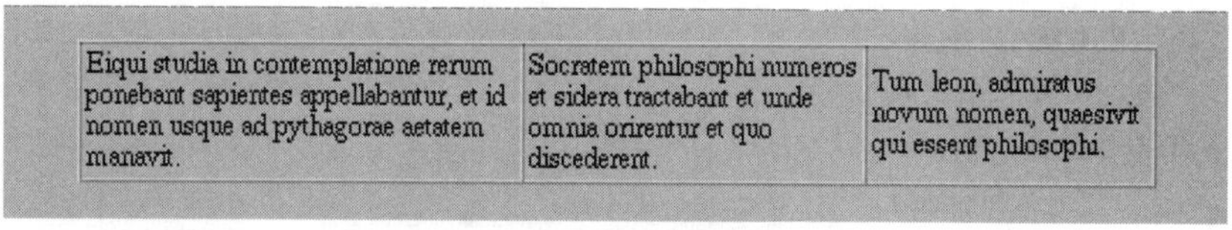

FIGURE 5.34

Table WIDTH set to 100 percent.

Eiqui studia in contemplatione rerum ponebant sapientes appellabantur, et id nomen usque ad pythagorae aetatem manavit.	Socratem philosophi numeros et sidera tractabant et unde omnia orirentur et quo discederent.	Tum leon, admiratus novum nomen, quaesivit qui essent philosophi.

```
<TABLE BORDER=1 CELLSPACING=0 CELLPADDING=2>
    <TR>
        <TD WIDTH=100>Eiqui studia in contemplatione rerum ponebant
        sapientes appellabantur, et id nomen usque ad pythagorae
        aetatem manavit.</TD>
        <TD WIDTH=100>Socratem philosophi numeros et sidera tracta
        bant et unde omnia orirentur et quo discederent.</TD>
        <TD WIDTH=100>Tum leon, admiratus novum nomen, quaesivit
        qui essent philosophi.</TD>
    </TR>
</TABLE>
```

When the table width values are included in each cell definition, control of cell widths is possible. Expansion occurs horizontally, though vertically constrained. The table accommodates larger font sizes or variances in amount of text, but each cell width will remain at the absolute pixel width.

Obviously, the amount of table cells may vary and each cell may vary its size in relation to others. Table design is largely dependent on the needs and requirements of the information being presented to the user.

A comparison of tables using pixels and percentage is shown in Figure 5.37.

```
<TABLE BORDER=1 CELLSPACING=0 CELLPADDING=2>
    <TR>
        <TD WIDTH=33%>Eiqui studia in contemplatione rerum
        ponebant sapientes appellabantur, et id nomen usque ad
        pythagorae aetatem manavit.</TD>
        <TD WIDTH=33%>Socratem philosophi numeros et sidera tracta
        bant et unde omnia orirentur et quo discederent.</TD>
        <TD WIDTH=33%>Tum leon, admiratus novum nomen, quaesivit
        qui essent philosophi.</TD>
    </TR>
</TABLE>
```

The top table in Figure 5.37 uses absolute pixels in the table cell; the bottom table uses percentage. The HTML shows the percentage val-

FIGURE 5.35

Table WIDTH set to 100 percent, browser resized.

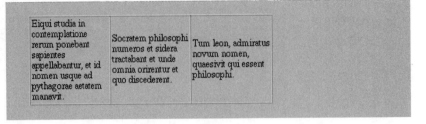

ues included in the table cell definition. Note how the table using absolute pixels retains its size.

When using percentages for tables, remember that the horizontal scale of the table will *always* change as the user resizes the browser window. Using absolute pixel values will lock the value when the user resizes the browser window *larger* than the table. However, when the browser window is sized *smaller* than the width of the table, the table will also shrink to fit within the new browser dimension, even when using absolute pixels. To completely lock-in the table dimension, a width value is also inserted in the main table definition, as seen in Figure 5.38.

```
<TABLE BORDER=1 CELLSPACING=0 WIDTH=300>
    <TR>
        <TD WIDTH=100 HEIGHT=100>This is cell #1</TD>
        <TD WIDTH=100 HEIGHT=100>This is cell #2</TD>
        <TD WIDTH=100 HEIGHT=100>This is cell #3</TD>
    </TR>
</TABLE>
```

The table will remain fixed in size regardless of browser resizing. Note the inclusion of the HEIGHT attribute. This attribute can be used for effectively controlling the vertical height of the table, but only when the content within each cell can be controlled or anticipated. The use of the HEIGHT attribute cancels out the ability for the table to expand vertically, accommodating content which may change due to font differences across platforms. This could also be

FIGURE 5.36

Table cell definition width set to 100 pixels.

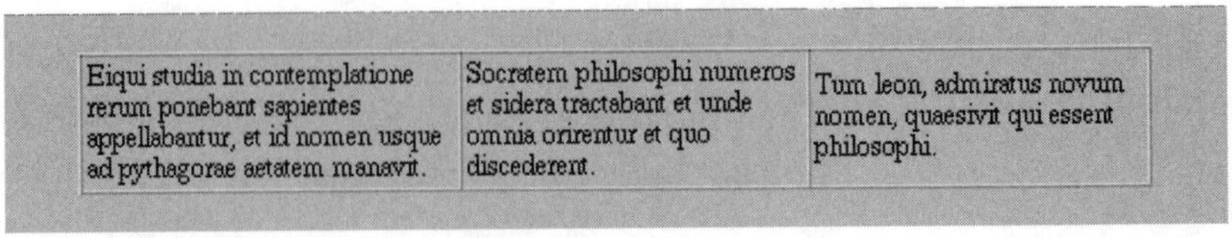

FIGURE 5.37

Table cell definition width set to 100 pixels (top) and percent (bottom).

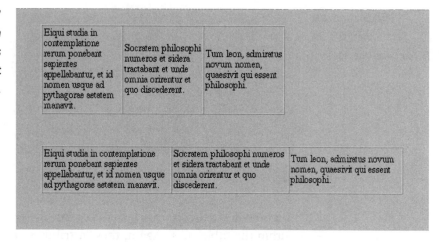

problematic when users view your page in a larger font size than your current development platform. However, in some instances, exact height control may be useful, as illustrated later.

Figure 5.39 ilustrates what happens when the content in a table cell exceeds the HEIGHT value.

Of course, one could either set the HEIGHT value to some very high number beyond the possibility of causing problems or simply remove the HEIGHT attribute altogether. In the latter case, the table simply expands vertically with the text, as shown in Figure 5.40.

Specific application and needs will determine the best method for table definition. However, the inherent quality of HTML is to support a logical translation of web pages across multiple platforms. Variances in font sizes and user-definable preferences means that any design should be tested across platforms for reasonable results.

FIGURE 5.38

Table size "locked" using absolute pixel dimensions in the <TABLE> and <TD> definitions.

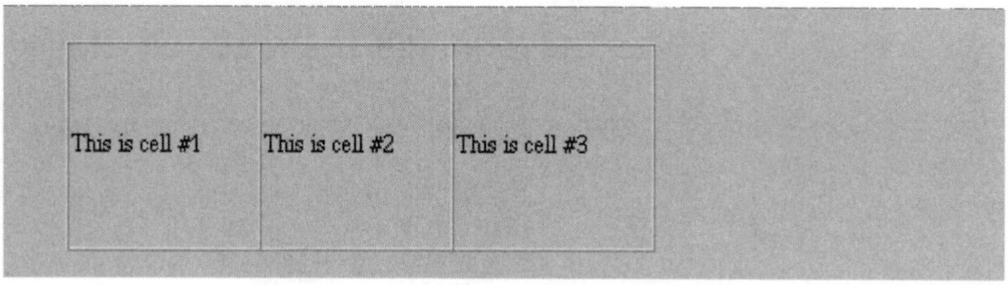

| This is cell #1 | This is cell #2 | This is cell #3 |

FIGURE 5.39

Text in the table cell flowing over the borders.

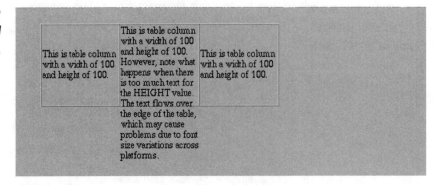

Alignment attributes exist which control the positioning of elements within the table cells. Again, these attributes can appear in various levels of the HTML table syntax—in the <TR> table row, <TD> cell, <TH>, close or table head definition. If no alignment values are included, the cell content will center vertically in each table cell by default. Text will appear flush left.

Since the <TR> table row definition functions as the wrapper for all <TD> tags, any alignment attribute included in this tag affects all cells in that row. If an alignment value which differs from the <TR> alignment value is included in the <TD> tag, the <TD> value will have precedence. Figure 5.41 is a table with a center alignment included in the table row tag.

```
<TABLE BORDER=1 CELLSPACING=0 CELLPADDING=4>

  <TR ALIGN=center>
      <TD WIDTH=100 HEIGHT=100 >This text is centered in the table
      cell.</TD>
      <TD WIDTH=100 HEIGHT=100 >This text is centered in the table
      cell.</TD>
      <TD WIDTH=100 HEIGHT=100 >This text is centered in the table
      cell.</TD>
  </TR>
</TABLE>
```

Figure 5.42 shows different alignment attributes within each table cell.

```
<TABLE BORDER=1 CELLSPACING=0 CELLPADDING=4>
  <TR>
      <TD WIDTH=100 HEIGHT=100 ALIGN=left>This text is flush
      left in the table cell.</TD>
      <TD WIDTH=100 HEIGHT=100 ALIGN=center>This text is
      centered in the table cell.</TD>
```

FIGURE 5.40

Text in the table cell vertically expanding the table.

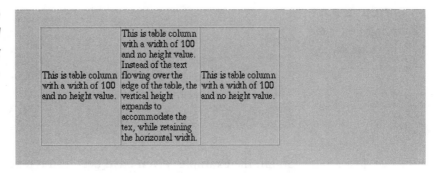

```
        <TD WIDTH=100 HEIGHT=100 ALIGN=right>This text is flush
        right in the table cell.</TD>
     </TR>
  </TABLE>
```

The VALIGN attribute controls the vertical position of content within the table cell. Again, this attribute may appear in the <TR> table row, <TD> cell, or <TH> table head tag. Its values are top, center, or bottom.

Figure 5.43 shows the VALIGN used in the table row definition to position all text at the bottom of the table.

```
  <TABLE BORDER=1 CELLSPACING=0 CELLPADDING=4>

     <TR VALIGN=bottom>
        <TD WIDTH=100 HEIGHT=100>This is valign set to bottom of
        the table cell.</TD>
        <TD WIDTH=100 HEIGHT=100>This is valign set to bottom of
        the table cell.</TD>
        <TD WIDTH=100 HEIGHT=100>This is valign set to bottom of
        the table cell.</TD>
     </TR>
  </TABLE>
```

Figure 5.44 shows the VALIGN set to different values in each table cell.

```
  <TABLE BORDER=1 CELLSPACING=0 CELLPADDING=4>
     <TR>
        <TD WIDTH=100 HEIGHT=100 VALIGN=top>This is valign set
        to top of the table cell.</TD>
        <TD WIDTH=100 HEIGHT=100 VALIGN=middle>This is valign set
        to middle of the table cell.</TD>
        <TD WIDTH=100 HEIGHT=100 VALIGN=bottom>This is valign set
        to bottom of the table cell.</TD>
     </TR>
  </TABLE>
```

FIGURE 5.41

*Center alignment in the
table row tag.*

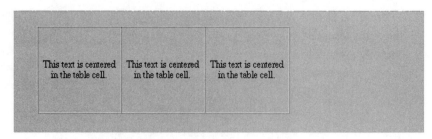

So far, the examples given have been using text. Images and form controls are also placed in tables. Positioning images and text within the table cell is just as simple and straightforward. The alignment attribute is placed in the image tag, as previously discussed when covering the Netscape HTML extensions. Figure 5.45 summarizes arrangements between image and copy in an HTML table.

```
<TABLE BORDER=1 CELLSPACING=0 CELLPADDING=4>
<TR>
    <TD WIDTH=100 HEIGHT=200 VALIGN=top><IMG ALIGN=left
    SRC="square.gif">This is an example of positioning a graphic within
    a table cell, and the relationship of text to this image.</TD>

    <TD WIDTH=100 HEIGHT=200 VALIGN=top><IMG ALIGN=left
    SRC="square.gif"><BR CLEAR=left><BR>This is an example of
    positioning a graphic within a table cell, and the relationship of
    text to this image.</TD>

    <TD WIDTH=100 HEIGHT=200 VALIGN=top><IMG ALIGN=right
    SRC="square.gif">This is an example of positioning a graphic within
    a table cell, and the relationship of text to this image.</TD>
    <TD WIDTH=100 HEIGHT=200 VALIGN=top><IMG ALIGN=right
    SRC="square.gif"><BR clear=right><BR>This is an example of
    positioning a graphic within a table cell, and the relationship of
    text to this image.</TD>
</TR>

</TABLE>
```

Since font style and size differ between platform and user-defined preferences, controlling exact line breaks column depth is impossible. However, the relationship of the image and text is controlled, as illustrated in Figure 5.45.

Tables are extremely useful for positioning groups of images and their hypertext link equivalent. In Figure 5.46, a table defines a position and label for each entry. If the user decides not to load images,

FIGURE 5.42

Various alignment attributes in the table cell definitions.

FIGURE 5.42

Various alignment attributes in the table cell definitions.

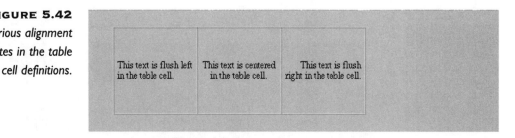

the hypertext equivalent is still visible. In such applications, it is usually better to set the table border to none, since the regularity of the elements already provides the needed structure to the layout.

```
<TABLE BORDER=0 CELLSPACING=0 CELLPADDING=4>
  <TR>
     <TD WIDTH=110 ALIGN=middle VALIGN=top><IMG VSPACE=4
     SRC="square.gif"><BR>Label 1</TD>
     <TD WIDTH=110 ALIGN=middle VALIGN=top><IMG VSPACE=4
     SRC="square.gif"><BR>Label 2</TD>
     <TD WIDTH=110 ALIGN=middle VALIGN=top><IMG VSPACE=4
     SRC="square.gif"><BR>Label 3</TD>
     <TD WIDTH=110 ALIGN=middle VALIGN=top><IMG VSPACE=4
     SRC="square.gif"><BR>Label 4</TD>
  </TR>
```

FIGURE 5.43

VALIGN set to bottom in the table row definition.

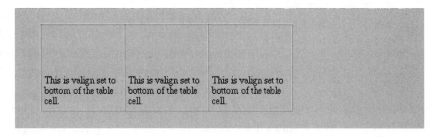

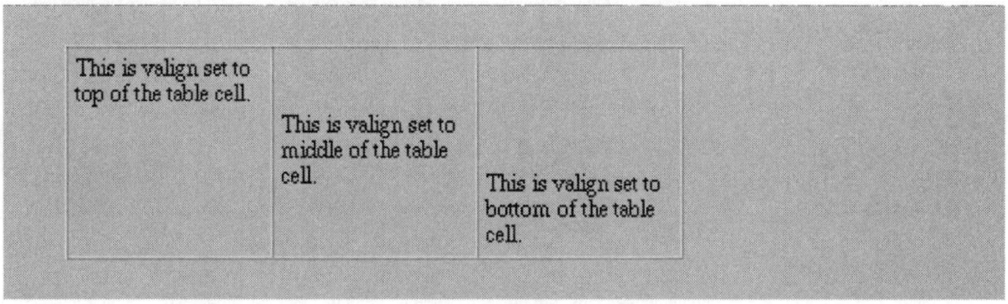

FIGURE 5.44

Various VALIGN attributes in the table cell definitions.

FIGURE 5.45

*Various image alignment
options in an HTML
table.*

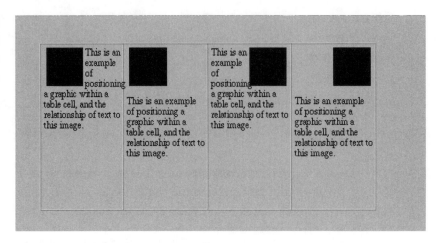

```
<TR>
    <TD WIDTH=110 ALIGN=middle VALIGN=top><IMG VSPACE=4
    SRC="square.gif"><BR>Label 5</TD>
    <TD WIDTH=110 ALIGN=middle VALIGN=top><IMG VSPACE=4
    SRC="square.gif"><BR>Label 6</TD>
    <TD WIDTH=110 ALIGN=middle VALIGN=top><IMG VSPACE=4
    SRC="square.gif"><BR>Label 7</TD>
    <TD WIDTH=110 ALIGN=middle VALIGN=top><IMG VSPACE=4
    SRC="square.gif"><BR>Label 8</TD>
</TR>

</TABLE>
```

Each cell entry has an image centered, with a VSPACE value to add
space between the image and the label. Using the <P> instead of

 produces a full-line space between the image and label, visual-
ly too much. Notice that table cell eight has a label which is longer
than others. Since absolute pixels are used in this table, the regularity
of the design is ensured and excess text will simply wrap to the next
line. If we removed all absolute pixel width tags, the table would
appear as in Figure 5.47.

FIGURE 5.46

*Using a table to position
an array of entries.*

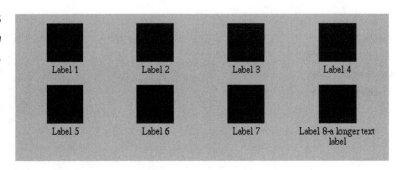

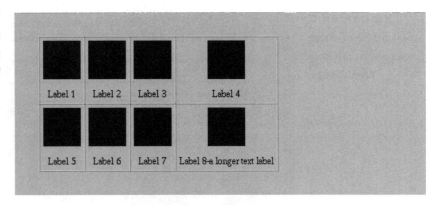

As shown, tables can provide the control for spatial arrangements which best suit the content and information presented on the web page. With an understanding of Netscape extensions and tables, effective table-based solutions for a variety of applications are possible.

A Basic Symmetrical Table-based Page

The series of three tables is used in all product pages for the on-line store example. Each table uses absolute pixel dimensions for the width, since the content is defined and controlled. No height value is given, which better anticipates differences in font style and size across platforms. This allows the table cell to vertically expand if needed.

At the very top of the page is an area designated for the identification head. Next, a small horizontal table defines the position of text and "paging" buttons for navigation. Next is the major table, composed of three cells, which defines the position of product images and text. A paragraph space is inserted between this table and the final one, which positions the navigation buttons. Figure 5.48 shows the HTML table in the browser window without any of the page contents.

The images are sized to common standard sizes, so the image width and heights tags are reused throughout all product pages (Figure 5.49). The same approach is taken with the navigational buttons.

```
<BODY BACKGROUND="gifs/tatami.gif">
<TITLE>Store</TITLE>

<IMG WIDTH=582 HEIGHT=34 SRC="gifs/head_clothing.gif">
```

FIGURE 5.48

The table-based design framework for the store product page.

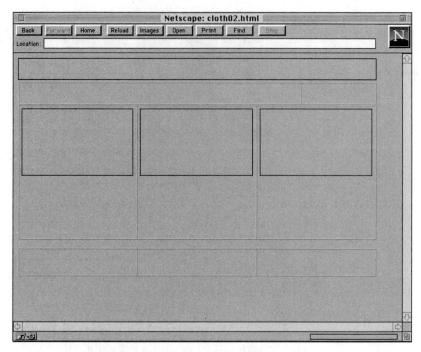

```
<TABLE BORDER=1 CELLSPACING=0 CELLPADDING=0>

<TR>
   <TD WIDTH=455 align=left>Page One</TD>
   <TD WIDTH=125 align=right><A HREF="cloth01.html"><IMG
      WIDTH=55 HEIGHT=32 SRC="gifs/prev.gif" BORDER=0></
      A><A HREF="cloth01.html"><IMG WIDTH=55 HEIGHT=32
      SRC="gifs/next.gif" BORDER=0></A></TD>
</TR>
</TABLE>

<TABLE BORDER=1 CELLSPACING=0 CELLPADDING=4>

<TR VALIGN=top>
   <TD WIDTH=184><A HREF="cloth02.html"><IMG WIDTH=18 HEIGHT=105
      SRC="gifs/fab04.gif" border=0></A><P><A HREF="cloth02.html">
      <I>Shirahama textile, Yamaguchi<I></A>
<P>
Eiqui studia in contemplatione rerum ponebant sapientes appellabantur,
et id nomen usque ad pythagorae aetatem manavit.
   </TD>
   <TD WIDTH=184><A HREF="cloth02.html"><IMG WIDTH=181
      HEIGHT=105 SRC="gifs/fab05.gif" border=0></A>
      <P><A HREF="cloth02.html"><I>Awatsuji textile, Kyoto</I></A>
<P>
      Hunc aiunt docte et copiose quaedam cum leonte disputavisse;
      et leon, cum illius ingenium.
   </TD>
```

```
                    <TD WIDTH=184><A HREF="cloth02.html"><IMG WIDTH=181
                        HEIGHT=105 SRC="gifs/fab06.gif" border=0></A>
                        <P><A HREF="cloth02.html"><I>Yuzen textile, hand
                        tie-dyed</I></A>
                        <P>
                        Eloquentiam admiratus esset, quaesivit ex eo qua arte maxime
                        uteretur. At ille dixit se artem nullam scire sed esse
                        philosophum.
                    </TD>

            </TR>
            </TABLE>
            <P>
            <TABLE BORDER=1 CELLSPACING=0 CELLPADDING=4 >
            <TR>
                <TD WIDTH=184><A HREF="japon.html"><IMG WIDTH=181 HEIGHT=32
                    SRC="gifs/jphp.gif" BORDER=0></A></TD>

                <TD WIDTH=184><A HREF="jpbag.html"><IMG WIDTH=181 HEIGHT=32
                    SRC="gifs/jpbag.gif" BORDER=0></A></td>
                <td WIDTH=184><A HREF="jpout.html"><IMG WIDTH=181 HEIGHT=32
                    SRC="gifs/jpout.gif" BORDER=0></A></td>
            </TR>
            </TABLE>
            <P>
            <H6>&copy 1995 Japonesque Designs</H6>
```

FIGURE 5.49

Store page and the HTML document.

An Asymmetrical Page Using a Table for Positioning Control

Tables allow the positioning of elements for asymmetrical page designs. When the outer table borders are also set to none, the page design gets closer to the quality of actual print documents. Figure 5.50 shows the table used for the positioning of the alternative asymmetrical design for the on-line store.

The table uses various alignment tags to carefully position elements on the page. The text occupies the second table cell and is, by default, centered. Note the amount of space above and below the text, to allow for expansion.

Figure 5.51 shows the actual page and the accompanying HTML follows.

FIGURE 5.50

Asymmetrical table for the on-line store.

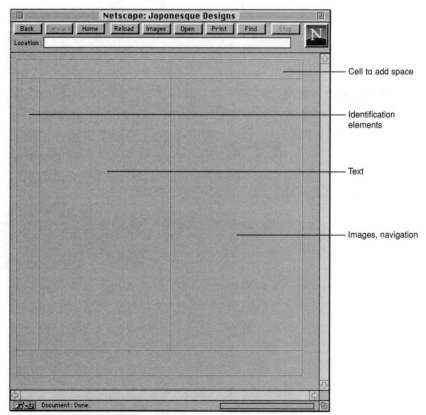

Cell to add space

Identification elements

Text

Images, navigation

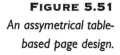

FIGURE 5.51
*An assymetrical table-
based page design.*

The far-right table cell will contain product photography and navigational controls, positioned using various HTML alignment tags. Note a horizontal table cell across the very top of the page, which functions simply to add empty space between the page contents and the border of the window.

```
<HTML>
<HEAD>

<TITLE>Japonesque Designs</TITLE></HEAD>

<TABLE BORDER=1 CELLPADDING=0 CELLSPACING=0>

<TR>
   <TD COLSPAN=3><BR><BR></TD> <!—this adds blank space—>
</TR>
```

```
<TR>
  <TD VALIGN=top><IMG SRC="gifs2/logotype.gif"></TD>
  <TD WIDTH=200 HEIGHT=400 ALIGN=right VALIGN=middle><I>The Art of
      Tea</I><P>Proscribes rules for the <P>tea ceremony date back
      to<P>Rikyu-Sen in the<P>Azuchi-Momoyama Period<P>late 15th
      century. Today I<P>enjoy the meditative, cleansing<P>moments in
      our restless world.<P><BR><I>More Information</I></TD>
  <TD WIDTH=200 ALIGN=right VALIGN=top><IMG SRC="gifs2/
      logo.gif"><P><IMG SRC="gifs2/b_prev.gif"><P><IMG SRC="gifs2/
      b_next.gif"><P><IMG SRC="gifs2/wisk.gif" ALIGN=left></TD>
</TR>

<TR>
  <TD COLSPAN=3><IMG SRC="gifs2/b_home.gif"> <IMG SRC="gifs2/
      b_bag.gif"> <IMG SRC="gifs2/b_chkout.gif"></TD>
</TR>

</TABLE>
<BODY>
</HTML>
```

Nesting Tables for a "Virtual Book"

Tables can be nested to actually construct a "Virtual Book" which
visually appears similar to traditional multimedia CD-ROM-based
products. A little planning and forethought, however, is required.
This is because the table must work with the exact dimensions of the
graphics. The page will require some "tweaking," just as one would
normally proceed when using a multimedia authoring tool, to get the
right fit for all visual elements.

In this example, the border elements of the book were completed
first. It was easy to draw the book in Adobe Photoshop, then separate out the individual elements needed. The purpose of designing
the pages this way is to avoid the production of swapping in large,
full-screen images with bit-mapped type. In this approach, all text is
still HTML, though appearing as if written on the book's surface.

Figure 5.52 shows the separate elements provide the illusion of a
book, when placed in an outer table.

Each of these graphic elements is reduced to the minimal amount of
colors possible, in order to reduce the file sizes.

Figure 5.53 is the table which encloses the entire book. The outer-
most rectangles form the table which holds each edge of the book.

The middle vertical table column holds the centerfold graphic. Exact absolute pixel dimensions for the tables correlate to the exact size of these graphic elements. The large left and right side interior table cells hold the page contents, which may be graphics or HTML text. Below this table is another table definition, which will accommodate five icons and associated hypertext equivalents centered in a regularly spaced interval.

Because the table uses exact pixel dimensions for all table cells, the book will retain its appearance no matter how large the browser window is sized by the user. As one can imagine, such a layout does require added planning to determine the optimal size for the page, along with noting dimensions for all graphic elements.

Figure 5.54 is the resulting HTML page, with the document listed below. Nested tables require extensive indenting for legibility while authoring, so as not to become confused by the many tags. Hopefully, authoring tools supporting direct manipulation of table-based pages in Figure 5.26 will soon appear.

FIGURE 5.52

Separate elements for placement in the outer table.

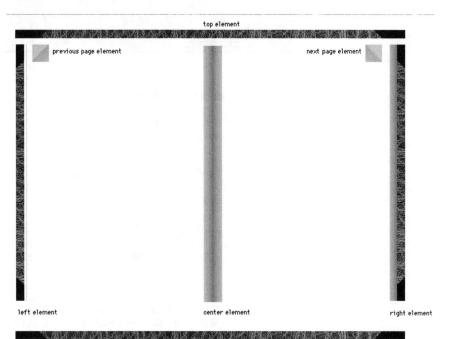

FIGURE 5.53

*The table for the book
page.*

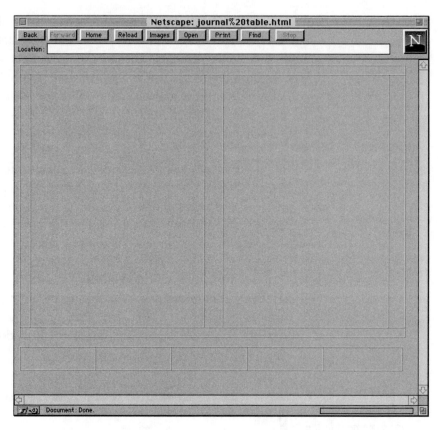

```
<BODY BGCOLOR="eee2d9">

<TABLE BORDER=0 CELLSPACING=0 CELLPADDING=0> <!—master table
which encloses all page elements—>

<TR>
    <TD COLSPAN=5><IMG WIDTH=582 HEIGHT=12    SRC="gifs/top.gif"></TD>
        <!—top edge—>
</TR>
<TR>
    <TD WIDTH=16 ALIGN=left><IMG WIDTH=16 HEIGHT=370 SRC="gifs/
        left.gif"></TD>          <!—column 1 holds left edge of book—>
    <TD WIDTH=264 VALIGN=top><TABLE WIDTH=264 BORDER=0
        CELLSPACING=0 CELLPADDING=0>

<TR>
    <TD ALIGN=left><A HREF="hp.html"><IMG WIDTH=25
        HEIGHT=25 BORDER=0 SRC="gifs/prev.gif"></A></TD>
</TR>

<TR>
```

```
   <TD ALIGN=middle>E  X  P  E  D  I  T  I  O  N<P></TD>
</TR>

<TR>
   <TD><CENTER><IMG WIDTH=160 HEIGHT=217 SRC="gifs/mystic.gif">
      </CENTER><P><BLOCKQUOTE>A mystic in Kathmandu. For 10 dinars,
      he poses for a photo. He takes advantage of the continuous
      source of tourist funds. Another day in Kathmandu.
      </BLOCKQUOTE></TD>
</TR>
</TABLE>
   </TD>

   <TD WIDTH=28 ALIGN=middle><IMG WIDTH=28 HEIGHT=370 SRC="gifs/
      center.gif"></TD>   <!-column 3 holds middle graphic->

   <TD WIDTH=251 VALIGN=top><TABLE WIDTH=251 BORDER=0
      CELLSPACING=0 CELLPADDING=0>

<TR VALIGN=top>
   <TD ALIGN=right><A HREF="page02.html"><IMG BORDER=0 WIDTH=25
      HEIGHT=25 SRC="gifs/next.gif"></A></TD>
</TR>

<TR><!-column 4 holds right page contents->
   <TD><CENTER><I>Nepal-Kathmandu</I><P>
      <IMG SRC="gifs/map_nepal.gif"></CENTER><P>
      <BLOCKQUOTE>Our feet are tired, hair matted with dust and
      earth, and senses overloaded by the smells and colors of the
      city. We slowly make our way to the hotel.<P>Dusk is
      approaching. Incense thickens the air with fragrance. The
      clear sky is magenta. </BLOCKQUOTE>

   </TD>
</TR>

</TABLE>
   </TD>

   <TD WIDTH=23 align=right><IMG width=23 height=370 SRC="gifs/
      right.gif"></TD> <!-column 5 holds right edge of book->
</TR>

<TR>
   <TD COLSPAN=5><IMG WIDTH=582 HEIGHT=12 SRC="gifs/
      bottom.gif"></TD> <!-bottom edge->
</TR>

</TABLE>
<P>
<TABLE BORDER=0 CELLSPACING=0 CELLPADDING=0 width=582> <!-table
for icons->

<TR>
```

```
<TR ALIGN=middle><IMG SRC="gifs/icon_log.gif"></TD>
<TR ALIGN=middle><IMG SRC="gifs/icon_atlas.gif"></TD>
<TR ALIGN=middle><IMG SRC="gifs/icon_passport.gif"></TD>
<TR ALIGN=middle><IMG SRC="gifs/icon_health.gif"></TD>
<TR ALIGN=middle><IMG SRC="gifs/icon_cash.gif"></TD>
</TR>

</TABLE>
```

FIGURE 5.54

The virtual book page.

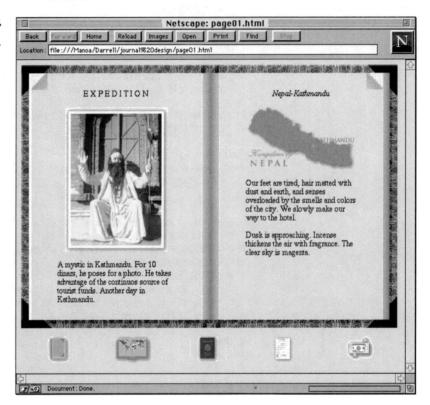

Designing Netscape FRAMESET Documents

Netscape 2.0 allows the content designer to use a new feature called "Frames." With Netscape frames, the single browser pane is subdivided into multiple regions referred to as frames, which can display a separate HTML document from any location on the Internet. An interesting design characteristic is the ability for an HTML document within a frame to reference another document in a different frame.

For example, when a user clicks on a graphic map of the United States, another frame may then display a document which provides details about the selected state. Selecting hyperlinks within the details document may also provide further specific information in another frame.

This capability extends the web browser beyond a single-page, paper-based model. Prior to frames, a user action would load an entirely new page in the browser window upon selecting a link, synonymous to turning the page of a magazine. Now, various frames on the page may load relevant content while preserving the central context for users. Frames may also provide dynamic information, such as a stock ticker, sports scores, news updates, and so forth, within a defined region of the window.

Frames may display anything a normal HTML document can, including text and images, and may also display content using server-push or client-pull. Frames may also display Java applets (executable Java applications, which may be animations or any other dynamic data).

ADVANTAGES OF USING FRAMES

There are several advantages when web sites use frames. A major benefit for users is the ability to preserve context during navigation. For example, a search query window could always be visible, with the results located in a different frame. This eliminates the traversal between query page and results. For large-scale web sites, frames can expose subsections of the organizational hierarchy, allowing the user access to finer details, while at the same time viewing the overall global picture.

Planning a web site to use frames also means that any URL located on the Internet is accessible within a frame. This is a powerful capablility that delivers related documents located anywhere on the Internet within a single browser window. Documents within a frame need not be limited to a closed set of information within a single web site. Taking advantage of the information available on the web with frames realizes the power of this new medium.

Frames also eliminate the need to redraw the entire browser window. For example, a frame may display a toolbar for navigating to specific areas within a web site. The toolbar is always present within a separate frame and is not redrawn. Only the frame located below or to the side of the toolbar updates with the appropriate content after a user selection. Many web sites prior to frames simulate this behavior, but require reloading the entire HTML page reflecting each selection.

The opportunities to design interesting user experiences are possible when using frames with technology such as server-push, client-pull, and the Java language. For example, specific frames may exhibit timely information, such as stock quotes or news headlines, while allowing the user to browse in another frame through various web sites. Animations or messages can be sent to specific frames—for example, as interactive advertisements. The possibilities are limitless and no doubt will be explored by those pushing the limits of web publishing.

CONSIDERATIONS WHEN USING FRAMES

Obviously, downloading multiple documents into separate frames will require more time than downloading a single document. The trade-off in using frames includes a performance factor, which also is largely dependent on the nature of the documents served (along with connection speed). The same considerations and sensitivity for using images mentioned earlier in Chapter 2 apply when implementing frames. Loading three text-oriented documents into three separate frames will be much faster than loading three graphics-heavy documents. Remembering the intended audience, available connection speed, and testing the frame-based document on a variety of platforms and connections will ensure that the results fall within expectations.

From a response perspective, the user can at least continue to browse information in other frames as a document is being downloaded. Tasks can be split among framed areas of the browser pane, allowing the user to move to other operations during document retrieval.

Displaying multiple documents in a single browser pane also infers the need for more screen real estate. This may be an issue if intended users have smaller displays or use notebook computers. Forcing users to scroll around a large window, which may display subordinate frames that may also require scrolling, is burdensome to the user. Frames should therefore enhance the user experience within a given web application and not detract from the overall usability.

Another consideration is that all browsers do not support this feature found in Netscape. If the target audience is an internal corporation using Netscape, frames can be used without hesitation. For the larger external audience, however, some planning and consideration for users without this capability are necessary. An HTML tag which sends an alternate HTML document to the user is available to accommodate browsers not supporting frames.

From a design production perspective, the use of frames requires additional planning and forethought before implementation. Frames must be named in order to allow hypertext referencing; this, along with the HTML documents, can potentially become confusing. A system for clearly naming frame windows and documents, along with an effective method for organizing documents and images, will save effort (and sanity) when using this capability. The frame document is referred to as the FRAMESET document.

PLANNING THE FRAMESET DOCUMENT

The first design objective is to develop an effective FRAMESET document, which will define the content areas of the browser window. This is very similar to designing a table-based layout, discussed in Chapter 4. The frame base determines the layout of the browser window, defining the areas of content. The frames within the document can be any size and have a variety of attributes, which will be discussed in detail later in this chapter. Once the base frame is defined, the appropriate HTML documents (which can be located anywhere on the Internet) are referenced into the designated frames.

Figure 5.55 illustrates the basic page layout of a FRAMESET document. The frame base is saved as an HTML document and two frames are defined and assigned unique names (frame 1 and frame 2) in this example. When the user loads the frame_base.html document, it references two URLs, which are then loaded into the appropriate frame. Once loaded, hypertext links in frame 1 may cause a new document to appear in frame 2 from within the web site, or alternatively, load a document located anywhere on the web.

Frames may be nested within one another; this provides the ability to load multiple documents in the browser with a single selection. Figure 5.56 illustrates the page layout of such a FRAMESET document.

In this example, frame_base.html defines the base frame, which determines the layout for all subsequent frames. A document called icons.html is loaded into frame 1. The user may select an icon "A," "B," or "C," which then loads the subsequent FRAMESET documents referenced by each specific icon. These FRAMESET documents are loaded into frame 2, in the frame_base.html document. The FRAMESET documents for each icon, representing different sections within the web site, vary in number of frames and in overall layout, which has been determined by the information needs specific to the content within each section. Notice that all frames are assigned unique names, so when a FRAMESET document is referenced, various HTML documents are then loaded into the individual frames.

As one can imagine, it is easy to become confused during the authoring process without a clear organization and structure of the infor-

FIGURE 5.55

Example page layout in a FRAMESET document.

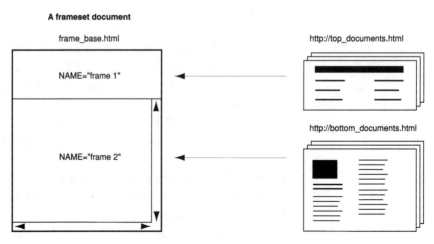

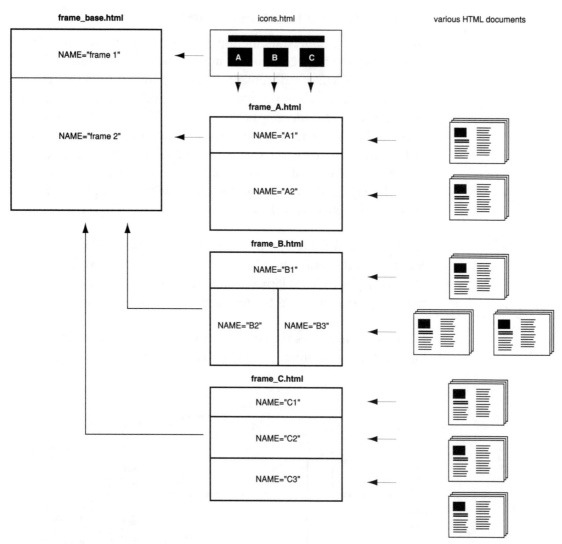

FIGURE 5.56 *Nesting FRAMESET documents.*

mation being presented. Changes to a design after frame names are assigned and HTML documents written may require additional time and effort. Planning ahead and utilizing the steps outlined in this book will help to alleviate some of the problems when ill-formed designs are quickly rushed into HTML production. The following examples will illustrate the exact HTML syntax for FRAMESET documents.

DESIGNING A **FRAMESET** DOCUMENT

An approach to understanding this feature is to correlate FRAME-SET documents to page layout templates, which define areas of content. The FRAMESET document defines separate frames that are window regions with which users interact. Each separate frame can be either an HTML document predefined within the service structure of the web site or referenced to any URL located anywhere on the web. In the latter case, the user may continue to traverse outside the confines of the orignal web site. Simply put, a FRAMESET document displays multiple HTML documents within a single browser window. (See also Color Plate 5.)

All frames, and the relevant information to display within each frame, should be identified in order to design an effective FRAME-SET document. This is largely related to the nature of the information being presented and the functionality of the web application.

Figure 5.57 illustrates the layout of a FRAMESET document displaying five separate frames. The layout is designed to support a user

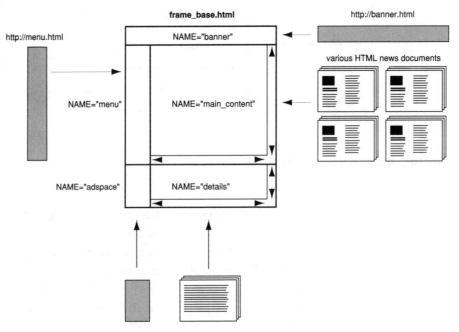

FIGURE 5.57 *A FRAMESET document using five separate frames to display information.*

FIGURE 5.58

Example of a FRAMESET document.

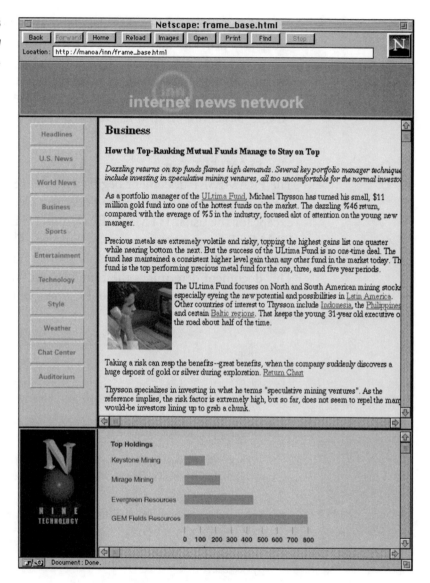

browsing through an information service provider. The design includes a frame named "banner," which will hold the graphic banner identification of the web site. The "menu" frame will contain an HTML document displaying an icon array for the various categories of information available to the user. A selection from this menu will cause the appropriate HTML document to display in the "main_content" frame. Selecting various hypertext links within the main content frame will allow the user access to finer detail or related information, displayed in the "details" frame. Finally, a frame named "adspace" provides an area for HTML advertising.

Figure 5.58 is the resulting screen image of the design illustrated in Figure 5.57. The complete HTML for the FRAMESET document "frame_base.html" is also listed. Each tag is discussed in detail.

The FRAMESET Tag

The FRAMESET document begins with the FRAMESET tag. This is the main wrapper for the frame document. No other HTML tags, except for the usual HTML, HEAD, and TITLE can precede the FRAMESET tag, or the frames are ignored. This document contains only tags associated with frames. No other HTML tags are included. This document determines the frame layout and initial URLs to load within each separate frame. The document in this example is therefore saved as frame_base.html:

```
<HTML>

<HEAD>
<TITLE>Frameset Demo</TITLE>
</HEAD>

<FRAMESET ROWS="55, 300, 100">

 <FRAME SRC="banner.html" NAME="banner" MARGINWIDTH=1
MARGINHEIGHT=4 SCROLLING=no NORESIZE>

<FRAMESET COLS="100, 400">
   <FRAME SRC="menu.html" NAME="menu" SCROLLING=no
NORESIZE>
   <FRAME SRC="headlines/headlines.html" NAME="main_content"
SCROLLING=auto NORESIZE>
</FRAMESET>

<FRAMESET COLS="100, 400">
   <FRAME SRC="adspace/ad1.html" NAME="adspace" SCROLLING=no
NORESIZE>
   <FRAME SRC="" NAME="details" SCROLLING=auto NORESIZE>
</FRAMESET>

</FRAMESET>

</HTML>
```

Sizing Attributes

Two sizing attributes for the FRAMESET tag are ROWS and COLS (columns). Like HTML tables, ROWS and COLS can take either absolute pixel or percentage values. The values for ROWS and COLS are separated by commas. The number of values in the comma-delimited list creates that number of ROWS or COLS in the layout. A third method of assigning values is to include an * (asterisk), which assigns the leftover space to this row or column. For example, a <FRAMESET COLS=100, 100, *> will assign three columns, two of which are 100 pixels wide and the third determined by whatever space is left over. This is contingent on the current size of the browser window.

In the example HTML, the ROWS attribute defines three vertical rows of various depths: 55 pixels (banner frame), 300 pixels (menu and main_content frames), and 100 pixels (adspace and details frames).

Using absolute values can be problematic, just as when defining HTML tables, especially since the user may resize the browser window to an unknown size or choose an extra large font size. For frames in which the content size is fixed, however, as in toolbars or image maps, absolute pixel values can be useful. In this example, the banner at the top of the page and the menu bar are graphic images with fixed sizes, so absolute pixel values are used.

The FRAME Tag

The FRAME tag defines the specific frame within the browser window and the URL to intially load into this frame. The example in Figure 5.58 has five frames and therefore includes five FRAME tags in the HTML.

The first FRAME tag defines the banner frame, which loads the banner.html document. This document simply references a graphic image to function as an identifier for the web site, much like a newspaper banner.

```
<FRAME SRC="banner.html" NAME="banner" MARGINWIDTH=1
MARGINHEIGHT=1 SCROLLING=no NORESIZE>
```

The SRC attribute determines what URL to load in the frame. The source can be any URL on the web, for example, http://www.foo. com/document.html. The URL will load into the frame when the FRAMESET document is served to the user.

NAME is the assigned name given to the individual frame, so it can be targeted by hypertext links in other documents located in other frames, as well as by any nested FRAMESET documents. This requires that each name given to frames in the same FRAMESET document remains unique.

MARGINWIDTH and MARGINHEIGHT specify in pixels a margin for the contents within the frame. Setting the margins to a value of one ensures the closest space between the frame edge and contents. If this attribute is not included, the browser decides the margin width.

SCROLLING has values as either "yes," "no," or "auto." For fixed-sized elements displayed in frames, such as a graphic toolbar or image map, scrolling is unneccesary. Auto will provide scrollbars when the content is too large for the current size of the frame, which depends on the size of the browser window. If the browser window is large enough, the scrollbars disappear. A yes value will always display scrollbars for the frame.

NORESIZE turns off the ability for the user to grab the divider lines of a frame and re-size them. Again, for frames containing fixed-sized elements, such as a toolbar, graphic ISMAP, or series of consistently sized images, resizing may be uneccessary. When resizing is available, the mouse pointer will change to arrows when positioned on the frame line, signifying that the frame border may be moved to enlarge or reduce the frame. By default, all frames are resizable. Making a frame NORESIZE will restrict the sizing for frame borders which are adjacent to other frames.

The NOFRAMES tag allows the content designer to include an alternative HTML document in the FRAMESET document for users who do not have the capability of viewing frames with their browser. Non-Netscape 2.0 browsers will ignore all FRAMESET tags and load the HTML included between the NOFRAMES tags, while

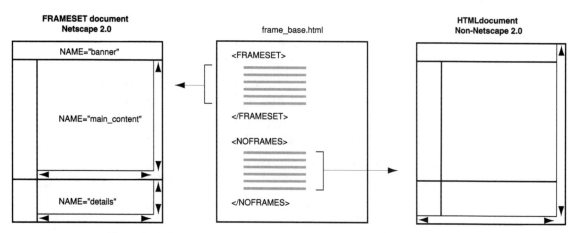

FIGURE 5.59 *Using the NOFRAMES tag allows browsers that do not support Netscape Frameset documents to display alternate content.*

Netscape 2.0 simply ignores the HTML between the NOFRAMES and loads the FRAMESET document. Figure 5.59 illustrates the use of the NOFRAMES tag, which is included in the FRAMESET HTML document.

The TARGET Attribute

In order to reference documents from one frame to another, the TARGET attribute must be included in the HREF tag in the HTML document. In the example in Figure 5.58, the frame "menu" displays the document "menu.html," which includes buttons for users to select a specific news category or activity. The particular home page for each specific category is then sent to the frame "main_content" by using the TARGET="name of frame" tag. Here is the HTML for the menu document:

```
<HTML>

<HEAD>
<TITLE>Main Menu</TITLE>
</HEAD>
<BODY BGCOLOR="e2dbcb">
<p>
<A HREF="headline_homepage.html" TARGET="main_content"><IMG
SRC="button_headlines.gif" WIDTH=80 HEIGHT=32 BORDER=0></A>
<p>
<A HREF="headline_usnews.html" TARGET="main_content"><IMG
```

```
SRC="button_usnews.gif" WIDTH=80 HEIGHT=32 BORDER=0></A>
<p>
<A HREF="headline_worldnews.html" TARGET="main_content"><IMG
SRC="button_worldnews.gif" WIDTH=80 HEIGHT=32 BORDER=0></A>
<p>
<A HREF="headline_business.html" TARGET="main_content"><IMG
SRC="button_business.gif" WIDTH=80 HEIGHT=32 BORDER=0></A>
<p>
<A HREF="headline_sports.html" TARGET="main_content"><IMG
SRC="button_sports.gif" WIDTH=80 HEIGHT=32 BORDER=0></A>
<p>
<A HREF="headline_entertainment.html" TARGET="main_content"><IMG
SRC="button_entertainment.gif" WIDTH=80 HEIGHT=32 BORDER=0></A>
<p>
<A HREF="headline_technology.html" TARGET="main_content"><IMG
SRC="button_technology.gif" WIDTH=80 HEIGHT=32 BORDER=0></A>
<p>
<A HREF="headline_style.html" TARGET="main_content"><IMG
SRC="button_style.gif" WIDTH=80 HEIGHT=32 BORDER=0></A>
<p>
<A HREF="headline_weather.html" TARGET="main_content"><IMG SRC="but-
ton_weather.gif" WIDTH=80 HEIGHT=32 BORDER=0></A>
<p>
<A HREF="headline_chatcenter.html" TARGET="main_content"><IMG
SRC="button_chatcenter.gif" WIDTH=80 HEIGHT=32 BORDER=0></A>
<p>
<A HREF="headline_auditorium.html" TARGET="main_content"><IMG
SRC="button_auditorium.gif" WIDTH=80 HEIGHT=32 BORDER=0></A>

</BODY>
```

Notice that the HREF tag for each graphic button includes the TARGET tag, which identifies the frame in which to display the HTML document listed before it. Each of the 11 graphic buttons sends a different URL to the same frame "main_content." In this example, the home page for each category is displayed in the main_content frame when the user selects a particular button. Any frame originally defined in the initial FRAMESET document can be referenced.

In this example, the user action of selecting a button from the menu updates a single frame with the appropriate HTML document. A FRAMESET document may also be loaded, providing the effect of displaying multiple windows when a user performs a single mouse click. The design illustrated in Figure 5.60 will deliver multiple frames on a single user selection from one of the five icons. This capability is accomplished simply by nesting the frame tags in the original FRAMESET document.

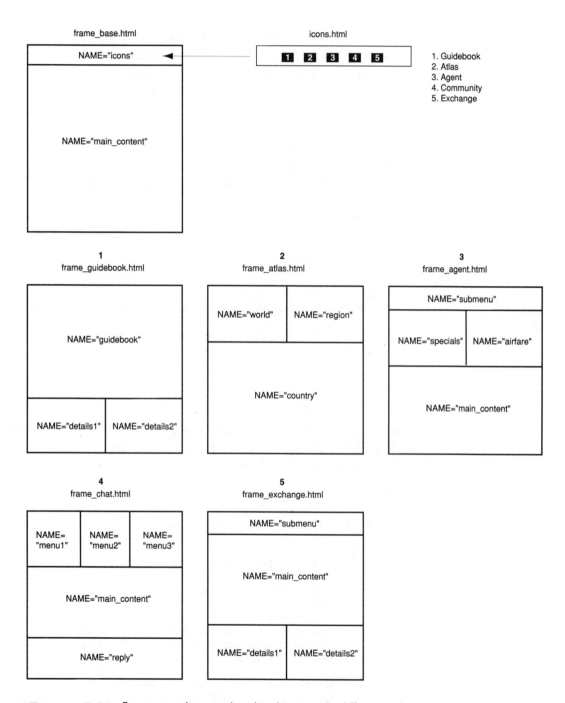

FIGURE 5.60 *Frames may be nested, and in this example, different in design, based on the information being presented.*

The design of this web site example has five distinct areas, each with a separate, unique frame base designed specifically for the information being presented. When a user selects an icon from the menu, the contents of the main area load the FRAMESET document specific to that category.

The initial home page is a FRAMESET document, which specifies only two frames: one for the icon menu named "toolbar," the other for the nested FRAMESET documents named "main_content."

```
<HTML>

<HEAD>
<TITLE>Travelars Corner</TITLE>
</HEAD>

<FRAMESET ROWS="40, 500">
  <FRAME SRC="icons.html" NAME="toolbar" SCROLLING=no NORESIZE>

  <FRAME SRC="intro_content.html" NAME="main_content" SCROLLING=no
NORESIZE>

</FRAMESET>

</HTML>
```

Selecting an icon from the menu in Figure 6.61 references another FRAMESET document, which is loaded into the main content area for the page. The HTML for the icon menu is shown:

```
<BODY BGCOLOR="eee2d9">

<TABLE BORDER=0 CELLSPACING=0 CELLPADDING=0>

<TR>
   <TD WIDTH=120><IMG ALIGN=right SRC="gifs/logotype.gif"></TD>

   <TD ALIGN=MIDDLE WIDTH=100><A HREF="guidebook/
      frame_guidebook.html" TARGET="main_content"><IMG
      SRC="gifs/icon_log.gif" BORDER=0></A></TD>
   <TD ALIGN=MIDDLE WIDTH=100><A HREF="atlas/frame_atlas.html"
      TARGET="main_content"><IMG SRC="gifs/icon_atlas.gif"
      BORDER=0></A></TD>

   <TD ALIGN=MIDDLE WIDTH=100><A HREF="agent/
      frame_agent.html" TARGET="main_content"><IMG
      SRC="gifs/icon_passport.gif"></A></TD>

   <TD ALIGN=MIDDLE WIDTH=100><A HREF="chat/
```

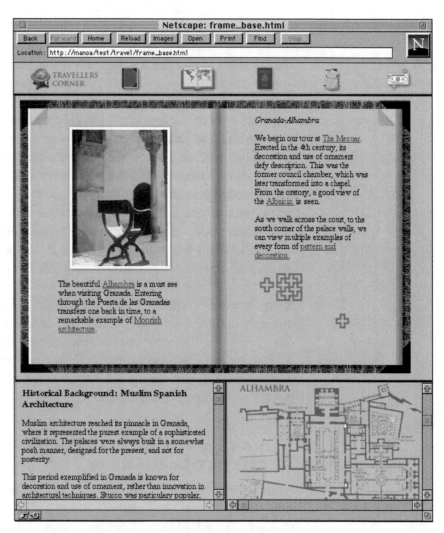

FIGURE 5.61

*Page after selecting the
Guidebook icon.*

```
            frame_chat.html" TARGET="main_content"><IMG
            SRC="gifs/icon_chat.gif"></A></TD>

        <TD ALIGN=MIDDLE WIDTH=100><A HREF="exchange/
            frame_exchange.html" TARGET="main_content"><IMG
            SRC="gifs/icon_cash.gif"></A></TD>

    </TR>

    </TABLE>
```

Selecting one of the icons loads a FRAMESET document into the
main content area of the page. For example, selecting the first icon,

the "Guidebook," displays the FRAMESET document for this area of the web site, shown in Figure 5.61. The book is the same HTML illustrated earlier in this chapter and now, simply referenced into a frame.

Since the book is fixed in dimension, the SCROLLING tag has a value set to "NO". Also, the NORESIZE tag is used to lock the frame width and height. The two smaller frames located at the bottom of the page do allow scrolling, since the content can vary in length. These frames display detailed or related information from the Guidebook. For example, additional historical information, site maps, hotel addresses, weather conditions, directions to get to a particular site, and so forth could be hyperlinked to these windows from the virtual Guidebook, without having to redirect the user to an entirely new page.

Each category of information will reference a frame document uniquely designed for that specific information group. In order to clarify naming, these documents always start with the term "frame," such as "frame_guidebook.html." This separates FRAMESET documents (which determine the layout) from the HTML documents (which are content) in the directory structure.

USING CLIENT-SIDE IMAGE MAPS IN FRAMESET DOCUMENTS

Graphic image maps are commonly found today on numerous web sites. The potential visual appeal and one-click access to information for users make ISMAPS a popular feature. A graphic image can be assigned hotspot regions, determined by coordinate information. Based on where the user clicks the mouse, HTML documents are displayed. The current method of implementing ISMAPS, however, requires the transmission of the coordinate information to the HTTP server for processing. Netscape 2.0 supports client image maps; this avoids the server round-trip by providing the coordinate values in the client HTML file. This also provides the image map functionality locally on the client, without the need to communicate with the server. Image map functionality would therefore work on a closed set of information, such as a CD-ROM archive of documents.

Selecting the Atlas icon in the icon menu loads the frame_atlas.html document into the main_content frame, shown in Figure 5.62. In this example, the individual frames are loaded with HTML documents displaying maps at various levels of resolution. The user is able to select various regions from the world map (top left), countries from the region map (top right), and districts from the country map (bottom middle), without losing context or redrawing the entire page with each selection.

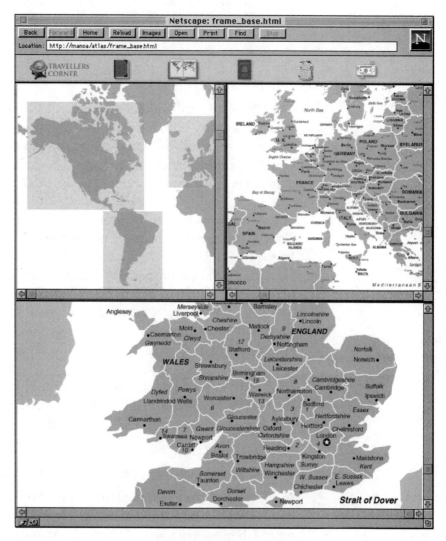

FIGURE 5.62

Client-side image maps in frames for an on-line atlas.

The image coordinate information in the HTML document for the world map (top left) is listed, with a discussion of each of the tags.

```
<BODY BGCOLOR="ffffff">

<MAP NAME="world_map">

<AREA SHAPE="RECT" COORDS="245,97,360,212"
HREF="map_europe.html"
TARGET="detail2">
<AREA SHAPE="RECT" COORDS="15,75,205,246"
HREF="map_northamerica.html" TARGET="detail2">
<AREA SHAPE="RECT" COORDS="138,248,230,371"
HREF="map_southamerica.html" TARGET="detail2">

</MAP>

<IMG SRC="gifs/map_world.gif" BORDER=0 USEMAP="#world_map">
```

The USEMAP attribute is added to the IMG SRC (image source) tag, which designates this document as a client-side image map. This argument specifies which map file to use—in this case, the world_map file. The cross-hatch character simply means that the map file is in the same document as the IMG SRC tag.

The coordinate information (or hotspots) is defined in the MAP tag. The NAME specifies the name of the map file, so it can be referenced by the IMG SRC tag. The AREA tag lists the coordinate information for each individual hotspot. The hotspot may be a geometric or irregular shape, determined by the SHAPE attribute. Various attributes for SHAPE supported by Netscape 2.0 include RECT (rectangle), CIRCLE, and POLY (polygon). For rectangles, the coordinates are given as left, top, right, bottom. Circle coordinates are given as x,y locations and the radius of the circle. Polygonal hotspots may have an arbitrary number of sides, defined by a list of x,y vertices. Following the COORDS tag, the HREF supplies the document to load when the region is selected and the TARGET specifies the frame.

PLAN AND ORGANIZE FRAMESET DOCUMENTS

It is helpful to plan an organizational method for all FRAMESET and HTML documents before production. Changes in a design can mean laborious renaming of frames, map references, and HTML

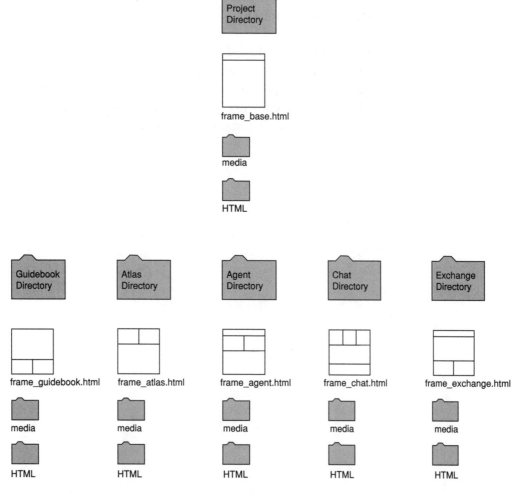

FIGURE 5.63 *Directory structure for organizing FRAMESET documents.*

documents. In Figure 5.63, the document structure for the "Travellers Corner" example is illustrated.

The organizational framework structure of the web site is reflected in the directory structure. Each category of the web site has an associated directory, containing its own FRAMESET document, image directory, and subordinate directories for HTML documents. This insulates each area of the web site within its own directory structure. Once created, edits and modifications to HTML documents and media files are placed into the appropriate directory.

The examples illustrated here only begin to explore the many design possibilities for using Netscape frames. The support of the Java language in Netscape 2.0, in conjunction with the capabilities in FRAMESET documents, will offer new opportunties for rich human-computer interaction across cyberspace.

BIBLIOGRAPHY

American Institute of Graphic Arts. 1981.
Symbol Signs. New York: Hastings House.

Apple Computer, Inc. 1992.
Human Interface Guidelines: The Apple Desktop Interface.
Reading, MA: Addison-Wesley.

Baecker, Ronald M., and William S. Buxton. 1987.
*Readings in Human–Computer Interaction: A Multidisciplinary
Approach.* Los Altos, CA: Morgan Kaufmann.

Barratt, Krome. 1980.
Logic and Design. Westfield, NJ: Eastview Editions.

Bertin, Jacques. 1989.
Graphics and Graphic Information Processing. Translated by P. Berg
and P. Scott. Berlin: William de Gruyter and Co.

Bertin, Jacques. 1983.
Semiology of Graphics. Translated by P. Berg, Madison, WI: University of Wisconsin Press.

Bringhurst, Robert. 1992.
The Elements of Typographic Style. Vancouver: Hartley & Marks.

Card, Stuart K., Thomas P. Moran, and Alan Newell. 1983.
The Psychology of Human–Computer Interaction. Hillsdale, NJ:
Lawrence Erlbaum Associates.

Carter, Rob, Ben, Day, and Phillip, Meggs. 1985.
Typographic Design: Form and Communication. New York: Van
Nostrand Reinhold.

Conklin, J. 1987.
Hypertext: An Introduction and Survey. *Computer* 20(9): 17–41.

Cotton, Bob, and Richard Oliver. 1993.
Understanding Hypermedia from Multimedia to Virtual Reality.
London: Phaidon Press, Ltd.

Diethelm, Walter. 1976.
Signet Sign Symbol. Zurich: ABC Verlag.

Dix, Alan, Janet Finlay, Gregory Abowd, and Russell Beale, 1993.
Human-Computer Interaction. Englewood Cliffs, NJ: Prentice-Hall.

Dondis, Donis A. 1973.
A Primer of Visual Literacy. Cambridge, MA: MIT Press.

Dreyfuss, Henry. 1972.
Symbol Sourcebook. New York: Van Nostrand Reinhold.

Foss, C. 1988.
Effective Browsing in Hypertext Systems. User-oriented content-based text and image handling. *Proceedings of the RIAO Conference*. March 21–24: 83–98.

Frutiger, Adrian. 1989.
Signs and Symbols: Their Design and Meaning. New York: Van Nostrand Reinhold.

Frutiger, Adrian. 1980.
Type Sign Symbol. Zurich: ABC Verlag.

Furnas, George W. 1986.
Generalized Fisheye Views. *CHI'86 Conference Proceedings*. 16–23.

Gerstner, Karl. 1986.
The Forms of Color. Cambridge, MA: MIT Press.

Gerstner, Karl. 1981.
The Spirit of Colors. Cambridge, MA: MIT Press.

Gerstner, Karl. 1974.
Compendium for Literates: A System of Writing. Translated by Dennis Q. Stephenson. Cambridge, MA: MIT Press.

Glushko, R. J. 1989.
Transforming Text into Hypertext for a Compact Disc Encyclopedia. Human Factors in Computing Systems. *CHI '89 Conference Proceedings*. ACM: New York. 293–298.

Glushko, R. J. 1989.
Design Issues for Multi-Document Hypertexts. *Hypertext '89 Proceedings*. 51–59.

GO Corporation. 1992.
PenPoint User Interface Design Reference. New York: Addison-Wesley.

Gray, Matthew, and Eric Richard. 1995.
Make Multimedia Friendly. *Internet World*. (March 1995): 26–28.

Grillo, Paul-Jacques. 1960.
Form, Function, and Design. New York: Dover. (Originally published as, *What is Design?* Chicago: Paul Theobold and Co.)

Hanks, Kurt, and Larry Belliston. 1980.
Rapid Viz: A New Method for the Rapid Visualization of Ideas. Los Altos, CA: William Kaufmann, Inc.

Hanks, Kurt, and Larry Belliston. 1977.
Draw: A Visual Approach to Thinking, Learning, and Communication. Los Altos, CA: William Kaufman, Inc.

Heller, Steven, and Seymour Chwast. 1988.
Graphic Style: from Victorian to Post-Modern, New York: Harry N. Abrams, Inc.

Herdeg, Walter. 1983.
Graphis Diagrams: The Graphic Visualization of Abstract Data. Zurich: Graphis Press.

Herdeg, Walter. 1981.
Archigraphia. Zurich: Graphis Press.

Hofmann, Armin. 1989.
Armin Hofmann His Work, Quest and Philosophy. Basel: Birkhäuser Verlag.

Hofmann, Armin. 1965.
Graphic Design Manual. New York: Van Nostrand Reinhold.

Hurlburt, Allen. 1978.
The Grid. New York: Van Nostrand Reinhold.

Laurel, Brenda, ed. 1990.
The Art of Human-Computer Interface Design. Reading, MA:
Addison–Wesley.

Martin, James. 1990.
Hyperdocuments and How to Create Them. Englewood Cliffs, NJ:
Prentice-Hall.

Martin, Douglas. 1989.
Book Design. New York: Van Nostrand Reinhold.

Mayhew, Deborah. 1992.
Principles and Guidelines in Software User Interface Design.
Englewood Cliffs, NJ: Prentice-Hall.

Müller-Brockmann, Josef. 1988.
Grid Systems in Graphic Design. Stuttgart: Verlag Gerd Hatje.

Müller–Brockmann, Josef. 1983.
The Graphic Designer and His Design Problems. New York: Hastings House.

Mullet, Kevin, and Darrell Sano. 1994.
Designing Visual Interfaces: Communication-Oriented Techniques.
Englewood Cliffs, NJ: Prentice-Hall/SunSoft Press.

Nejmeh, Brian A. 1994.
Internet: A Strategic Tool for the Software Enterprise.
Communications of the ACM. 37, no. 11: 23–27.

Nielsen, Jakob. 1995.
Multimedia and Hypertext the Internet and Beyond.
Boston: Academic Press.

Nielsen, Jakob. 1993.
Usability Engineering. San Diego: Academic Press.

Nielsen, Jakob, ed. 1989.
Coordinating User Interfaces for Consistency.
Boston: Academic Press.

Norman, Donald A. 1988.
The Psychology of Everyday Things. New York: Basic Books
(paperback edition titled, *The Design of Everyday Things*).

Parunak, H. Van Dyke. 1989.
Hypermedia Topologies and User Navigation. *Hypertext '89 Proceedings*, 43–49.

Press, Larry. 1994.
Commercialization of the Internet.
Communications of the ACM 37, no. 11: 17–21.

Rand, Paul. 1993.
Design: Form and Chaos. New Haven, CT: Yale University Press.

Rand, Paul. 1985.
Paul Rand: A Designer's Art. New Haven, CT: Yale University Press.

Ruder, Emil. 1981.
Typography. New York: Hastings House.

Rüegg, Ruedi. 1989.
Basic Typography: Design with Letters. New York: Van Nostrand
Reinhold.

Spencer, Herbert. 1983.
Pioneers of Modern Typography. Cambridge, MA: MIT Press.

Spiekermann, Erik, and E.M. Ginger. 1993.
Stop Stealing Sheep and Find Out How Type Works. Mountain
View, CA: Adobe Press.

Strunk, William, Jr., and E.B. White. 1979.
The Elements of Style. 3rd ed. New York: Macmillan.

Tufte, Edward R. 1990.
Envisioning Information. Cheshire, CT: Graphics Press.

Tufte, Edward R. 1983.
The Visual Display of Quantitative Information. Cheshire, CT: Graphics Press.

West, Suzanne. 1990.
Working with Style, New York: Watson-Guptill.

Wilbur, Peter. 1989.
Information Graphics. New York: Van Nostrand Reinhold.

Samuelson, Pamela. 1995.
Copyright and Digital Libraries.
Communications of the ACM. 38, no. 4: 15-21, 110.

Smedinghoff, Thomas J. 1994.
Multimedia Legal Handbook: A Guide from the Software Publishers Association. New York: John Wiley & Sons.

Stefanac, Suzanne. 1994.
Multimedia Meets the Internet.
New Media. (November): 56–63.

Strangelove, Michael. 1995.
The Walls Come Down: Net Age Advertising Empowers Consumers.
Internet World (May 1995): 40–44.

Thüring, Manfred, Jörg Hannemann, and Jörg M. Haake. 1995.
Hypermedia and Cognition: Designing for Comprehension,
Communications of the ACM. 38, no. 8: 57–66.

Tognazzini, Bruce. 1989.
Achieving Consistency for the Macintosh. In, *Coordinating User Interfaces for Consistency*, ed. J. Nielsen, 57–73.
Boston: Academic Press.

Weiss, Jiri. 1995.
Digital Copyright Who Owns What?
New Media (September) 38–43.

Wiggins, Richard. 1995.
Publishing on the World Wide Web.
New Media (February) 51–55.

INDEX

Index Notes

Page references followed by lowercase Roman i indicate illustrations.
Page references followed by lowercase Roman t indicate tables.

Symbols and hard-to-classify

8, 16, and 24bit color displays, 51

14,400 and 28,800 modems, 47. *See also* connection speed

<!comment here> tag, 220

@home service (Kleiner Perkins Caufield & Byers), 49